An etching of Elisabeth Stopp by Edgar Holloway, R.E.
[Reproduced by kind permission of the artist]

GERMAN ROMANTICS
IN
CONTEXT

Selected Essays 1971-86
by

ELISABETH STOPP

Collected by
Peter Hutchinson   Roger Paulin   Judith Purver

Bristol Classical Press

First published in 1992 by
Bristol Classical Press
an imprint of
Gerald Duckworth & Co. Ltd
The Old Piano
48 Hoxton Square, London N1 6PB

A catalogue record for this book is available
from the British Library

ISBN 1-85399-334-4

Printed in Great Britain by
The Cromwell Press, Melksham, Wiltshire

Contents

Acknowledgments

The Editors would like to express their gratitude to a number of editors of journals and *Festschriften* for permission to reprint the following material:

" 'Ein Sohn der Zeit': Goethe and the Romantic plays of Zacharias Werner", *Publications of the English Goethe Society,* 40 (1970), 123-50

"Brentano's 'O Stern und Blume': Its Poetic and Emblematic Context", *Modern Language Review,* 67 (1972), 95-117

"Eichendorff und Shakespeare", *Festvortrag zur Jahresversammlung der Eichendorff-Gesellschaft,* 7 April 1972, *Aurora,* 32 (1972), 7-23

" 'Übergang vom Roman zur Mythologie': Formal Aspects of the Opening Chapter of Hardenberg's *Heinrich von Ofterdingen, Part II", Deutsche Vierteljahrsschrift,* 48 (1974), 318-41

"Joseph Görres' Metaphorical Thinking", in *Literaturwissenschaft und Geistesgeschichte, Festschrift für Richard Brinkmann,* edited by Jürgen Brummack et al., Max Niemeyer Verlag, Tübingen, 1981, 371-86

"Carus' *Neun Briefe über Landschaftsmalerei (1831).* Werk und Form in romantischer Perspektive", *Vortrag auf dem Internationalen Eichendorff-Kongreß,* Würzburg, 15 July 1982, *Aurora,* 43, (1983), 77-91

"Ludwig Tieck and Dante", *Deutsches Dante-Jahrbuch,* 60 (1985), 73-95

"Arnim's *Luisen-Kantate* as Romantic Occasional Verse", *Aurora,* 46 (1986), 87

A Note on the Plates

The frontispiece is taken from an etching of Elisabeth Stopp by Edgar Holloway, R.E., which was completed during the war years and which is now reproduced by kind permission of the artist. The original was displayed in the Ashmolean Museum, Oxford, in 1991, coinciding with Elisabeth's eightieth birthday.

The four plates accompanying the article on Brentano's "O Stern und Blume" are:

I: *Scala coeli et inferni ex divo Bernardo*, from a broadsheet by Johann Bussemacher, Cologne, *c. 1595*. Reproduced by courtesy of the Herzog August Bibliothek, Wolfenbüttel, where its index number is: Cod. Guelf. 31.8 Aug. 2° folio 26/7.

II: Philipp Otto Runge's *Die Nacht,* a pen drawing from the cycle *Die Tageszeiten,* 1803.

III: "O Stern o Blume nach Runge mit St. Edwardsstuhl u. dem Schnitter." J.F. Böhmer's title for lithograph XIV in Brentano's *Gockel, Hinkel und Gackeleja*, 1838.

IV: Edward von Steinle's "O Stern und Blume", 1852. Reproduced by courtesy of the Kösel Verlag, Munich.

The plate accompanying the article on Carus is a self-portrait by the author completed in 1822.

FOREWORD

Elisabeth Stopp has been associated with Cambridge for over sixty years - with its libraries, colleges, undergraduates and research students. Together with her husband Freddy she was a pillar of German teaching there, and numerous careers in *Germanistik* were directly launched by their joint and unstinting efforts. The editors of this volume themselves all owe much to her scholarship, her friendship, and her generosity, and the surprising length of the *Tabula Gratulatoria* proves they are very far from alone. Although those editors have done their best to select the most important of Elisabeth's writings in a particular area, it must be emphasised that they have done partial justice to only one side of her creative output. She remains active - and distinguished - in areas of scholarship unrelated to German Romanticism, and in her personal life, too, she plays a number of very different roles. These are reflected in the diversity of names associated with this project: as expected, former pupils, colleagues, fellow scholars and teachers; but it is surely unusual to have Fellows of the Royal Society in among the Fellows of the British Academy and the Royal Society of Literature, a Nobel Prizewinner for physics, not to mention clergy of the higher ranks and also Heads of Houses here in Cambridge.

In honour of her eightieth birthday, the editors have brought together some of Elisabeth's essays on German Romanticism, a series which began with an important article published over fifty years ago in 1939, just before the beginning of the Second World War. Born in London, though of multiple European origin - Austrian, Czech, German and French - Elisabeth was educated at the Camden School; from 1929 she was an undergraduate at Girton College, Cambridge, then a research student and Research Fellow there until 1937. She completed her Ph.D. thesis on *The Place of Italy in the Life and Work of Ludwig Tieck*, although - and it is now difficult to understand this - because Cambridge women students were not full members of the University until 1948, she was not able to graduate officially. Her thesis and her whole attitude to learning and scholarship in the Cambridge tradition of the Modern Languages Tripos, modelled on that of Classics, was inspired by her research supervisor, Professor Edward Bullough of Gonville and Caius College, Professor of Italian in Cambridge. Like Elisabeth, he was a European in outlook and affinity, at home in diverse fields of study. After Bullough's untimely death, Francis Bennett, also of Caius College, directed Elisabeth's work, as he had, at an earlier stage, supervised that of her fellow student, Frederick John, whom she married in 1937. (In those days, of course, marriage was likely to have severe repercussions on a woman's academic career.) Freddy, as he was universally known, was at that time one of the three English Lectors at the University of Heidelberg, all of whom, unable to go on facing the political stress there, came back to England the following year.

Elisabeth, whose dissertation involved archival work in the State Libraries of Berlin and Dresden, had spent some months of her final year of research at the University of Tübingen so as to work with Paul Kluckhohn, the eminent Romantic scholar, whose name, together with that of Richard Samuel, will always be linked with the great edition of Friedrich von Hardenberg (Novalis). This course of action was, in fact, suggested to Elisabeth by Richard, at that time in exile in Cambridge where he was Lector in German. Kluckhohn was under Nazi surveillance, prevented from travelling abroad, and glad to have foreign contacts and intellectual exchange. This meant a great deal to a young scholar, and it was Kluckhohn who, as co-editor of one of the leading German periodicals, as yet untainted by political expediency, encouraged Elisabeth in that first article on Tieck's changing image in German literary consciousness. Kluckhohn encouraged her in the scrupulous integrity and independence of judgement that have been the hallmark of her scholarship. Indeed, many of the issues raised in that article were not fully registered by Tieck studies, or Romantic studies in general, until some decades later.

War meant separation from Freddy, on active service in the "Black Cats", the 56th London Division, in Iraq, Africa and Italy, and who was abroad without leave for years; this brought Elisabeth, alone in war-time London, little opportunity for academic work. However, she greatly enjoyed teaching, for a time, in the upper forms of St Paul's Girls' School, more often than not in air-raid shelters. On the Stopps' return to Cambridge in 1947, she renewed contact with Girton (the college of which, in retirement, she is now a Life Fellow); she also taught in the Faculty of Modern and Medieval Languages. During these years there came the first unfolding of the Stopps' joint, yet individually so different, scholarly careers. Freddy's wide-ranging work ultimately led him to a Readership in German Renaissance Studies, a career cut short by years of illness and an untimely death in 1979. Elisabeth embarked on a series of writings on seventeenth-century French moralists and mystics, St François de Sales and Madame de Chantal, work which led to wide recognition and to her election to a Fellowship of the Royal Society of Literature in 1963. It was essentially not until her appointment to a full University Lectureship in 1966 that she was able to resume her Romantic interests, though she had continued to review widely in this field. Reviewing was work to which she was devoted throughout her career, not least in the course of her close collaboration with Freddy during his years as Germanic Editor of the *Modern Language Review.*

And yet her theological and literary interests have never led independent lives, separate from each other. The interplay of body and spirit, the power and limits of the human imagination, the sense of our beginning and end, the power of human religious language to compass the inexpressible, the common iconography of spirituality and poetry, these - not abstractions or theoretical constructs - have been central to her work on Romantics and mystics alike. Her concern throughout has been the close analysis of poetical and pictorial structures in the overall context of Novalis' imperative for the Romantic poet, philosopher, mystic and artist that the whole world, the whole of creation as it manifests itself to the inner eye, must be "poetisirt", "romantisirt".

Elisabeth's seminar on the literature, thought and art of German Romanticism - alive in the memories of several subscribers to this volume - was in its time the real centre of Romantic studies in this country. It was also so successful that it was permitted to continue beyond the period customarily allotted to Special Papers in the Cambridge Tripos. The idea came primarily from her teacher and friend, Trevor Jones, who had begun work on Arnim before turning to the great lexicographical work for which he is best remembered. Elisabeth's work on Novalis, Brentano, Werner and Eichendorff largely dates from this period. Later, often as a result of invitations to speak and write, she found her way to Arnim, Görres, Sailer, Carus, and also back to Ludwig Tieck in his relationship to Dante and Italy.

In 1975 Elisabeth was, for a time, acting Head of the Department of German. She retired after her husband's death in 1979 and was then in a position to resume her scholarly work more intensively. In the course of a Salesian tour in the States she lectured on the literary work of St François de Sales and the influence of his spirituality on iconographical work in his century. Then in 1982 the Eichendorff-Gesellschaft, the International Association for Romantic Studies, awarded her the "Eichendorff Medaille" in recognition of her work in the field of Romanticism. She was the first woman to receive this distinction and is, to date, its only recipient in this country. A further honour was to follow when, in 1986, she was awarded the degree of Doctor of Letters for her publications in the German and French fields; and now, for the first time, she was able to take a Cambridge degree in person in the University's Senate House.

The essays collected in the present volume demonstrate the importance, originality, scope and quality of Elisabeth's contribution to Romantic studies. She practises critical interpretation as the German Romantics themselves believed it should be practised: as an art form in its own right. At the same time her writing embodies the best features of the British scholarly tradition. Exemplary in its clarity and sensitivity to nuance, it shuns prolixity and the merely speculative in favour of patient, careful and penetrating analysis, condensing a great deal of substance into a small compass. A gifted and inspiring teacher, for whom teaching and research have always gone hand in hand, Elisabeth has also encouraged good writing in others: as well as shedding new light on Romanticism she was, and is, deeply concerned to hand on the torch of scholarship to future generations. Her essay "Zur bibliographischen Erschließung der Romantik" bears particular testimony to this concern, but it underlies the present volume as a whole; indeed, Elisabeth agreed to the enterprise not least because it would enable articles drawn from a wide range of learned publications, now difficult of access, to be made available once more as a resource for fellow scholars and students of Romanticism, and especially for the younger ones among them. Thus this volume, while conceived as a gift to Elisabeth, is really a gift from her to others, and as such is typical of her whole attitude both to life and to scholarship. This attitude is characterised by a healthy dash of humour (including the self-deprecatory kind) and an even larger portion of courage, a quality which enabled her to carry on at times of great personal difficulty and to uphold German studies, and in particular the study of German Romanticism, during a period when these were not regarded with special favour. Increasing acknowledgment of the continued relevance of German Romanticism bears witness to her insight and sheer tenacity of purpose in holding to the course on which she had embarked. Space has prevented us from including as many of her articles as we would have liked, but we have tried to achieve a sense of balance by selecting pieces which are representative of Elisabeth's interests as well as represening a broad range of Romantic studies. No author features more than once, and most are seen in a wider, sometimes European, setting. Two items are in German: these were actually lectures delivered on important occasions, and it seemed to us appropriate that these should feature in their original form.

As ever, Elisabeth continues to work and to write in both the German and French fields, to consult and to discuss with younger colleagues. Her home at 4, Drosier Road - Caius territory - remains a place where scholars and friends go in and out and find the stimulus of her company and conversation.

The Editors

"Ein Sohn der Zeit": Goethe and the Romantic Plays of Zacharias Werner[1]

At a time of humiliation after Napoleon's triumph in Germany, Goethe looked towards the state as an artistic rallying point well suited to improve national morale. In May 1807 he therefore encouraged his actors of the Weimar Hoftheater, in spite of all the difficulties involved, to accept an invitation for a summer tour in Saxony and he decided that something new and inspiriting should be put on for their début in Leipzig - a first staging of *Don Carlos* in its verse form. For this occasion Goethe wrote a Prologue which stressed in a special way the actors' need for new stimulus and fresh ideas at a time of national and personal depression:

> Denn keiner ist von uns, der sich vollendet,
> Der sein Talent für abgeschlossen hielte;
> Ja, keiner ist, der nicht mit jedem Tage
> Die Kunst mehr zu gewinnen, sich zu bilden,
> Was unsre Zeit und was ihr Geist verlangt,
> Sich klarer zu vergegenwärtigen strebte.
> Drum schenkt uns freien Beifall, wo's gelingt,
> Und fördert unser Streben durch Belehrung.[2]

Goethe was not only speaking for his actors on this occasion; in stage matters, and in spite of his own frequent depression and of intrigues on the part of the actors, he himself tried to move with the times, as he understood them, and to keep an open mind for "Belehrung", till he finally gave up directing the theatre at Weimar.

His most notorious failure in this respect and at about this time was with Kleist; one of his most interesting experiments, now little remembered and never as yet explored in any detail, was with the Romantic, Zacharias Werner, who stayed with him for several months on end two years running: from December

1807 to March 1808 and from the December of that same year until June 1809. Goethe staged Werner's *Wanda, Königin der Sarmaten* on 30 January 1808, the gala night celebrating Herzogin Luise's birthday. The letter to Kleist refusing *Penthesilea* in hurtful terms is dated two days later. He seriously considered three other plays by Werner for his theatre - *Das Kreuz an der Ostsee, Attila, König der Hunnen*, and *Cunegunde die Heilige* - but eventually only staged a fourth play, the one-act tragedy, *Der vierundzwanzigste Februar*, written at Weimar and at Goethe's suggestion. This was in 1809, but the performance was not till a year later, "an seinem Tage", when Werner had already left Germany for Rome. Although a few letters and messages passed between him and Goethe after that, their relationship deteriorated and they never met again. After his conversion in and to Rome Werner practically ceased writing for the stage; he became an extraordinarily successful preacher in Vienna where he died on 17 January 1823 at the age of 54.[3]

I should like to explore Goethe's attempt to understand "Was unsre Zeit und was ihr Geist verlangt" as represented in the Romantic art and personality of Zacharias Werner. "Seine Tendenz möchte ich, wenn ich auch könnte, nicht ändern", Goethe said; "Er ist ein Sohn der Zeit und muß mit ihr leben und untergehen; und was von ihm übrig bleibt, ist allenfalls auch nicht schlecht" (Letter of 7 March 1808 to Jacobi; WA, iv, xx, 29). How far did Goethe, in fact, succeed in this attempt to compromise with the times, and with this particular manifestation of the Romantic spirit?

Quite apart from the national situation, the three or four years before Goethe met Werner had been a time of ill-health and personal depression because of the apparent drying up of his artistic powers. He had not yet recovered from the blow of Schiller's death and the increased sense of solitude it brought him; he felt out of step with the times and also with himself as he faced the process of ageing - he was 58. A break-through had come in Jena in May 1807, when he was suddenly able to continue work on the *Wanderjahre* with "Sankt Joseph der Zweite", the strange story of the carpenter who had turned the dead world of painted religious frescoes into a real life of the present. *Pandora*, expressing the problematical relationship between old and young, between the backward-looking introvert and the violent man of action, was begun in Jena in the Advent of that same year and completed when Werner was already his guest. During Werner's second visit in 1809 Goethe was at work on *Die Wahlverwandtschaften.* Looking back at this time, Goethe said: "*Pandora* sowohl als die *Wahlverwandtschaften* drücken das schmerzliche Gefühl der Entbehrung aus, und konnten also nebeneinander gar wohl gedeihen" (*Tag- und Jahreshefte,* 1807-8; WA, i, xxxvi, 28). During the summer of 1807, when he was at Karlsbad, he noted repeated conversations on religious topics in his *Tagebücher*; he was reading the manuscript of Adam Müller's lectures on the Spanish drama, given at Dresden the previous year, and in connection with this, Goethe turned his renewed attention to Calderón, whose *Andacht zum Kreuze*, and especially *Der standhafte Prinz*, were already familiar to him through A. W. Schlegel's translations. He himself had plans for a Christian play in Calderón's manner which has survived as "Bruchstücke einer Tragödie", set in the age of Charlemagne and bearing on the theme of Christianity versus paganism, as expressed in an insoluble opposition between the young generation and the old. This was first mentioned in the *Tagebücher* in August 1807, but was still occupying Goethe's mind three years later. It is clear, then, that during the years when Werner and his work made their impact on Goethe, his mind was already predisposed to receptivity for what might be called Werner's particular line; Goethe was feeling his way towards new themes, exploring fresh possibilities, and the direction he was taking was, in the widest sense of the term, religious.

By the time he met Werner, Goethe had read the three plays Werner had already published. First of all, *Die Söhne des Thals* (1803-4), a sequence of two dramas about the decline of the "Templerorden", in which Werner, a freemason like Goethe (they used to go to the Weimar Lodge together) saw the origin of freemasonry. In this play Werner tries to work out a theory of the relationship between the individual and the community, of the power of the many invested in the one, the mystical body, as it were, of the masonic order. The order seems to perish to the outward eye, but it is in fact saved by the freely accepted death and martyrdom of its outstanding individual member. Werner's second play, *Die Weihe der Kraft* (1806), was a Luther drama, and like the first, was staged in Berlin by Iffland who took the chief part. Again, this is a study of society, with emerging protestantism to replace freemasonry; the great individual, Luther, only succeeds in redeeming the group after he himself has been redeemed by accepting love in the person of Catherine de Bora. After reading this play and before he knew Werner personally, Goethe wrote to ask Cotta for "eine recht gute Rezension . . . es ist der Mühe wert, dieses nicht verdienstlose aber monstrose Werk zu würdigen" (7 March 1807). There is no direct evidence to prove that Goethe had, before their meeting, read *Das Kreuz an der Ostsee*, Part I, "Die Brautnacht", published 1806 but never staged; in view of its main theme, however, closely analogous to Goethe's own plans for a Christian tragedy in the Calderón manner, it is more than likely that he was already familiar with it. It was Werner's favourite and most characteristic play, telling of the love, renunciation and martyrdom of a Polish princess, a Christian, and her Prussian husband who has been converted, while his family and tribe continue to stand out in bitter combat against the cross. " . . . der Kampf ich möchte sagen der dämonischen Menschen gegen die Heiligen ist der große Grundstoff des Ganzen", as Werner says in his preface to the play (DLER, XX, 19). A similar theme, and in fact Werner's own basic personality problem, preoccupied him in *Attila, König der Hunnen* (1806, published in 1812), where through love, the pagan Attila, who, like Napoleon, called himself "die Geißel Gottes", is ultimately converted to Christianity and a new "life", in this case, death. The play was also meant as a parable and a prophetic mime for the conqueror of Europe and, not unnaturally, the censors in Berlin did not risk staging such inflammable material.

Werner was at that time a convinced but quite unorthodox Christian. He did not become a Catholic till 1811, was ordained three years later and thereafter devoted his talents to preaching and spiritual direction instead of the stage. But in a sense, he had not really changed his vocation at all, for in all his plays he considered "Proselytenmacherei", the attempt to convert people to his own point of view, whatever it happened to be at the time, as the poet's sacred trust and the only right use of god-given talents :

> . . . da wir im protestantischen Deutschland keine Tempel haben, [ist] die Bühne noch der einzige Ort, von welchem herab der Priester der Gottheit zum Volke sprechen kann. Viva vox, Anschauung! (Letter to Scheffner, 12 May 1805; *Briefe*, I, 358)

He saw the poet as God's mediator, "Mittler" in Novalis' sense, especially in a right understanding of love:

> Alle meine Arbeiten sind nur Variazionen dieses himmlischen Thema's . . . Vergöttlichung der Menschheit durch die Liebe . . . Wahrhaft Liebende sind sich gegenseitig Heyland. (Letter to Tina, Gräfin von Brühl, May 1806; *Briefe*, II, 22)

But at this earlier stage, religion was not so much personal conviction, *Glaubenssystem*, as "eine wieder aufgegrabene mythologische Fundgrube" for artistic purposes (*Briefe*, 1, 100).

> Heyland, Kunst, Liebe, Tod, jedes [ist] in seiner Art für uns Mittler, es sind beinahe Synonima, die uns ins Universum, aus dem wir genommen, für das wir da sind, wieder mit mütterlichen Händen versenken. (Letter to Peguilhen, 5 December 1803; *Briefe*, I, 218)

These mystical theories, not always completely fused with the historical and strikingly unfolded realistic plane of action, were not an extra thrown in as an after-thought; as far as Werner was concerned, they *were* the drama, the very action itself, and any attempt to make him divide up his plays, rescuing, as it were, the realistic plane from the mystical, as Goethe would have liked, was doomed to fail. What Goethe was in fact trying to do was to save the Romantic playwright of Schillerian excellence from what he considered his mystical aberrations, that is, his essential Romanticism.

Iffland had openly hailed Werner as Schiller's natural successor,[4] and in Goethe's eyes, Iffland's patronage of the Romantic in Berlin was probably the greatest single factor in his favour and the reason why he invited him to Weimar. There was an element of rivalry between the two theatres which worked in

Werner's interests; talent spotting in view of an almost permanently depleted repertoire of suitable contemporary plays was as important in Weimar as in Berlin.[5] Werner's visit to Weimar was, then, no mere chance social occasion. He had been thrown out of work by the national crisis. Now aged 39, he was by profession a civil servant, first stationed in Poland, later in Berlin. His private life had also been disrupted when his third wife, a Pole, left him in 1805. He was trying to create a new career for himself as a dramatist, and when he finally reached Weimar it was at the end of a long tour which included Dresden, Prague, Vienna, Munich. Like Kleist who followed practically the same route two years later, he had tried to sell his plays to the highest bidder, indeed to any bidder.

Werner arrived in Jena late at night on 2 December 1807, marking the final stage of his journey by a dramatic sonnet in dialogue form, "Der Weg";[6] the next day, at the house of the publisher, Frommann, he read out to Goethe and a select circle which included Minna Herzlieb, the first three acts of *Wanda, Königin der Sarmaten*, begun that summer in the course of his tour. In his *Tag- und Jahreshefte* Goethe reports :

> Mit großer Kraft und Wahrheit las er vor. . . Es war das erste Mal seit Schillers Tode, daß ich ruhige, gesellige Freuden in Jena genoß; die Freundlichkeit der Gegenwärtigen erregte die Sehnsucht nach dem Abgeschiedenen und der auf's neue empfundene Verlust forderte Ersatz. Gewohnheit, Neigung, Freundschaft steigerten sich zu Liebe und Leidenschaft, die, wie alles Absolute, was in die bedingte Welt tritt, vielen verderblich zu werden drohte. (WA, i, xxxvi, 391)

Werner, the gifted dramatist, then only a few years younger than Schiller at the time of his death, was associated in the general context of loss and compensation implied in Goethe's first veiled reference to his strong feelings for Minna Herzlieb. Goethe goes on to say that he then sought solace in poetry :

> In solchen Epochen jedoch erscheint die Dichtkunst erhöhend und mildernd, die Forderungen des Herzens erhöhend, gewaltsame Befriedigung mildernd. Und so war diessmal die . . .von Werner ins Tragische gesteigerte Sonettenform höchst willkommen.[7]

In the first weeks of December he began work on *Pandora* and wrote his cycle of seventeen sonnets in close consultation with Werner whom he regarded as an outstanding exponent of the form: " . . . eben von ihm rühren einige Sonette her, die man wohl unter das beste wird zählen müssen, was in deutscher Sprache gedichtet worden" (to Cotta, 9 April 1808; WA, iv, xx, 44-5).

Advent is, by definition, a time of heightened expectation, and Goethe initially saw Werner within the aura of strong feeling aroused by this "Epoche" of Advent 1807, which, according to the sonnet entitled "Epoche", was written into his heart with letters of flame:

Mit Flammenschrift war innigst eingeschrieben
Petrarcas Brust, vor allen andern Tagen,
Karfreitag. Eben so, ich darf's wohl sagen,
Ist mir *Advent* von Achtzehnhundertsieben.

(JA, II, 12)

The same concept of "Epoche" was used for Werner himself:

> . . . man kann nicht läugnen, daß er [Werner] Epoche in unserem Kreis gemacht. Er mußte sogleich als merkwürdiger Mensch betrachtet werden. Ein sehr schönes poetisch-rhetorisches Talent hatte sich in dem wunderlichsten Individuum verkörpert. (WA, i, xxxvi, 391)[8]

To begin with, at any rate, personal affection and literary stimulus were mutual between the two men, and Werner's name occurs almost daily in Goethe's diaries over the next few months. He calls him "dieser wunderlich bedeutende Mann" who has become "lieb und angehörig" to him after their first meeting which actually took place at Frommann's house. "Werner, der Thalsohn, ist auch bald vierzehen Tage hier. Seine Persönlichkeit interessiert und gefällt uns", he writes to Zelter. His brilliant reading has opened all eyes to his true quality :

> . . . und so kommen wir über die seltsamen Außenseiten dieser Erscheinung in den Kern hinein, der wohlschmeckend und kräftig ist. . . er ist in jedem Sinne eine merkwürdige Natur und ein schönes Talent. . . durch seinen Vortrag, seine Erklärungen und Erläuterungen ist manches ausgeglichen worden, was uns schwarz auf weiß gar schroff entgegenstand. (16 December 1807; WA, i, xix, 475 ff.)

A description by E.T.A. Hoffmann, Werner's close friend, his countryman, collaborator and fellow civil servant in Poland, may serve to supplement the picture of the man Goethe found so attractive. Werner has just been made an honorary *Serapionsbruder in absentia*:

> In jener schönen Zeit... mußte ich ihn für den gemütlichsten und liebenswürdigsten Menschen anerkennen, den es nur geben mag, und all die seltsamen fanatischen Schnörkel seiner äußeren Erscheinung, seines ganzen Wesens, die er selbst mit feiner Ironie mehr ins Licht zu stellen als zu verbergen suchte, trugen nur dazu bei, dass er in der verschiedensten Umgebung, unter den verschiedensten Bedingnissen, auf höchst anziehende Weise ergötzlich blieb. Dabei beseelte ihn ein tiefer, aus dem Innersten strömender Humor . . . ein göttlicher Spaß - ein fulminantes Witzwort schwebt auf den Lippen.[9]

Werner, who had a sophisticated, nonsense type of humour, and a strong power of "attrativa", apparently could always, even after their estrangement, make Goethe laugh.

It is striking, too, that Goethe did not, at that time, object to Werner's undisguised defence of the cross. Goethe, who called himself "der letzte Heide", paid Werner (and Christianity) the following ambiguous compliment: "Werner [ist] der erste und letzte Christ".[10] But in a less ironical vein he wrote to Jacobi:

> ...besonders hat Werner, der Sohn des Thals, den du ja auch kennst, uns durch sein Wesen, sowie durch seine Werke unterhalten und aufgeregt. Es kommt mir, einem alten Heiden, ganz wunderlich vor, das Kreuz auf meinen eignen Grund und Boden aufgepflanzt zu sehen, und Christi Blut und Wunden poetisch predigen zu hören, ohne daß es mir gerade zuwider ist. Wir sind dieses doch dem höheren Standpunct schuldig, auf den uns die Philosophie gehoben hat. Wir haben das Ideelle schätzen gelernt, es mag sich auch in den wunderlichsten Formen darstellen. (Letter to F.H. Jacobi, 11 January 1808; WA, iv, xx, 5)

Whatever may have been the tenor of the private conversations between Goethe and Werner - according to Goethe, religion was a constant topic - *Wanda* was the only play where the setting was incontrovertibly pre-christian. In the course of December, Werner read out *Wanda* again, then both parts of *Das Kreuz an der Ostsee* (on 7, 8 and 12 December, on this last occasion in the presence of Charlotte von Schiller); all these plays were then read aloud again at court when Goethe returned to Weimar with Werner at the end of the month. By the first week in January, Goethe had settled for *Wanda:*

> ... ob man gleich das Abstruse des Ganzen nicht billigen konnte, so fanden sich doch so schöne Stellen in einem untadelhaften, dramatischen Gange, daß man die Vorstellung des Stücks wohl beschließen konnte... [besonders da] auch der...hohe Geburtstag unserer verehrten Fürstin bis jetzt noch eines bedeutenden Feststücks ermangelte. (*Tag- und Jarhreshefte*; WA, i, xxxvi, 392)

The last two acts, unfinished but fully sketched in, were completed at lightning speed before Epiphany and no doubt in general consultation with Goethe as soon as he made the commission definite. "Die Zeit ging hin", says Goethe, "und man hatte genug zu thun, die zwei letzten Acte von Wanda seinem beweglichen Talent zu entreißen" (ibid.). On 10 January Goethe notes a lunch party followed by a *Leseprobe* with Werner and the two principal actors, Pius and Amalie Wolff.[11] By 19 January Goethe had extracted music for the choruses from Destouches; day by day the director and the author conducted rehearsals together. Werner had considerable experience of stage craft, both from his days as *Theaterintendant* in his native Königsberg, and from his close co-operation with Iffland in Berlin. On 23 January Goethe writes: "Diese Woche macht mir der Hof- und Leichenstaat unsrer sarmatischen Königin viele Noth; doch geht es ganz lustig dabey her und zuletzt kommt etwas Seltsames zur Erscheinung" (to Knebel; WA, iv, xx, 10), and again, "... je toller, je besser!" He considered *Wanda* less difficult to stage than *Die Jungfrau von Orleans* (WA, iv, xx, 14).

The final performance on 30 January, the actual birthday, was an unqualified success and two more followed on 3 and 15 February; the play was taken on tour and also repeated in Weimar in 1811 and 1812. Goethe's labour had not been wasted on an unworthy object; he considered the play "bretterrecht", not just written "für die unsichtbare Bühne", as he said of Kleist's plays. In later years Eckermann asked him "wie ein Stück beschaffen sein müsse, um theatralisch zu sein. 'Es muß symbolisch sein', antwortete Goethe. 'Das heißt: jede Handlung muß an sich bedeutend sein und auf eine noch wichtigere hinzielen'" (26 July 1826). *Wanda* satisfied Goethe's requirements in that it was "symbolical" in his sense, having a carefully structured chain of events, each pointing forward and cumulatively working up to a grand finale, an impressive opera-like tableau at the end. Werner had taken great pains, even before his contact with Goethe, to make this play "... kurz, opernhaft, unmystisch und beziehungslos" (*Briefe*, II, 101). In another letter he says :

> Es ist mit Gesangchören *kurz!* mit einfacher, klarer, fortschreitender Handlung, ohne Episoden, fast im Genre des bessern französischen Trauerspiels, und, da es in ganz heydnischer Zeit und unter Heyden spielt, auch nicht catholisch, noch weniger politisch und so wenig mystisch, daß kein einziger Heiland darin vorkommt! (to Tina, Gräfin Brühl, 27 January 1808; *Briefe*, II, 111).

a description from which it would be difficult to recognize what one imagines to be a "Romantic" drama. But these were precisely the qualities which commended it to Goethe, the coating which sugared the pill of "das Abstruse". Nevertheless, this element remained; there was no getting away from it.

The theme of the play is that love cannot be fulfilled except in death, which is the only true marriage. "Wanda stellt den Tod als Geburt zum Leben dar. Was soll diese nackte Idee in der unreifen Welt? Sie bedarf eines Schleyers, und das nennen sie Mystik", said J.D. Falk who reviewed the play for the periodical *Prometheus*.[12] Werner himself said that he was trying to describe "einen... wichtigen Lebensmoment der Liebe, nehmlich den: wie sie, freywillig sich zerstörend, sich verklärt" (*Prometheus*, II, 42). The play is set in the dark ages, the half mythical, half historical past of Poland, the Sarmaten being the original inhabitants of that land. The heroine is the unmarried warrior queen of her tribe, Wanda, the hero is a Prussian prince, Rüdiger, who has sailed down the Vistula from the Baltic islands to Cracow with the idea of marrying Wanda and annexing her country as his own. This is not mere empire building - he loves Wanda whom he had met some ten years previously at Libussa's court in Prague. He had won her love in return but never revealed his identity. At the beginning of the play Rüdiger swears to his men that he will win Wanda or else die; meanwhile Wanda, who thinks that her lover died long ago, vows to her people to remain unmarried for their sake. The tragic conflict is based on these two mutually exclusive vows, the situation coming to a head in Act III when Rüdiger says: "Ich halte was ich mir und dir geschworen!" and Wanda answers: "Ach, weil ich schwur, bin ich für dich - verloren!" (DLER, XX, 241). Their troops engage in battle, and after an inner struggle in which the lovers finally manage to integrate their vows into their personality and freely accept their tragic fate in model Schillerian fashion, Rüdiger prevails on Wanda to kill him. In the last act Wanda stages a marriage ceremony with death: at the moment of sunrise she runs through a sacrificial fire which has been kindled on the high rock of Krakus overlooking the river Vistula, and she casts herself down into the water. Out of this river of death - it is that throughout the play - there arises a "kolossale, durch den klaren Morgenhimmel strahlende Lilie", a Jakob Böhme symbol of resurrection and transfiguration.

The whole action only lasts "dritteinhalb Stunden", on the stage - two and a half hours, in the linguistic usage of the time - and is concentrated, within the play, to the space of an evening, then the following day and night, until sunrise. The five acts of the play divide the action into logically grouped units moving in a mounting crescendo towards this grand finale tableau. The first two acts match one another in a parallel exposition of the two main characters, their entourage, their respective vows; the third act describes their meeting, recognition and the clash of tragic opposition between them, Act IV brings the conflict to a head and ends with Rüdiger's death at Wanda's hand and her own inner destruction; the last act leads on from this apparently final crisis through the yet greater tension and mystery of Rüdiger's burial, on stage, to Wanda's own marriage with death.

There is no secondary action; the remaining characters are grouped round the two main ones. Wanda has her court and her high priest; her confidente is Ludmilla, a Czech peasant girl who looks after Wanda's garden and mourns for her dead lover, killed in battle. Rüdiger is accompanied by his knights and by

Balderon, a poet-minstrel. Linking the two main figures and a significant factor within the experience of each, is the spirit of Queen Libussa who stands for the harmony and mystical understanding of all things that the lovers will finally experience in death - and at the same time she points the way there, bridging the present world of suffering and the metaphysical realm beyond appearances. She warns, directs, explains, appearing on the stage enthroned on her lion-drawn carriage and heralded by thunder or soft woodwind music, as occasion demands. There is also a chorus. Blank verse alternates with three-foot trochaics, rhymed stanzas, alexandrines, free rhythms. Werner was a master of versification. An even rhythm, he thought, is only suitable for "die Ruhe des Epos", but it works

> ...schnurstracks entgegen... der wechselnden, thätigen, unruhevollen Gegenwart des Dramas... so scheint es nicht nur der Natur des Gegenstandes höchst angemessen, sondern auch der Schauspieler wegen nöthig, dem Drama ein *wechselndes* Metrum, d.h. jeder wechselnden Leidenschaft auch die ihr angemessene wechselnde *Form* zu geben. (Letter to Iffland, 15 June 1805; *Briefe*, I, 383)

One need hardly stress the appeal of all these features to the author of *Proserpina*, with its final tableau (WA, i, xl, 113 ff.), of *Pandora*, with its detailed staging effects, and later, of *Faust II*. It is perhaps legitimate to associate Werner's rhythmic expertise and his stimulating example not only with Goethe's sonnets but with the rhythmic experimentation evident in *Pandora*, the work of that "Advent von achtzehnhundertsieben".

A contemporary critic said of *Wanda*:

> Der opernartige Glanz dieses Stücks besticht, ja berauscht zugleich jedes Auge und jedes Ohr... vorüberziehend wie eine Welt von Schatten. (*Prometheus*, II, 12)

Werner knew all the places he was describing: the river banks at Cracow, the royal castle and its flower garden. Flowers, stars, the river of time and death, are the leading symbols of the play. Werner's explicit aim was to produce a "Gesamtkunstwerk" in the Romantic sense, appealing, to use Goethe's term, as an "Ensemble": to the emotions and the intellect by a conflict tragically solved, to the eye, by colour and striking gestures and plastic grouping effects, to the ear by the music of strings, flutes and hunting horns. The musical effect was enhanced throughout by carefully calculated variations in speech rhythm.

With *Wanda* as a whole, then, a well constructed drama on the French model, having operatic radiance, a brief, exciting action, no religion, precise characterization and good rhythms, Goethe found himself on familiar home ground, that is, in all except for "das Abstruse". This referred, presumably, to Werner's idea that love is perfected and thus transfigured by its freely willed self-destruction. This theory is explained by Libussa when she makes known to the lovers "des Lebens Zweck" (Act III; DLER, XX, 251-3). Human beings flow out from the primeval wholeness of the universe in a divided form, male and female, "Kraft und Zartheit"; in the course of this earthly life, they are destined to unite in wholeness again in a relationship of love with one specific, preordained partner, the *Urbild*, in order to flow back into the eternity of nature and love from which they came. The only gateway back into this wholeness is death which is therefore inextricably linked with love and with the torture of apparent separation by death. Man's function as a human being is to become fully aware of this mysterious pattern and its rhythm, and to make "...die Macht und Pracht der Qual, / Offenbar im Tränental" (p. 252), however terribly he may suffer in the process.[13]

The whole play is enacted in the shadow of death, the reality which dominated Werner's thinking and was so deeply fused with his theories of love. In the first act, Libussa prophesies to Rüdiger that he can only possess Wanda in death, not in life. She warns him not to pursue his enterprise: "Deine Sterne ziehen dem Abgrund zu!" In answer to his plea, "Gib mir Wanden!", she replies:

> . . . Es erblühn
> Liebesmyrten, wo die Sterne glühn;
> Nur im Tode wird das Leben kühn! -
> (DLER, XX, 217)

that is, love will not blossom till it reaches the other realm, that of the stars, and until the flowers of love, the bridal wreath of myrtle, which also makes up the *Totenkranz*, has changed into a star; there is no true life except in death. But Rüdiger ignores this prophecy and warning, and this is, in a sense, his tragic guilt: he is still full of confidence and the pride of life.

Whatever Goethe may have thought of what Werner later came to see as his "aus platonisch scholastischen Fetzen zusammengeflicktes Lumpensystem", its artistic and moral possibilities did not remain unexplored as a try-out model at the end of the *Wahlverwandtschaften,* nor did the theme of self-willed death, even martyrdom, in close association with love. The idea of death as an analogy of self-renunciation, especially in the sexual sphere, haunted all Werner's writing and thinking. If, in *Wanda*, the dramatic necessity for the lovers' death seems so classically motivated on a rational plane by their separate, conflicting vows, as to make death as a Romantic metaphor less conspicuous than in Werner's other plays, one is perhaps justified in seeing the *genius loci* of Weimar at work there. The death of Achilles and Penthesilea in that other play which Goethe spurned for the Weimar stage was not neatly motivated except at the more hidden, image level; it remained a blind and violent confusion of misunderstanding, Romantic by its very irrationalism and perhaps by this very fact more powerful as drama. Goethe could not place Kleist, as he could Werner, by assigning his apparently "Romantic" vagaries to any tangible category, such as false mysticism; but between Goethe and Werner there still seemed to be enough common ground for the latter to be judged and finally condemned on apparently rationally argued grounds. As drama, *Das Kreuz an der Ostsee*, especially the second part of it, now lost,[14] and also *Attila*, were undoubtedly finer than *Wanda*; but with their greater stress on the irrational, the daemonic and even the absurd, they were as totally inaccessible to Goethe as was, in its different way, *Penthesilea.*

After the success of *Wanda*, Goethe did, however, give serious consideration to the possibility of staging *Attila* and even *Weihe der Kraft*, getting as far as discussing the distribution of parts (*Tagebücher*, 5 and 10 February, and 2 March). By 21 March Werner had finished a stage version of *Das Kreuz an der Ostsee*, combining both parts into one play. In a sonnet,

"Kunstloseinfältige Bitte an Helios um Aufführung des... Kreuzes an der Ostsee am bevorstehenden Ostermondtage", Werner pleads with Goethe for the stage realization of "Was freudig er für Gott und Dich vollbracht".[15] He added an actual "Projekt zur Rollenbesetzung", also preserved in the archives. And in a last letter from Madame de Stäel's Coppet, before his departure for Italy the following year, Werner repeated his plea for the performance of this play after his death, should he not return from his travels (21 October 1809; SGG, XIV, 57). The intensity of his feeling for *Das Kreuz an der Ostsee* was not caused by an artist's vanity but by the poet-preacher's concern for the salvation of souls, according to his conception of the writer's function. In this drama, and also in *Attila*, theatrical expertise could not, as in *Wanda*, tone down "das Abstruse", here a nexus of mysticism, martyrdom, *agape* and *eros* in close Romantic juxtaposition, if not confusion; in fact, all that Goethe found most distasteful about the ideas of the younger generation. One might also say that in spite of his efforts, Werner, for his part, found himself unable to compromise sufficiently with Goethe's known desires for less emphasis on the "message", which, as far as he was concerned, quite simply *was* the play.

"Allein", said Goethe, revealing a misunderstanding that went deep, "es war ihm nicht gegeben, sich zusammenzufassen ..." (WA, i, xxxvi, 392). But it was not only a question of outward form, as Goethe continued to think:

> Unter allem diesen ward offenbar, daß er sich einer gewissen realistischen Ansicht, wodurch allein das Ideelle zur Erscheinung gebracht werden kann, nicht fügen, noch weniger dieselbe sich aneignen könne. (ibid., p. 393)

After Goethe's express statement in 1808 that he was not trying to change Werner and his plays, the use of the verb "sich fügen" is interesting; the gulf between this proselytizing Romantic son of the times and his well-intentioned but deeply pedagogic patron was too wide ever to be bridged: both men resisted conversion, yet each desired, in his own way, to convert. Goethe goes on to describe how he did his best to help Werner in every way:

> ... und ihn für den wahren aesthetischen Kreis zu gewinnen, allein vergebens, denn sein Beharren auf der eigenen Weise zeigte sich immer deutlicher, seine hartnäckigen Bemühungen, andere in seinen wunderbaren Zauberkreis hineinzuziehen, immer entschiedener... ohne daß von beiden Seiten irgend etwas wäre gewonnen worden. Wir schieden mit Wohlwollen von einander, unsererseits in Hoffnung ihn bei einem zweiten Besuche mehr der hiesigen Denk- und Bestrebensweise anzunähern, er aber gewiß im Stillen der Meinung, uns zu seiner Art und Weise zu bekehren. (ibid.)

Goethe, of course, sees the insoluble dilemma, and not without humour, but whereas *his* desire to convert Werner to the point of view of the establishment is unconsciously assumed to be legitimate, Werner's similar, though certainly more tactless aspirations, in view of his position as a petitioner, are seen as illegitimate and even furtive ("im Stillen").

Werner arrived at Weimar for his second visit just before Christmas in that same year, 1808, when intrigues against Goethe's manner of directing the theatre were at their most unpleasant. The situation was only saved by the tactful intervention of Herzogin Amalie herself who persuaded Goethe to carry on the work, but Goethe's sense of strain expressed itself in a general touchiness from which Werner was by no means exempt,[16] and by a renewed determination not to risk experiments, as in the previous year. Instead of *Cunegunde*, a martyr drama of a novel kind, which Goethe had commissioned from Werner and which he read aloud in Weimar early in January, Goethe put on the unexceptionable adaptation by Rochlitz of Sophocles's *Antigone* for the gala night of 30 January. Werner was, however, allowed to recite his poem, "Lied der heiligen drei Könige aus der Nibelungen Land",[17] a witty and laudatory comment on Weimar personalities in the Nibelungen strophe. Werner did not improve his position with Goethe when, towards the end of March, he moved to the house of the actress Caroline Jagemann, who led the anti-Goethe faction in the theatre and was Karl August's mistress. The move took place at the duke's suggestion, and it is probable that Werner was a mere pawn in the struggle, but certainly an innocent one; the truth was that lodgings at the "Schwan" were costly, that Werner was poor and that he could not afford to spurn a suggestion coming from Karl August, who in fact remained his benefactor for life.

Before this move, Werner had written at Goethe's suggestion and at speed (27 February to 10 March) a short "Schweizer Tragödie", *Der vierundzwanzigste Februar*, to illustrate "die Folgen des Fluchs", and to which Goethe himself apparently intended to write a "Nachstück" showing "die Folgen des Segens" (SGG, XIV, 320). It is probable, though this has not been pointed out in connection with Werner's work, that the idea of a modern fate tragedy preoccupying both Goethe and Werner at that time was the immediate result of the production of the *Antigone* in January; the newspaper story of the *Mordeltern* was merely a further stimulus to treat anew "die Triebfeder der griechischen Tragödie: den Fluch" (*Briefe*, II, 196). The play, of course, as has by now been sufficiently stressed, is not about fate at all, or else it is about the idea of fate in modern dress; it concerns the effect of a belief in fate, that is, the effect of superstition on character, and the possibility of redemption from this evil by faith. The tragedy, to use Kluckhohn's term, is an "Erlösungsdrama", and not a "Schicksalsdrama".

Werner, as is evident from this play and many letters, had an absorbed interest in the whole religious and ethical thought-complex, "fate-superstition-character", and so, of course, did Goethe, whose *Wahlverwandtschaften* was first mentioned in his *Tagebücher* on 16 April that year, and was already in print by October. "Der Aberglaube", he said to Riemer, "ist die Poesie des Lebens"; the poet is fully justified in the imaginative use of superstition, "da er ihm, wie jeder anderen Phantasie, blos mentale Giltigkeit verleiht".[18] This is the way in which Werner gave "mentale Giltigkeit" to the idea of fate in his tragedy. Goethe goes on:

> Mir erscheint es als eine unsichtbare Intervention, als das Dazwischentreten einer gleichsam gespenstisch wirkenden Macht, die den freien, natürlichen Decurs des menschlichen Wollens hemmt, es von seinem beabsichtigten Ziele ablenkt und dennoch wie ein Correctiv zu einem andern nützlichen oder nöthigen hinführt.

In the Greek fate drama, Antigone considers her own and her brother's tragic fate to be the direct result of the curse laid upon her father, Oedipus; she knew for certain that there could be no release from this curse except in death, and that all she could do was to accept and to suffer. Her belief was valid within the Greek context. In Werner's play, the Swiss innkeeper, Kunz, merely *believes* that all his material misfortunes and also his young son's inadvertent killing of his sister, resulted from the curse laid upon him by his own cruel father. The focus of his superstitious belief is the seemingly fateful date on which terrible things happen, and also the knife, the instrument of terror, with which he finally murders, on the stage, the stranger who turns out to be his own son. Kunz allows himself to be hypnotized by the idea of fatality after freely consenting to its influence in order to do evil. Madame de Stäel said of Werner's play which had its first private production at Coppet:

> La fatalité des Anciens est un caprice du destin; mais la fatalité dans le christianisme, est une vérité morale sous une forme effrayante. . . la conscience repoussée se change en un fantôme qui trouble la raison. (*De l'Allemagne*, Part 2, ch. 24)

As these horrible events occur within a Christian context, the son Kurt, guilty of hubris in his own way but at the same time a believer who forgives his murderer with his dying breath, can be the means of laying what his father can only see as an unredeemable curse. But what he sees as fate is, in fact, almost entirely the outcome of his own character failings. The son can - and does - redeem both his parents and himself from the remnants of a false superstition which is at variance with a Christian belief in God's providence, a mere projection of an inward failure of character and lack of true faith.

In the same way as the sea and the hills form the living background of the *Antigone* through the descriptions by the chorus and the messenger, so in Werner's tragedy the icy solitude of the mountains dominates the consciousness of the three people, father, mother, son, whose tragedy is played out in a frozen, timeless realm: "La description des Alpes est de la plus grande beauté; . . . on se demande pourquoi du temps dans ce lieu; pourquoi la division des heures . . . " (Mme de Stäel). The idea of the play is underlined throughout, and especially at the end, by the contrast made between man's time and God's timelessness. At the moment of understanding, and before the father walks out of the house to give himself up for murder, he says, referring to the "fateful" date which he has never stopped talking about: "*Ein* Tag ist's ! - Gottes Gnad ist ewig! Amen! - " (my italics). He has already moved into another time dimension, the eternal present of the realm of faith, where earthly dates and days and hours - the clock in the solitary house is continually emphasized, as is, of course, the date of the title - cease to have any significance.[19]

Although Goethe refused to stage the play during the difficult months while Werner was still in Weimar - on 28 April he wrote to him: "Wir dürfen uns nicht leugnen, daß die Aufführung des Stücks einige Gefahr hat. Deswegen lassen Sie mich so lange zaudern, bis ich mit Muth und Überzeugung daran gehen kann . . ." (SGG, xiv, 38) - he believed in its oustanding quality as drama and devoted much care to its presentation "an seinem Tage" in 1810. In his *Tag- und Jahreshefte* he says that it was "vollends ein Triumph vollkommener Darstellung. Das Schreckliche des Stoffs verschwand vor der Reinheit und Sicherheit der Ausführung; dem aufmerksamsten Kenner blieb nichts zu wünschen übrig" (WA, i, xxxvi, 58). To guard still more against the impression of horror - the murder was actually on stage, rendered more vivid by the division of the stage into two rooms where the murderer and his victim could be seen in their separate spheres at the moment of highest tension - Goethe put his own Singspiel, *Jery und Bätely,* first on the bill.[20] By this juxtaposition of his own light and cheerful Swiss love story with the terror and gloom of Werner's alpine tragedy, Goethe was, in a sense, making a nice commentary on the latter. He was also, though with a work written earlier (1799), fulfilling his part of the literary bargain. He was showing the happy "Folgen des Segens", as it were, in the reluctant Bätely's acceptance of her lover when she suddenly realizes his sterling qualities at a moment of danger and her own real love of him. At the end Bätely and Jery kneel to ask her father's blessing on their union, and the father says: "Nehmet den Segen", whereupon all three sing in chorus: "Segen und Glück" (*Werke*, VIII, 64-5). After this introductory piece of his own to mitigate the coming horror, Goethe was immensely satisfied with the performance of

Werner's play and really felt that he had achieved something like a Greek tragedy on the modern stage. To quote the actor Genast:

> Goethe kam, was höchst selten geschah, nach der Aufführung auf die Bühne, um den Darstellern seine Zufriedenheit persönlich auszusprechen. Seine Züge drückten ein stolzes Bewußtsein aus, als er sagte: "Nun sind wir da angekommen, wohin ich Euch haben wollte; Natur und Kunst sind jetzt auf das Engste verbunden".[21]

The final formula, "Natur und Kunst", went for the play as well as the acting; it sounds reassuringly familiar, having an aura of the eighteenth century and of Lessing, but hardly of revolutionary Romantic tenets. Werner's tragedy was, in fact, one of which Goethe could fully approve because, again, in its own way, it might perhaps be described as only peripherally "Romantic". True, its mood was Romantic, it was lyrical as well as dramatic in inspiration, it had extraordinarily skilful metrical forms, and it was, after all, an "Erlösungsdrama". That is, it looks like one now, but this original version of the play, of which Goethe had "eine Copie sowie die ausgeschriebenen Rollen" (his letter to Werner of 28 April 1809), no longer exists. It may have been somewhat different from the only version we now have, that first printed by Werner in 1814.[22] After his conversion he is known to have made additions, as for instance the motto, "Führe uns nicht in Versuchung", and the long "Prolog an deutsche Söhne und Töchter" (Reclam, pp. 5-10) which is heavily loaded in the Christian direction.

> Eisernes Schicksal nannten es die Heiden;
> Allein seitdem hat Christus aufgeschlossen
> Der Höllen Eisentor den Kampfgenossen,
> So schafft das Schicksal weder Lust noch Leiden
> Den Weisen . . . (p. 7)

> . . .die alte Kunde
> Vom Fluch, gottlob, ist uns ein Märlein worden;
> Ein Kind, ein Christenkind, kann drüber spotten...
> (p. 8)

There may well have been other slight shifts of emphasis in

the same direction within the actual body of the play, once the eye of "Helios" was no longer on Werner. This, however, is a matter for conjecture only.

The fact remains that Goethe's compromise with the times, as represented by this particular "Sohn der Zeit", was after all more apparent than real, and looking back in later years, he seems to have rued it, that is, if the following reflection, probably made with his initial enthusiasm for Werner and others in mind, is any guide: "Leichtsinnige leidenschaftliche Begünstigung problematischer Talente war ein Fehler meiner früheren Jahre, den ich niemals ganz ablegen konnte" (1823, *Maximen und Reflexionen*). Perhaps Goethe's basic unwillingness to enter into "Was unsre Zeit und was ihr Geist verlangt", in spite of his conscious preparedness to do so, and his unconscious involvement in certain respects, is proved by the selection he made among Werner's plays: he chose *Wanda* and *Der vierundzwanzigste Februar* but refused to have anything to do with *Das Kreuz an der Ostsee* and *Attila*, both more truly representative of what he himself had called Werner's "wunderbaren Zauberkreis".

[1] This is the first of two papers dealing with the relationship between Goethe and a notorious Romantic. The present inquiry centres on Goethe's attitude to Werner and his plays, the second, "A Romantic reaction to *Die Wahlverwandtschaften*. Zacharias Werner and Goethe", *Literaturwissenschaftliches Jahrbuch*, Neue Folge, Vol. XI, 1970, considers how Werner reacted to Goethe's works, expecially to the novel written while Werner was the Romantic on Goethe's own doorstep in Weimar. What has interested me throughout is the interaction of two conflicting points of view which are, however, in some ways paradoxically cognate to one another.

[2] "Prolog bei der Eröffnung der Darstellungen des Weimarischen Hoftheaters in Leipzig. Den 24. Mai 1807, gesprochen von Madame Wolff"; JA, IX, 282.

[3] For letters exchanged between Goethe and Werner, see *Goethe und die Romantik*. Briefe mit Erläuterungen, ed. by Carl Schüddekopf and Oskar Walzel, *Schriften der Goethe Gesellschaft*, XIII and XIV, Weimar, 1899. Vol. XIV, pp. 1-66 and notes, pp. 305-27, contains much additional information, some of it from the Weimar archives (abbr. SGG, XIV). Goethe's letters and diaries will be quoted from the Weimar Ausgabe (WA), the works from the Jubiläums Ausgabe (JA).

Werner's letters are quoted from *Briefe des Dichters Friedrich Ludwig Zacharias Werner*, ed. by Oswald Floeck, 2 vols., Munich, 1914-18, and the same editor's *Die Tagebücher*, Bibliothek des literarischen Vereins, Stuttgart, Vols 289 and 290, Leipzig, 1939-40 (abbr. *Briefe*). For a modern edition of *Wanda, Königin der Sarmaten* and *Das Kreuz an der Ostsee*, see *Dramen von Zacharias Werner*, ed. by Paul Kluckhohn, Deutsche Literatur in Entwicklungsreihen, Reihe Romantik, Vol. 20, Darmstadt, 1964 (abbr. DLER, XX).

The relationship between Werner and Goethe has never been studied in any detail except in a dissertation by Trude Undesser, *Goethe und Zacharias Werner*, Unpubl. Diss., Vienna, 1944, who does not deal specifically with the plays concerned. More relevant comments from the point of view of Werner can be found in: *Das dramatische Werk Zacharias Werners*, Gerard Kosielek, Wroclaw, 1967; and from Goethe's angle in: *Pandora - zu Goethes Metaphorik*, Gottfried Diener, Frankfurter Beiträge zur Germanistik, vol. 5, Bad Homburg, Berlin, Zürich, 1968, esp. p. 38 ff. Swana L. Hardy, in her dissertation, *Goethe, Calderón und die romantische Theorie des Dramas*, Heidelberger Forschungen, Heft 10, Heidelberg, 1965, pp. 49-52, has missed an opportunity of considerable importance by her superficial coverage of Werner. Gretl Carow, *Zacharias Werner und das Theater seiner Zeit*, Theater und Drama, vol. 3, Berlin, 1933, gives illuminating details about contemporary methods of staging at Weimar.

[4] *Schiller und die Romantik*, Briefe und Dokumente, ed. by H. H. Borcherdt, Stuttgart, 1948, pp. 105-9 and also p. 641 and p. 645.

[5] See "Goethe and the Theatre" by W. H. Bruford in *Essays on Goethe*, ed. by William Rose, London, 1949, pp. 76-95.

[6] *Zacharias Werners Sämmtliche Werke*, 13 vols, Grimma, n.d. [I840]; I, 147-8 (abbr. *Werke*).

[7] It is interesting that Goethe did not himself publish the above passages of direct self-revelation in the main body of his work; they appeared later in the "Lesearten" of the Weimar Ausgabe as "Paralipomena für 1807-8". These passages, apparently at first discarded, contain Goethe's longest and most revealing account of Werner.

[8] See Gottfried Diener, op. cit., pp. 31-47, "Begriff der 'Epoche'", for the connotation of this word in Goethe's usage at this time.

[9] *Die Serapionsbrüder*, Sämmtliche Werke, Serapionsausgabe, Berlin and Leipzig, 1922, XIV, 111-12.

[10] Biedermann, *Gespräche*, Leipzig, 1911, V, 72.

[11] Pius and Amalie Wolff, a husband and wife team, were Goethe's special protegés. Amalie was the daughter of the Weimar actor, Malcomi; it was she who took the part of Johanna at the first performance of *Die Jungfrau von Orleans* in 1803. In later years, after the Wolffs had moved to Berlin in 1816, one of her most distinguished performances was that of Sappho in Grillparzer's play (1819) which has a number of striking analogies with *Wanda* (see *Grillparzer und Zacharias Werner*, by Harald Görtz, Unpubl. Diss., Vienna, 1947). For portraits of Pius and Amalie Wolff see *Theatergeschichte der Goethezeit* by Heinz Kindermann, Vienna, 1948, p. 592, plate 49 (Amalie as Johanna) and p. 614.

[12] *Prometheus. Eine Zeitschrift*, ed. by Leo von Seckendorf and Joseph Ludwig Stoll, Vienna, 1808, Heft 2, p. 31. The first number contained Goethe's *Pandora*, the second, "Sonette eines Reisenden", pp. 29-34, by Werner, and an essay known to be by Werner but published anonymously on Goethe's advice, "Über die Tendenz der Wernerschen Schriften", pp. 35-50. Excerpts from the play, similar in scope to Kleist's "Organisches Fragment" of *Penthesilea*, *Phöbus*, January, 1808, appeared in Cotta's *Morgenblatt für gebildete Stände*, 6 February 1808, pp. 126-8. A later number of this periodical, 23 February, p. 181 f., had a perceptive and laudatory review of *Wanda* which, on internal evidence, I consider to be Werner's own work. The same applies to the attractive essay, "Wandas Grab", a "Stimmungsbild" of the Polish landscape that Werner loved,

Morgenblatt, 16 March 1808, pp. 257-8, signed by the pseudonym "Dr Usener". Useful information about *Wanda* and its sources can be found in *Das dramatische Werk Zacharias Werners* by Gerard Kosielek, ed. cit., pp. 228-52, though Franz Stuckert, *Das Drama Zacharias Werners*, Frankfurt am Main, 1926, pp. 107-20, still provides the best analysis of the play. See too *Das Prinzip von Form und Sinn im Drama Zacharias Werners*, by Herbert Greyer, Breslau, 1933, especially pp. 57-62.

[13] Paul Kluckhohn, *Die Auffassung der Liebe im 18. Jahrhundert und in der Romantik*, Halle, 1931, pp. 592 ff., gives a full explanation of Werner's theories. - The alternative sonnet which Werner supplied instead of Libussa's original poem is a far better vehicle of thought. In its very structure it reflects the sharp dichotomy of the human condition (according to Werner), followed by resolution and synthesis. In his last letter to Goethe, Werner calls this theory "Eine alberne Mystik, ein verrücktes aus platonisch scholastischen. . . Fetzen zusammengeflicktes Lumpensystem, das ich auf nichts als leere Träume begründet, mit dem Nahmen eines Systems der Liebe ! (von der ich eigentlich so wenig verstand) taufte . . . " (23 April 1811, from Rome; SGG, XIV, 63).

[14] For a full account, see *Geschichte und Mythos in Zacharias Werners Drama, "Das Kreuz an der Ostsee"*, Diss., Göttingen, 1960, by Birgit Heinemann, and the same author's article "Ein Fragment des Dramas, *Der Ostermorgen* von Zacharias Werner", *Jahrbuch des freien deutschen Hochstifts*, Tübingen, 1962, pp. 409-21. E.T.A. Hoffmann wrote an account of this lost play (DLER, XX, 275-7) and music for the overture and choruses of *Das Kreuz an der Ostsee.*

[15] SGG, XIV, 309 f., from the MS. in the *Goethe-Schiller Archiv* in Weimar.

[16] Goethe's mood at this moment is well reflected in the unhappy, bewildered expression evident in the portrait Kügelgen painted of him at this time. See *Goethes äußere Erscheinung*, by Emil Schaeffer, Leipzig, 1914, plate 42 and p. 60. Goethe notes in his *Tagebücher* (WA, iii, III, 406) that he invited Werner to lunch with Arnim and Kügelgen on 22 December. - For an account of the notorious incident at lunch on 31 December, when Werner roused Goethe's wrath by a comparison, in one of his sonnets, of the moon with the elevated communion host, see H. Steffens, *Was ich erlebte*, 6, p. 265, "...'Sie haben mir meine Mahlzeit verdorben' sagte er [Goethe] ernsthaft".

[17] *Werke*, I, 182.

18 *Mitteilungen über Goethe*, Berlin, 1841, I, 110 ff.

[19] For a full bibliography and a good commentary on the play as a whole, see Johannes Krogoll's edition in Reclam's Universalbibliothek, Stuttgart, 1967. The following articles, to both of which I am indebted, are additions to the bibliography in the Reclam edition: Lee B. Jennings, "The Freezing Flame. Zacharias Werner and the Twenty-Fourth of February", *Symposium*, XX (1966), 24-42, a perceptive analysis, especially of the images, and Heinz Moenkemeyer's "The Son's Fatal Homecoming in Werner and Camus", *MLQ*, XXVII (1966), 51-67, a convincing juxtaposition of analogies and differences. - Mr Jennings points out that the murder, in fact, takes place after midnight, that is, on 25 February, according to the earthly time dimension; the idea of fateful repetition thus finally breaks down in any case. It would, I believe, have been in character for Werner to have consciously intended this ultimate piece of irony as a silent witness to the point he was trying to make. In the same way he probably also intended the spectator to think about the significance of the number "24" in the title: there are twenty-four hours in what we, here on earth, call a day - but what is our day in the light of God's eternity?

[20] See the text of the "Theaterzettel" given by G. Carrow, op. cit., p. 128 - Werner's name was not given, in accordance with the usual Weimar practice for first performances (though an exception seems to have been made for *Wanda*), the identity of the son, Kurt, was not revealed, so as not to give away the plot. This part was played by Wolff; Amalie Wolff took the part of the mother. Although the bill bears the information: "Zum Erstenmahle", the play was actually first performed on the private stage at Mme de Stäel's house, Coppet, on 13 October 1809; cf. Werner's description of this in a letter to Goethe, 20 October, SGG, XIV, 51-8. Werner himself acted the son's part and A. W. Schlegel the father. Benjamin Constant and Mme de Stäel prevailed on Werner to add about fifty lines to strengthen the psychological likelihood and motivation of the murder. In December of the same year, Werner read the play aloud to the German colony in Rome at the salon of Frau von Humboldt where he was a well-liked guest.

[21] Quoted by Heinz Kindermann, *Theatergeschichte der Goethezeit*, Vienna, 1948, p. 682, from the memoirs of the actor, Eduard Genast.

[22] *Urania. Taschenbuch für Damen auf das Jahr 1815*. Leipzig [1814], pp. 305-84. It is not known, either, whether Goethe accepted the fifty extra lines added at Coppet but in view of their traditional function as motivation, it seems likely; the MS. no longer exists (SGG, XIV, 322). It is certain that Werner revised the work again for its publication in 1814, for it appeared, according to the publisher, "mit den neuesten Verbesserungen", cf. Krogoll's Reclam edition of the play, "Nachwort", p. 92.

Brentano's *O Stern und Blume:* its Poetic and Emblematic Context

Eichendorff described Clemens Brentano (1778-1842) as being at the same time "einer der reichstbegabten deutschen Dichter" and "ein schlechthin unerklärlicher Proteus, ein innerer Widerspruch", whose greatest problem as an artist was "geistiger Überschuß".[1] His apparently simple but in fact highly complex work, only about half of which has as yet been published,[2] is so diverse in scope, so densely allusive, so closely interrelated, that it is hardly possible to treat even a single poem in isolation. One cannot afford to ignore his earlier poetry when dealing with the later, nor yet neglect the man behind the poet: in Brentano's case, critical generalizations based on aesthetic criteria alone are often fallacious. One also needs to follow out a complex variety of aspects in different but related art fields if oversimplification, even plain error, is to be avoided. The most fruitful inquiries into Brentano's work all show the need for this total kind of approach even when dealing with what may at first appear to be a circumscribed problem : an essay soon assumes the aspect of a monograph. There is, for instance, Emil Staiger's comprehensive analysis of "Auf dem Rhein" and Wilhelm Fraenger's of "Alhambra", both relatively short poems; Wolfgang Frühwald surveys the few pages of the mystifying dedication of the revised "Gockelmärchen" to Marianne von Willemer, while Hans Magnus Enzensberger traces the genesis of a few poems among many hundreds by which to reveal Brentano's poetical method over a life time. In each of these works a limited point of entry has necessarily widened out into a survey of considerable scope and coverage.[3]

When considered in isolation, or even in one only of their various settings, the two most famous lines that Brentano wrote, and which have come to be regarded as his device,

O Stern, und Blume, Geist und Kleid,
Lieb, Leid und Zeit und Ewigkeit

must remain enigmatic. One can, however, examine them in a rather wider context than has as yet been envisaged and this will, perhaps, help to solve the riddle they still seem to present.

Brentano's couplet appears in facsimile under the engraved frontispiece portrait of him by Emilie Linder in the first volume of his posthumously edited *Gesammelte Schriften* (1852), and one may take it that it was chosen for this prominent position because it was thought to represent, in some way, the essential Brentano. The couplet makes its first appearance in his work as the refrain of a poem addressed to Emilie, "20 Jenner [1835] nach großem Leid". Then, as a kind of leitmotif it winds its way through the latter part of the revised "Gockelmärchen" and its conclusion, "Aus dem Tagebuch der Ahnfrau", where it makes its last appearance as the climax of the poem which ends the whole work. It also features centrally in the last of the fourteen lithographs which Brentano designed for the illustration of this work.[4] These lines have constantly been quoted in connexion with Brentano and, as an isolated entity, they have more recently been the object of a special kind of mystique on the part of critics. In the past it was assumed that this couplet, admittedly "meaningless" as it stands, not only had numinous quality as poetry but also corresponded to a specific, though hidden meaning on a conceptual level. It was taken to be an example of what Gundolf in a similar context called Brentano's "Wortsymbolik".[5] Now it is more commmonly held that its poetical quality resides in its ambiguity alone, in "dem Schwankenden und Ungewissen", in its "inständige Rätselgestalt" as a "bündige Chiffre"; any attempt to decode it and give it a rational equivalent explanation destroys it as poetry. A procedure of this kind, it is argued, "greift nur eine von unendlich vielen Möglichkeiten heraus" and thus limits the possibility of a valid poetic response to this magical poetic formula.[6] This opinion is based, in part, on a view of Brentano as a forerunner of modern lyrical tendencies, a view which has cast much light on his earlier lyrics but must be applied with discrimination, more especially to the later ones. In part, however, this opinion has also been supported by something which Brentano's fictional character, the "Ahnfrau", herself says about the couplet when she first hears it. But this supporting quotation has been used without reference to its total context and to the specific situation of the fictional character concerned. Brentano's Ahnfrau - not, as anyone unfamiliar with the story might suppose, some gruesome ghost à la Grillparzer, but simply a young girl of medieval times - recalls the words as she first heard them after awaking from a striking dream:

> In meinem Schlafgemach hörte ich immer jene Worte noch um mich tönen. Ich verstand sie durch und durch und konnte sie doch nicht erklären. Ich verstand ihr Wesen und hatte keine Worte für sie als sie selbst.
>
> (III, 857)[7]

Taken in isolation, this can, of course, be seen as a most apt description of the nature of poetry and of its effect, of the relationship existing between the mode of operation of poetry and the rational content of the words which are its vehicle. But the significance of the girl's actions immediately preceding and following these reactions, and of the dream itself has then been ignored. This is the vital context if her reaction is to be rightly understood and if the riddle couplet itself is to be seen as something more than a poetical joker-card produced whenever the story seems to require an atmosphere of vague poetical incantation. In a quarter where one would hardly expect critical oversimplification of this kind, Brentano himself has been identified with his character, Amey, regardless of her imaginary situation; the girl's words are taken to be the poet's own personal definition and therefore as a proof that his couplet cannot have a rational correlative.

It is, of course, perfectly true that in his early lyrics some of Brentano's refrains and melodic repetitions in the folksong mode or in his own idiom do not make sense. Walther Killy has, for instance, analysed a poem from *Godwi*, "Sprich aus der Ferne / Heimliche Welt, / Die sich so gerne / Zu mir gesellt", with this idea in mind. But he is not entirely convincing, and one cannot, in any case, generalize about Brentano as a whole from such instances.[8] He rarely used poetical jingles of this kind in his later verse, and even earlier on, his use of them seems to me conscious and contrived: if it is nonsense, it is, as it were, meaningful nonsense, not just a mindless musical meandering, as is so often the case with Tieck. Staiger's idea that language is in control of Brentano, not he of language, now seems rather suspect: Brentano was always a highly conscious, formally precise artist. His greatest desire, admittedly, was to be less conscious, to be carried away mindlessly on the wave of emotion - but he rarely was. In this, as in other ways, such as the at times overwhelming piling up of verbal conceits, his affinity was to the baroque with its riddle sonnets and puzzle poetry, and not to what is popularly conceived of as the German romantic style: Brentano's wit was essentially Latin.

It is the object of the present essay to suggest that poetic ambiguity and precise conceptual meaning and intention, far from being mutually exclusive in Brentano's case, can and do exist side by side, more especially in his later poetry; this juxtaposition constitutes the form of Brentano's thinking and is an essential feature of his artistic work. Encoding and mystification, that is, consciousiy intended poetic enigmas, were part of his technique at all times, more particularly in the poems, letters and stories of his last Munich years: he was torn between an almost compulsive desire to communicate intensely personal experience but at the same time to hide it from all except the initiated for whom it was primarily meant. He felt that the mystery of the poetical cypher was the nearest approach to truth and his only possible response to the false immediacy of a materialistic civilization. The mystification tendency is at work throughout his last story, beginning with the complex dedication, actually a non-dedication, to Marianne von Willemer, "Keiner Puppe, sondern nur / Einer schönen Kunstfigur", and culminating in the last lithograph and the final refrain, "O Stern und Blume".[9] Denying meaning to Brentano's poetical productions, and especially to this "Wahlspruch", at the expense of aura or musical magic, impoverishes his art by a whole important dimension.

Brentano's use of this couplet is complex and he gives it a varying function: it can be the chorus-like refrain of a poem, as in "20. Jenner [1835] nach großem Leid", an isolated invocation, almost a prayer, as in the leitmotif use of it in the "Gockelmärchen" as a whole, and finally it can function as an integral part of the meaning of a poem, as in the dream poem at the end of the "Märchen", "Alle patschten in die Hände", in the last verse of "Es ist ein Schnitter, der heißt Tod", and in "Was reif in diesen Zeilen steht" at the end of the "Tagebuch".[10] Both these poems and the couplet are illustrated in the final lithograph as in an emblem, a picture conditioned by Philipp Otto Runge's ideas and to some extent also by baroque pictorial models. The only way to achieve some sort of clarity about the couplet is to look at the way it is used in at any rate some of these poetical contexts and also in the lithograph with its emblem and Runge background. An analysis of the final poem together with the discussion of a water-colour by Edward von Steinle will conclude the inquiry.

It is a well attested opinion that the couplet first took shape in connexion with a dream of Emilie Linder's which Brentano, an eager amateur analyst of the unconscious, described and interpreted for her in the poem "20. Jenner [1835] nach großem Leid".[11] Emilie's dream itself does not go beyond the opening antithesis, "Stern und Blume", an image familiar to Brentano himself and to romantic thinking as a whole in the wake of Calderón. The imagery of Zacharias Werner's *Wanda, Königin der Sarmaten*, for instance, centres on this antithesis, which represents the extremity of tension between the metaphysical and the vegetative spheres. Goethe uses it at the end of the *Wahlverwandtschaften*, and *Stern und Blume* is also, as it happens, the title of a recent study of Hölderlin.[12] Each of the eighteen verses of Brentano's poem ends with the couplet as a refrain. The "suffering" of the title is Emilie's and would seem to be a spiritual and emotional difficulty. An orphan child, mute with grief is standing in her flower garden at sunset when the stars begin to appear; because they ask no questions, she can commune with flowers and stars in a wordless language (verses 2-4). As the shadows deepen, she falls asleep and dreams, while the poet, seeing her as another of the flowers all around her, asks angels to protect and bless her sleep (verses 6-7). All colours fade in the darkness of night and dream until an angel shows the child a group of radiant white lilies underneath a lime tree (verses 8-9). In terms of a star-like light coming down from heaven upon one of the lilies growing among thorns, the angel tells the dreamer the story of the Annunciation and of the Word made flesh (verses 10-13):

Der Engel sprach: mein Kind, o sehe,
Die Lilie unter Dornen dort,
Das Licht wird Fleisch, horch: "Es geschehe
Der Magd des Herrn nach deinem Wort!"
    O Stern und Blume, Geist und Kleid,
Lieb, Leid, und Zeit und Ewigkeit.

Die Lilie spinnt nicht, doch es webt
Aus ihr das Wort sich einen Leib,
Zur Jungfrau ist das Licht geschwebet,
Und Mutter Gottes ward das Weib.
    O Stern und Blume, Geist und Kleid,
Lieb, Leid und Zeit und Ewigkeit.
(I, 603)

The angel leads the child right up to this lily, she kneels, but as she herself can find no words for the prayer she longs to say, the lily speaks, calling her by name: Mary invites her to join in her Magnificat, to "awake" to her in the sense of believing in her (verses 14-15). The poet cannot tell whether, in her dream, Emilie then actually did join in the Magnificat, but certainly she gave him some sign of assent: "Sie hat mich träumend angeblickt". This seemed to indicate that she had to some extent yielded her independent, coldly conceptual religious position: "Das kalte Wissen war ermattet, / Das milde Fühlen war erwacht", (16-17). The final verse, like the opening one, is a kind of envoi.

The narrative content of the poem proceeds in the quatrains while the refrain, typographically distinct from the rest of each verse by a full stop and also by reason of the rhyme, acts as an insistent chorus reinforcing the significance of the dream story as it gradually unfolds. It would seem, therefore, that the chorus must contain, in this juxtaposition of antithetical and apparently a-logical terms, some meaning fully known to both the poet and the dreamer of the dream. It is also legitimate to assume that this haunting no-statement is meant to act as an incantation in the poetical sense, along with its meaning: it is to support "das milde

Fühlen" as against "das kalte Wissen". All this fits in with the known background facts: Brentano was devoting his total persuasive powers to the conversion of Emilie Linder, whether by poem, story, letter or picture. On her conversion depended the possibility of a marriage between them, for neither could envisage marriage on any other terms. But Emilie reacted to this barrage of suggestion by postponing her conversion until after Brentano's death. In the meanwhile Brentano busied himself giving artistic shape to her fantasies, writing them up and drawing them, slanting them according to his ideas of what she ought to want, and very probably did somehow want. He added his own fantasies to hers, hoping all the time to influence her attitudes at a level deeper than that of intellectual argument, a manoeuvre which had every chance of success with Emilie who was herself an artist responsive to symbols.[13]

In the present instance, her dream of the lily flooded with starlight was turned into a tableau of the Annunciation. It was an idea in the Nazarene idiom which, to judge by Emilie's own paintings, may well have been her own personal dream association. Brentano wanted to follow up this promising dream insight by stressing to the waking Emilie the important role of the Immaculate Virgin Mary in the general plan of the Redemption and thus in Catholic doctrine, a point on which a Swiss Calvinist, even a wavering one, might well need some persuasion. "Alhambra", too, an earlier poem revised for Emilie, is designed to show her a way back to the lost paradise of spiritual childhood and simplicity which no realm of art and imagination - that is, no Alhambra, can replace. Here too it is Mary who shows the way back, this time on the back of Joseph's donkey and holding the Christchild, described here as "das Ewige der Zeit" (I, 585). "20. Jenner" is not of the same high artistic quality as "Alhambra", but both represent special pleading in artistic form and therefore carry specific argument and meaning; it would be quite out of keeping for the chorus-refrain alone to be of the nature of sound without sense. Enzensberger, starting from the conviction that the refrain has no meaning but only a wide-spread ancestry of associations, ignores the punctuation of the poem and cannot see the clear progression of the narrative describing the stages of the dream. He thinks that star, dream, the poem itself, angel and lily "nacheinander unterschiedslos" repeat the refrain which is thus "bis zur Sinnlosigkeit entleert" (p.92). In the poem as a whole he sees nothing more than a meaningless juxtaposition of Brentano's leading "Bildkomplexe": "In sich selbst schon mehrdeutig, treten sie hier zu einem einzigen unübersehbaren Riesen-Komplex zusammen, der als Chiffre gar keinen Wert mehr haben kann, weil innerhalb des Ganzen jedes Element beliebig seine Stelle wechselt" p. 93. Tracing out "Bildkomplexe" as isolated units divorced from their logical context can be an illuminating critical exercise, and can lead to enlightening discoveries, as is evident from some of Enzensberger's analyses ; but it does not, as he of course realizes, "explain" a poem or do justice to its actual form. Enzensberger's procedure can, however, and in this case definitely does, lead to a failure to see the wood for trees.

In Emilie's star-flowered antithesis turned into an allegory, Brentano first paired "Stern und Blume" with "Geist und Kleid" through a chain of scriptural associations developed in the poem as a whole : the spirit takes on the garment, "Kleid", of a human body woven from the substance of the flower joined by the star, the lily which does not itself toil or spin but consents to receive the creative light from above. Brentano then for the first time, it would seem, added the further sequence of opposites in assonance: love and suffering, time and eternity. They were already present by implication in this first poem through the basic mystery of the Incarnation of Christ ("das Ewige der Zeit" of "Alhambra"), and of its inextricable mingling of love and suffering ("die Lilie unter Dornen"). At the same time, "Lieb und Leid" are traditionally linked quite apart from any specific connotation, while "Zeit und Ewigkeit", too, apart from the meeting point between them in the mystery of "Stern und Blume", are of themselves of a more generally accepted nature. Even at the very beginning, then, Brentano has devised a prayer-like invocation of paradoxical ambiguity which may elicit an aesthetic response in the uninitiated and combine with it a particular spiritual one in Emilie and himself as the sharers of a secret. The clues to its meaning are, however, already there and they become more evident in Brentano's last prose work and its illustration.

I should now like to look at the passage in *Aus dem Tagebuch der Ahnfrau* mentioned by both Staiger and Enzensberger where the rhyme is introduced in its most significant context. If it can be shown that Brentano also intended it to have a specific meaning in this instance, even though Amey herself could not explain it except in its own terms, that is, had not as yet been able to make a bridge between unconscious and conscious, then this cypher can also correspond to a rational notion whenever it occurs.

Brentano was at work on the revision of his "Gockelmärchen" from about 1835 onwards.[14] It is generally held that his attempt to fuse the Märchen with the "Tagebuch" was not an artistic success, but if one judges it on its own extraordinary terms the work can be seen to have a strong inner coherence of its own. Both Märchen and "Tagebuch" are based on the structural principle of the arabesque; in this their many excursions and themes are analogous to marginal arabesques, that is, to ornamental excursions round the edge of the page and surrounding a centre that remains enigmatically hidden. This is the centre where, as Brentano wrote to Runge in explaining his requirements of the arabesque, ". . . die Gestalt unaussprechlich ist und das Symbol eintritt".[15] But even on a more conventionally acceptable level, Brentano has, I think, achieved a convincing structural integration of the two stories. He uses a carefully planned foreshadowing technique in the latter part of the first story and also a striking parallelism of theme and events, sometimes in the grotesque mode, more generally as play. While the "Herzliche Zueignung" joins the various levels of the two stories in a comprehensive fantasy, the title-page lithograph of the book, and more particularly the final illustration (see Plate), combine and fuse elements from both stories at the pictorial level. The last lithograph is an attempt to express the "inexpressible" hidden centre of the whole with the help of the refrain "O Stern und Blume" placed in a directly central position.[16] The refrain itself acts as a leitmotif linking the fantastic toy world of Gackelaia with the more realistic adolescent world of Amey, one of her ancestors.

The impoverished but noble family of Rauhgraf Gockel becomes rich and poor in turn through the possession and loss of a magic wishing ring, his daughter, Gackelaia, being the means of both the loss and regaining of the ring. The fortunes of this family are linked with an equally noble breed of cock and hen, Alektryo and Gallina, the former being descended from the "conscience" cock who crowed when Peter betrayed Christ. The story ends with Gackelaia's marriage and with herself and all her wedding guests being turned into children by the magic power of the ring now rightly used by her. Before this happens she discovers something about the time immediately preceding the marriage of her forebear, Amey, who lived in a past century. Her diary with its background of fantastic stories and the account of a benign and penitent ghost, "das Büblein", in her poultry shed, forms the second part of the Märchen. Both stories are an extraordinary mixture of magic, play, sober realism and also of nonsense fantasy practically unknown outside the pages of *Alice in Wonderland* and certainly unique in German.

In his "Herzliche Zueignung" Brentano says that the "Tagebuch" belongs to the same sphere ("Umfang") as *Die Chronika des fahrenden Schülers,* one of his earliest works dating from about 1802 onwards when he and Arnim, together with the Grimm brothers and Görres were immersed in the study of old German material of every kind for their collections. With its insistence on traditional lore and folk customs, lightly ironized this time, the "Tagebuch" clearly shows its relationship to the earlier work. It is also related to the *Chronika* by the title with its emphasis on the time structure, and finally, by its theme. The theme of both works taken as a whole might be stated in the words of Blake's title as that of "Innocence and Experience", of transgression which leads to the loss of paradise, and of a time of grief and trial that finally shows the way back to a different kind of Eden. In their diverse ways, the Beautiful Beggar of the *Chronika,* Gackelaia, Amey and the boy of the "Tagebuch", all yield to the romantic thrall; they get lost in a world of dream and fantasy, be it Thule, Vadutz, Midsummer Night, and are then helped by the sacrifice of others to find their way back to their own integrity, whether in this world or the next. The Beggar loses all sense of reality by reading the love stories in the siren's glittering chronicle, the small boy steals and wastes corn so as to have a chance to read and travel. Gackelaia's transgression is in the miniature mode and on a toy scale: she is punished by loss for playing with the forbidden doll, "keine Puppe, sondern nur / Eine schöne Kunstfigur", and in her journey to the grotesque mouse-town to retrieve the wishing ring of Solomon, she learns the wisdom of true childhood. Amey, as a child, steals her mother's bridal ornament of pearls, a "Paradiesgärtlein", and when she is grown up she recklessly follows the lure of the red fires on Midsummer Night, then the fascination of the deep amaranth colour in the green fields at sunset. But in the end she too is won over to the ultimate good by following out the pattern, as she came to understand it, of the mystery implicit in her chosen motto, "O Stern und Blume".

Amey is full of good will and good works - she founds a lay-order for herself and her friends to look after poor children - and she keeps an honest record of her doings from Good Friday to "Sonnenwende" (summer solstice) of the year 1317, describing her reactions, her dreams, and her quest for her true self: "Was willst du, wer bist du, wer ich ?" she cries out at a tense moment to Klareta who acts as a conscience figure to her (III, 867). But all the time she keeps a core of hard adolescent independence "Es ist ein Hang nach Unabhängigkeit in mir, der mich verschließt, wenn er gefesselt ist", she says, and she has a great fear "irgend eine Gewalt über meine Seele zuzugestehen" (III, 901-2), or of being unduly swayed by any deep emotion connected with the supernatural: "Ich habe einen eignen Abscheu vor Wunderbarem, das meine Freiheit stört" (871-2). Thus repelled, "das Wunderbare" soon catches up with her in dreams. During Whitweek she is helping to look after the newborn child of one of her friends. She dreams that the lilies in her garden have flowered and that she is standing near a rosebush close by. She plucks a rose, finds that it is full of deadly mildew which only vanishes when a shining figure pours over it a stream of light from the flower cup of one of the lilies. She puts the healed rose back into its place in the bush and then wakes up out of her dream. This mime of baptism and the reintegration of the purified soul into the Mystical Body has been so vivid to Amey that she runs out into her garden expecting to find some trace of the dream vision. But all is still and dark until she comes to the lilies whose whiteness causes a strange light phenomenon when she looks from flower

Plate 1 *Scala coeli et inferni ex divo Bernardo*, c. 1595.
[Reproduced by courtesy of the Herzog August Bibliothek, Wolfenbüttel]

Plate 2 *Die Nacht* by Philipp Otto Runge.

Plate 3 'O Stern o Blume nach Runge mit St. Edwardsstuhl u. dem Schnitter.'

Plate 4 'O Stern und Blume', by Edward von Steinle, 1852. [Reproduced by courtesy of the Kösel Verlag, Munich]

to star:

> sie dufteten Licht und ich sah Strahlen von den Sternen in sie niederschießen und von ihnen wieder empor . . . Und wie ich so sinnend stand, hörte ich eine Menschenstimme, fern und doch nah mit wehmütigem Tone die Worte sprechen:
>
> O Stern und Blume, Geist und Kleid,
> Lieb, Leid und Zeit und Ewigkeit!
> (III, 857)

Her first and immediate reaction is one of fear and of flight: "Bang hüllte ich mich dichter ein und eilte aus dem Garten." She at once runs away and will not listen to what she feels to be the message which yet haunts her. She is fully awake when she first hears these words and it is as though a human voice is pleading with her. Run as she may, there is something here that will not be denied, that actually clutches at her: a bramble of thorns catches her dress as she runs,

> erschreckt rief ich laut: "Wer faßt mich?" und stand. Niemand zeigte sich, so riß ich dann schneller eilend die Ranke mit fort.

Back in her room, she continues to hear the echo of those words:

> Ich verstand sie durch und durch und konnte sie doch nicht erklären. Ich verstand ihr Wesen und hatte keine Worte für sie als sie selbst. Immer wiederholte ich sie, immer sah ich die leuchtenden Lilien und die Sterne vor mir, die sie grüßten.

When this reaction is seen as immediately related to Amey's evasive action, it takes on a rather different aspect and can no longer be read only as an aesthetic response to a poetic formula. It is a psychological reaction to a mystery understood to be threatening the independence of a particular fictional character. Like the bramble, the message of the words has caught her in spite of herself, has followed her to her own house, to the inward recesses of her personality. She washes her eyes and her face in cold water and then she can see more clearly: it is as though there is someone beside her,

> als sehe ich ein Haupt so deutlich neben mir, daß ich die Ranke von meinem Kleide löste und das Haupt mit ihr bekränzte.

Immediately she has done this, a gesture acknowledging and confirming her understanding of what is required of her, she hears the words of the refrain again, and this second time she is no longer afraid:

> Da hörte ich jene Worte wieder und erschrak nicht, und legte die Hand auf das Haupt und fühlte: diese Worte sollen mein Wahlspruch sein.

By the symbolism of this gesture she has made a free election to accept the challenge offered by these words and to take their message as a pattern for her own life. In her diary up to this point Amey has shown herself to be a believing and even devout Christian but also as one who has by no means yielded unconditionally to the possibility of pain, to the crown of thorns, the cross and the suffering that love must be prepared for ("Lieb und Leid"). She has shirked the mystery of the Passion, but now, fully awake to the meaning of her action, she commits herself: it is her own head that she crowns. Her incapacity to find any other words for the mysteries of her religion except the human terms in which they are necessarily presented ("und hatte keine Worte für sie als sie selbst"), and her inability to explain them ("und konnte sie doch nicht erklären") does not prevent her from understanding the essence of these mysteries ("ich verstand sie durch und durch"). But this kind of understanding, even when she is fully committed to it, must necessarily remain an act of faith which is untranslatable into vision ("und hatte keine Worte für sie als sie selbst"). Understanding a mystery in the realm of faith is a parallel, *mutatis mutandis,* to the process of understanding a metaphor in the poetic dimension: both mystery and metaphor remain basically inexplicable except in their own terms. This is, perhaps, what Brentano, a mystic as well as a poet, was trying to convey as a model by the very structure and nature of this motto, as also by Amey's commentary on it within the context of her personal situation.

As sleep draws near, Amey is again overtaken by fear, for unconsciously she is greatly afraid of her conscious election and wants to withdraw it, to hide away again from its implications:

> Entschlummernd aber hörte ich eine klagende Stimme: "Ach, wer nimmt mir von der Stirne den Traum?" Da versteckte ich mich und hörte zum erstenmal in meinem Leben mein Herz heftig pochen und entschlief.

The complaining voice is her own. The crown of thorns was a symbol deeply imprinted on Brentano's consciousness and continually before his eyes in a picture of St Catherine of Siena crowned in this way.[17] In his mind he now associates this symbol with the despairing question in the opening stanza of Hölderlin's "Menons Klage um Diotima" which he had first read as far back as 1802. Hölderlin describes Menon's grief-stricken wandering and his attempt to flee sorrow: "so flieht das getroffene Wild in die Wälder . . . Jammernd und schlummerlos treibt es der Stachel umher . . . und niemand / Kann von der Stirne mir nehmen den traurigen Traum?" (compare III, 1125). In the same way, Amey, having accepted the full implication of what she has understood in her "Wahlspruch", would rather, on the natural level, be rid of it. Her dream and her waking reactions to it had taken place on the feast of St Silverius, a martyr pope of the Dark Ages, who died for his witness to the cross; one of the figures in her dream, "eine gekrönte Matrone mit einem Kreuz in der Hand", was clearly St Helena, a practical Englishwoman who insisted that there must somewhere be a real wooden cross to discover in Jerusalem, not just her Emperor son's *labarum,* a jewelled parody of it, not a toy of the imagination, but a hard, unglamorous, painful cross. The newborn child that is baptized the day following Amey's dream, and to whom she tells it "im Herzen" as she carries it round in her garden, seems to understand this message of sorrow and joy much more readily than Amey as yet does herself, for it both weeps and smiles "und es schien es besser zu verstehen als ich" (III, 857).

Amey's confrontation with this realistic view of her religion came just before "Sonnenwende, des Täufers Tag [24 June], da die Sonn nicht höher mag; da hat sich auch meine Sonne gewendet, und ist vieles anders geworden mit mir" (III, 858).

The night before her wedding not long after the turning point of Midsummer Day, she has a second important dream which shows her, as in a single point, all the years of her life, her past and present, her effort of charity in trying to help redeem the thieving boy with whose fate her own is mysteriously connected, her marriage, her death and burial, her rising from the dead. This kaleidoscopic dream is the more impressive as the reader is already familiar with much of its substance from a different perspective. In the Märchen, which is chronologically centuries later, Amey's "irdisches Kleid im Blumensarge" (III, 796), her undecayed body, had been exhumed by her descendants, the Gockel family; part of her diary was read, her life outlined and the substance of her great dream told in the poem that ends the Märchen, "Alle patschten in die Hände". By means of Amey's own vivid narration and by the pictorial representation in the last lithograph (see Plate), the dream is now rounded off. The climax of both stories is thus seen in different perspectives, each lending depth and relief to the other. In this second dream in the "Tagebuch", Amey and her nurse, Verena, wearied out with their "Jahrhunderte von Meilen lange Traumreise" come to the final place of encounter at midnight:

> ... in ein weites Erntefeld. Wir zogen dem Sensenklang und dem Schalle der Schnitterlieder nach; Verena las Ähren, und ich sammelte Blumen zum Erntekranz. Endlich kamen wir mitten in dem Ährenfeld auf einen kleinen freien Raum, wo der Kranz sollte geflochten werden, da sahen wir Seltsames. St. Eduards Thronstuhl, in dessen Sitz der Schlummerstein Jakobs bewahrt ist, stand zwischen zwei hohen Lilien vor den Ähren. Aus dem Sitze des Stuhles strahlte eine Mohnpflanze von Licht mit acht Blumen zum Nachthimmel hinauf. In der Mitte der Pflanze unter dem Monde saß die Nacht, eine liebe mütterliche Frau, und ihr zur Rechten und Linken auf den acht Mohnblumen acht Sterne als sinnende Knaben. Es schwebte aber von dem Thronstuhle an dem Mohnstengel ein ernstes kleines Mägdlein zum Sternhimmel empor, und zwei Engeln senkten Sterne in die beiden Lilien zur Seite des Throns; dazu sangen die Knaben auf den Mohnblumen oben:
>
> O Stern und Blume, Geist und Kleid,
> Lieb, Leid und Zeit und Ewigkeit.
>
> Die Sense des Schnitters sauste immer näher durch die Halmen, und da ich

mich niedersetzte, den Kranz aus den gesammelten Blumen zu flechten, sah ich zu meinen Füßen dicht vor dem Thronstuhl einen Knaben schlummernd sitzen. Er hatte eine Feder hinter dem Ohr und schlief, den Kopf auf den Arm lehnend, auf dem scharfen Rande des Thronstuhls.

(III, 916-17)

In her dream, Amey with Verena walks into the last poem of the "Gockelmärchen" (III, 826-31). This accounts for the two children, for Night and her attendant angels on the poppy flowers, for the presence of the English coronation chair in the middle of a cornfield instead of at Westminster Abbey. The star-lily candles on either side, Brentano's emblem for the Virgin at the Annunciation, suggest that this throne is also *"sedes sapientiae",* one of Mary's attributes in her litany. The stone of Scone contained in the chair is reputed to be part of Jacob's pillow when he dreamt of the angel's ladder which formed a link between earth and heaven. So in this sense too it is the seat of wisdom, forming the point of departure to heaven of an earnest blue-stocking given to historical research work in antiquities. This character in the Märchen is a "würdige Märtyrin der Ernsthaftigkeit", but at Gackelaia's wish at her wedding this solemn woman has been turned into a child, no longer subject to the laws of gravity. Once she has given up her pretensions to esoteric knowledge, she can say:

Mir ist, als verstünde ich jetzt erst den Stein Jakobs recht, mir ist, als stiege ich mit den Engeln auf der Himmelsleiter, die er auf diesem Steine schlafend im Traume gesehen, auf und nieder.

(III, 820)

By means of this ladder she has discovered the secret of how to live on earth and in heaven at the same time, a two-way traffic is now possible for her. In the dream poem she soars to heaven by the poppy-ladder, "Blatt vor Blatt gleich Leitersprossen" (III, 828) and joins the star children in their song, "O Stern und Blume". This journey to heaven is not death but a mystical realization of the essentials hidden and revealed in the paradox of the song. Poem and Märchen end with the poet himself in his own person singing the refrain at the end of time:

Ja dann ist selbst auf ein Härchen
Dieses Märchen mehr kein Märchen
Und bis so das Märchen aus,
Sing ich in die Nacht hinaus:
"O Stern und Blume, Geist und Kleid,
Lieb, Leid und Zeit und Ewigkeit!"
(III, 831)

As at the end of the Tagebuch, the refrain is to be the poet's last word at the end of the tale of his life as well as of the tale he has told.

While the girl ascends in the freedom of her newly found centre of gravity, the boy takes her place on the child's chair "vor Sankt Eduards Thronstuhl dicht" (III, 828). The quill pen behind his ear and Amey's diary in front of him, designate him as the actual author of the whole work, as the poet himself. This work which he has fashioned at a time when he is close to his open grave and coffin (seen on the left of the picture), and to his own day of harvest reckoning, is his own particular small sheaf of corn. It is what he will be able to declare when he is asked to give an account of himself; and indeed, Amey's big book was a diary at one end only and an account book at the other, as can be seen from the entry of a legacy, "item 12 fr. der gold. Amey". "Es hat sein Sach vollbracht", Verena's final answer to Amey's insistent question, "Was macht's Bübli?", is written on the banner in Verena's basket; she is kneeling in prayer while Amey winds her garland of flowers, her own personal contribution to the harvest festival.

If the repentant boy and in some sense Amey, too, represent the author himself who has tried to make good by writing the "account" of this book, then Verena is in a way Anna Katharina who helped him by her prayer, and the serious bluestocking now of a size to climb the ladder of "O Stern und Blume" is Emilie Linder, for whose benefit the story was written. Yet she is also, of course, Amey herself. For the sake of Emilie's conversion to spiritual childhood Brentano had elaborated a complex multiple mime in story, poem and picture, as he had also done in his drawing, "Der Lebensbaum". While critics have not failed to point out these personal equivalents, they are by no means fixed quantities, and for anyone who knows Brentano's methods, all apparently static equations are, in fact, complex and mercurial. While the key is useful for a critical inquiry it is not essential for enjoying the story and seeing in it a general human situation, that of the soul learning to co-operate with grace on its way to the final day of harvest and reckoning, a *Pilgrim's Progress* in miniature. Brentano himself was only too painfully aware of the personal element in all his work; he had said to Runge as far back as 1810 that he hesitated to go on with his writing because the whole of it was "die geheime heiligere Geschichte meines Herzens" (Seebaß, II 4). It was his intention to blur personal equivalents and to give his characters a general application outside the merely personal. In this story he has to a great extent succceded. When in her last dream Amey asks Verena whether the boy by the throne is really the same as the one she had helped in the past and who had stolen so much corn, Verena answers: "Ach, warum dasselbe Büblein ? Alle tun so und auch wir" (III, 917). At the end of the dream all is merged into one great mystical unity: in answer to the prayers of Verena and Amey the boy's book bears fruit a hundredfold, all their tears turn into corn[18] which rapidly shoots up in a rich golden harvest burying the grave and the coffin, flowing over, almost hiding the throne itself, "und alle Ähren wehten durcheinander und keines sah das andere mehr: denn Alles war nur Eines." (III, 919). In Amey's dream vision, all human beings, by virtue of Christ's Redemption of which the angels sing in their chorus, have passed from time into eternity where "Alles ist nur Eines". Brentano's lithograph is an attempt to picture the point of intersection between "Zeit und Ewigkeit".[19]

The lower half of the picture, then, shows death's harvest field at the time of personal judgement. Death himself is a reassuringly simple everyday figure, a kind of peasant "Freund Hain" in a straw hat that shades his face so that one cannot really recognize him for what he is. The harvest proceeds at midnight by the light of the full moon and of the lily candles, night's throne in heaven corresponds to the one on earth:

Oben in dem Strauße thront

Mild ein Weib in ernster Feier
Thront die Nacht in weiter Hülle,
Schauet, tauet durch den Schleier
Mutterstille, Mutterfülle
Träumerisch vom blauen Zelt
Auf das goldne Ährenfeld.

(III, 828)

Eight rungs of the flower ladder between earth and heaven are inscribed in ascending order with the four dialectically opposed terms of Brentano's refrain, an attempt to render antithesis by diagram, paradox by picture. Each of the eight star-children holds or incorporates the attribute corresponding to its word on the ladder from which each stalk emerges in a poised balance of symmetry. For the first antithesis, the child on the right holds a flower, the one on the left, like the rest, has a star above his head. In alternating sequence, left and right, the children then have the emblems of "Geist", a dove, "Kleid", a shroud-like garment, "Lieb", a heart, "Leid", a crown of thorns, "Zeit", an hour-glass, "Ewigkeit", an ouroboros, or the coiled snake ring of eternity. This last pair is the climax of contrasts, held up aloft on either side of the moon and thus forming the summit of both the pictorial and verbal pattern of the rhyme.

In this illustration of his rhyme in word and emblem Brentano was creating a kind of rebus riddle where pictured concepts are to be read and interpreted in a logical sequence in conjunction with words. It is still a riddle, however, for he is not explaining the words, just presenting them in another medium. In the world of the *Pia Desiderea* or *The School of the Heart,* namely that of spiritual emblems, the idea that a flower ladder reaching from earth to heaven should directly represent doctrinal or moral concepts, is nothing in the least out of the way.[20] But where the emblem would have stated its meaning openly in allegorical terms, Brentano concealed his in a further enigma of word-picture correspondence. At the same time there can be little doubt that emblematic models and their basic conventions of symmetry and contrast were always at the back of his mind. He had, at one time, owned many broadsheets and emblem books, as is evident from the catalogue of the remnant of his library sold by auction in Cologne in 1853, and the theme of a ladder to heaven, particularly in association with Jacob's stone, was well known as a subject of emblematic illustration.[21] There is, for instance, the "Scala coeli et inferni ex divo Bernardo" (see Plate) published c. 1595 by Johann Bussemacher of Cologne.[22] This shows Free Will, the central figure, making an election between the broad way to hell offered by Pride of Life in the flowery valley of vice, and the straight and narrow ladder to heaven offered by Grace and resting on the thorny mountain of the cross and of virtue. The twelve rungs of each ladder are labelled with vices and virtues respectively, and while the devil's hell mouth yawns in wait on one side, the sun-symbol of Jahve shines on the other, with the heavenly thrones of "delectatio" and "sublimitas" prepared for the blessed. The chair, and the idea of being seated, is the sign of possession, as "*sedere*", the etymological root of this word, implies. Another instance of a ladder emblem would be the " Scala Vitae Aeternae" , a broadsheet poem by Christian Plack printed in the shape of a ladder, the theme being that Christ is the way, the ladder to heaven which he has made available to mankind by his work of redemption.[23]

While the allegorical representation of contrast is more striking in Brentano's "Lebensbaum" drawing for Emilie, emblematic proprieties such as ladder, throne, heart, hour-glass, cock,[24] flowers, "Spruchband", and the general symmetry of construction, are clearly evident in his lithograph as well. And yet it is immediately obvious that Brentano's "Versuch zu sinnbilden" (II, 1051), as he calls it, moves also in a much more mysterious world than that of the emblem; it is the world of the symbol as opposed to that of allegory. In its pictorial aspect, this world had been opened to him by the art of Philipp Otto Runge (1777-1810). As far back as 1812 Brentano had written a striking analysis of the mythological cover drawings of a periodical called *Hesperus,* a Runge type of design for which Brentano himself may well have been responsible.[25] He characterizes thc pictorial symbol thus:

> Das Symbol soll nur ein Wink sein, der sich zugleich wieder selbst deutet, es ist gewissermaßen eine vor unseren Augen vorgehende

> Metamorphose in ein Bild ihres Sinnes. Es liegt eine Bewegung, ein Werden in dem Symbol, kein Nachmachen, Vorstellenwollen, keine handelnde Abspiegelung, welche letztere Eigenschaften mehr der Allegorie, die etwas Dramatisches hat, zugehören, so wie in dem Symbol mehr das Epische vorherrscht. (II, 1051)

This precisely expresses the sense of symbolical process that Brentano was aiming at, and which he in fact achieved, in his lithograph more than twenty years later.

It is well known in a general way that the upper half of this picture was modelled on the last of Runge's "Tageszeiten" sequence, "Die Nacht", that is, except for the incorporation of the motto (see Plate). Runge's thinking, too, was emblematic though he was not, like Brentano, familiar with Renaissance and baroque models; he had, however, a basically religious and allegorical view of the world and of art:

> So ist die Welt eine Stufe zum Himmel, die wir ersteigen müssen, sonst können wir die ewige Klarheit hier nicht sehnsüchtig verlangen. . .Die Religion ist nicht die Kunst; die Religion ist die höchste Gabe Gottes, sie kann nur von der Kunst herrlicher und verständlicher ausgesprochen werden.[26]

The lower part of the lithograph, too, is cognate with Runge's symmetrically balanced arrangement, the throne surrounded by the waving mass of corn corresponding to Runge's central fiery sunflower with the "smoke" of violas all round it; the figure grouping on either side and the central angels are also analogous. But the interesting point here is surely not just the known fact that Brentano modelled himself on Runge, but why he did so, why he selected "Die Nacht", and what the extraordinary flower and figure arrangement in the sky really meant to Brentano against the background of Runge's ideas. For it is here that he so intricately placed his own central concern, "O Stern und Blume", grafting it, as it were, into Runge's poppy flower.

Brentano knew Runge's work well, both through personal study and indirectly through Görres and other friends in close contact with the artist. Early in 1810 Brentano wrote him a long lettter asking him to illustrate his verse epic, *Die Romanzen vom*

Rosenkranz, with marginal arabesques because he felt close kinship between his own vision of the world and that of Runge. This was, at least, the main purpose of the letter, but Runge's pictures affected Brentano in such an extraordinary way that the letter turned into a searching self-analysis of his own attitude to art, indeed of his psychology in general. Though Runge agreed to do the work, the plans for illustration never matured as he died in December that same year; Brentano himself never published the *Romanzen.* While he was working on the revision of the "Gockelmärchen", he was again preoccupied in various ways with Runge, and in a letter of 1837 he says of him: "Er ist doch der *tiefsinnigste* Künstler, der *unmittelbarste* der neueren Zeit gewesen, der eine Tiefe, ein Inneres, das vielleicht nie Gestalt gewonnen, zu Tage hat gebären müssen" (Seebaß II, 358).[27]

I would now like to give some idea of Runge's theories and aims as they appear from a reading of his letters and essays. In his "Die Tageszeiten" which were wholly mystical in inspiration, Runge wanted to depict the eternal rhythm of life and death, procreation and birth, flowering and fading, by presenting this ever changing process in an ordered system of natural symbols:

> Es soll zeigen, wie unser Leben unter der Herrschaft des dreieinigen Gottes in ewig gleichbleibendem Rhythmus dahinfließt; und soll uns dadurch auf diesen Gott hinlenken.
>
> *(Schriften,* II, 210)

All growing things in nature, especially flowers and children, were for Runge interpreters of God's purpose in the times and seasons of man's earthly existence; flowers, in particular, were close to God's original design for man in paradise and therefore capable of showing him the way back to God when rightly contemplated in their carefully structured beauty. It was in the flower that he himself first came to realize the interrelationship of all phenomena in nature. When we study this miracle of design,

> dann erweitert sich der Raum in unserm Innern, und wir werden zuletzt selbst zu einer großen Blume, wo sich alle Gestalten und Gedanken wie Blätter in einem großen Stern um das Tiefste unserer Seele, um den Kelch wie um einen tiefen Brunnen drängen . . . . In den Blumen fühlt unser

Gemüt doch noch die Liebe und Einigkeit selbst alles Widerspruchs in der Welt. *(Schriften* II, 220)

The medium through which the flower is made manifest to man is light, which, by its very nature and origin, leads man out of the confines of his own immediate being and connects him with the cosmic sphere. Hence the importance for Runge of the changing media of light, of the sun, moon and stars which dictate the aspect of times and seasons, of morning, noon, dusk and night. But even night itself, as he wanted to show in his "Die Nacht", was to be radiant with a light of its own, through the fire of flowers from below, and by moon and stars from above:

. . . [die Nacht] sollte unten in Feuer brennen, das aus Blumen bestände, die in den stillen Schlafenden gesammelt waren, welche von Rauch und Thau bedeckt liegen, der Liebe und des Schutzes gewiß, die von oben kommen, erwartend die Klarheit des Unendlichen, das über uns ewig und ruhig ist, und aus welchem von neuem in ewigem Cirkelschlag alles aufblühen, zeugen, gebären und wieder versinken wird.

(Schriften I, 69)[28]

While in the heavens star and moon reflect the light of the sun, as of God, so on earth light is reflected in the radiance and life of the flower. When God became man, light, as of the star, was joined to its reflected radiance in the flower, as of the earth; and the continually renewed process of divine creation, redemption and sanctification of the world of nature, presided over by light, is symbolically manifested in the rhythm of days, seasons, the ages of man and of history. The rhythm of change in the cosmic sphere corresponds to the changing life-cycle of man between birth and death. By incorporating his "O Stern und Blume" into the ideological and pictorial pattern of Runge's "Tageszeiten", Brentano wanted to associate Christ's redemptive act immediately with the universal rhythm and process of man's life presided over by "die Klarheit des Unendlichen".

Runge's "Tageszeiten", then, were meant to show, as if in essence, the actual process of human existence in a cosmic dimension and relationship. He intended them for a large-scale wall decoration, in a specially constructed building, with a poetical commentary by Tieck and music as well: the whole cycle was to be a "Gesamtkunstwerk" in colour, but it never got beyond drawings and a few paintings for "Der Morgen" with extraordinary radiance in their light effects. He wanted to show people not only an end-result but a dynamic process within a static picture; this was to be done by the effect on the onlooker of pattern, design, correspondences between light and the living organism of the plant, and of human beings seen in close relationship with both flowers and light. He was intent on communicating his own personal experience,

> nicht was ich mir denke und was ich empfinden muß . . . sondern, wie ich dazu gekommen bin, und noch dazu komme, das zu sehen, zu denken und zu empfinden, so den Weg, den ich gegangen bin, und da müßte es doch curios seyn, daß andere Menschen das so gar nicht begreifen sollten.
> *(Schriften, I,* 27, letter of 1 December 1802 to Tieck)

The English reader will often find himself reminded of the kind of vision and even of the language rhythms of Runge's contemporary, William Blake, of his prophetic zeal for spiritual values, of his flower and child symbols, of his sense of personal relationship with light, sun, moon and stars. Among those who really did understand what Runge was trying to convey was Goethe; he could not always agree with Runge but he continually encouraged him and he reserved a room specially for the large engravings of the "Tageszeiten", which are still on show now in the Goethehaus at Frankfurt.

At the time of life when Brentano was writing his last story it was natural for him to concentrate on the harvest season, the moon - "Der Mond ist der Tröster, der heilige Geist" - and on night, which Runge called "die gränzenlose Klarheit und Tiefe der Erkenntniß von der unvertilgten Existenz in Gott' *(Schriften, I, 41*, and I, 82).[29] Brentano himself saw the moon as pointing to

> den steten ruhigen Wechsel, auf die ewig gleichmäßige Bewegung der Natur von dem Anfange der Lebenssaat bis zu ihrem Ausgange in den Samen, der ewig ist, auf den ruhig wiederkehrenden Pulsschlag des

> allgemeinen Seins, der die Sekunden der ewigen Zeiten mißt, und wer ihn so, kindlich und fromm anschauend, versteht, den wird er leicht trösten und beruhigen. (II, 1052, "Erklärung der Sinnbilder", 1812)

In Runge's picture, the queen of night is enthroned immediately under the moon which in turn is presided over by the Holy Ghost from the arabesque frame outside the picture. Both Runge and Brentano intended the motherly figure to humanize and personify in some sort these abstract concepts about night. In the same way, the star-children on the flowers spread out like a fan in the sky were to bring the idea of cosmic constellations within man's ken. In Runge's words:

> Auf jeder Blume sitzt ein Knabe, der still und schnurgrade vor sich weg sieht; alle sind sie ganz en face und ernst, über jedem steht ein Stern, so daß diese obere Regularität ganz den Eindruck macht wie das Himmelsgewölbe. *(Schriften I,* 33)

The attitude of these star children had already impressed Brentano years before. In 1810 he had written to Runge:

> . . . vor allem erfreu ich mich an dem Mond und vor allem an den geisterhaft bewegten Sternkindern zu seiner Seite; diese sind mir oft in einsamen Stunden strenge, gute Geister vor den Augen. (Seebaß, II, 5-6)

In the dream poem of the "Gockelmärchen" he describes them as

> Sterne, Kinder aller Launen
> Die da sinnen, harren, staunen,
> Beten, sehnen, prophezeien
> Wenig wohl um uns bekümmert
> Schweigen und ins Herz uns schreien.
> (III, 828)[30]

In his lithograph he makes them his emblem-bearers; as in a constellation, they write Brentano's metaphorical refrain across the night sky and thus place the mystery of its meaning in a universal context. Like Runge, Brentano wanted to depict not just the result, but the actual process by which he himself had reached understanding, and thus to influence people towards sharing in the same development. In a similar way, Novalis communicates by means of simple, transparent events the inward process itself which turns Heinrich von Ofterdingen into a poet and opens his inner eye. Brentano too saw the operation of word, and in this case, picture, as "magisch"; he never intended the process to take place, in the first instance, at a fully conscious level but, as it were, by the light of the moon. It was not in Brentano's nature to underpin his artistic work with theory, as Novalis did, but he too saw the poet's mode of influence as magical and the poet himself, as having, in Hofmannsthal's phrase "die Gebärde des Magiers" ("Ein Traum von großer Magie"). Brentano had himself come under the spell of Runge and he therefore made use of his pictorial methods and their implications as an adjunct to the effect of the words, rhythm and rhyme, the method of poetical operation of his own riddle refrain. By reading his story and looking at his picture people were to become, like the wedding guests at the end of the Märchen, as children in their attitude of faith to the Christian mysteries.

Brentano's intention is equally evident in the last poem of the Tagebuch "Was reif in diesen Zeilen steht". This lyric was called "Eingang" by the first editors of his works, a title which may or may not go back to the poet but was in any case adopted by later editors and anthologists. The poem itself has become widely familiar while its actual context is as good as unknown. In spite of its adoptive title, it is put last in most selections and is thus made to look like a total summary; but the "in diesen Zeilen" of the opening line here refers only to Brentano's last work and not to his lyrical poetry in general, let alone to his work as a whole. Brentano has, as he hopes, led the reader of his "Gockelmärchen" to a point of child-like affirmation of mystery: the concluding poem describes the spirit in which he wrote his story and how he thinks his reader will react to it, what his inward experience will be as a result of reading it. It can be called a prophecy of what Brentano thinks will happen after he himself is dead - "Und ist das Feld einst abgemäht" - or at least, he would like all this to happen by a process of sympathetic magic.

Was reif in diesen Zeilen steht
Was lächelnd winkt und sinnend fleht,
Das soll kein Kind betrüben,
Die Einfalt hat es ausgesäet,
Die Schwermuth hat hindurchgeweht,
Die Sehnsucht hat's getrieben;
Und ist das Feld einst abgemäht,
Die Armuth durch die Stoppeln geht,
Sucht Ähren, die geblieben,
Sucht Lieb, die für sie untergeht,
Sucht Lieb, die mit ihr aufersteht
Sucht Lieb, die sie kann lieben,
Und hat sie einsam und verschmähmt
Die Nacht durch dankend im Gebet
Die Körner ausgerieben,
Liest sie, als früh der Hahn gekräht,
Was Lieb erhielt, was Leid verweht,
Ans Feldkreuz angeschrieben
O Stern und Blume, Geist und Kleid,
Lieb, Leid und Zeit und Ewigkeit!
("Gockelmärchen", 1838)

An earlier but shorter parallel poem addressed to Emilie Linder with a letter in June 1834 will help to make the structure and meaning of the final poem clearer:

Was heiß aus meiner Seele fleht
Und bang in diesen Zeilen steht,
Das soll dich nicht betrüben.
Die Liebe hat es ausgesäet
Die Liebe hat hindurchgeweht,
Die Liebe hat's getrieben.
Und ist dies Feld einst abgemäht,
Arm Lindi durch die Stoppeln geht,
Sucht Ähren, die geblieben,
Sucht Lieb, die mit ihr untergeht,
Sucht Lieb, die mit ihr aufersteht,
Sucht Lieb, die ich mußt lieben.
(III, 1129, and I, 546, with slight variants)

The letter, now lost, to which this latter poem is an envoi, must clearly have been important. In the metaphor of the field of growing corn he identifies both the letter and his own life immediately with the plea he has made to Emilie. He then goes on to a favourite fantasy - the loved one's actions once he himself is dead.[31] She will wander across the bare stubble field of her memories of him looking for what endures: the Redeemer's love which also, in the past, forced his own love in return. According to his method, he puts a concrete fantasy before her which is to move her will and finally command her allegiance.

"Was reif in diesen Zeilen steht" is the boy's last entry in his diary-account book which he leaves behind at the end when he himself has vanished. He has cleaned himself and his quill-pen out of existence in a final gesture of irony: ". . . das Papier mit einem Tintenfleck fiel mir zu Füßen", says Amey as she is about to read this last poem, "Das Büblein war fort, es war als habe es sein eigenes Dasein aus der Feder geputzt." (III, 929). The personal context of Emilie and the letter to her has now been extended to the wider context of the book as a whole, and "arm Lindi" has become all mankind in its neediness, "die Armut", any reader of the story who is truly poor in spirit. The basic rhythmic and rhyme pattern is the same in both poems: two four-foot iambic lines with a stressed rhyme on "steht" (a), are followed by a three-foot line with a feminine rhyme on "betrüben" (b). With the exception of the refrain, "a" and "b" are the only rhymes in the poem, the lines being arranged in an internal three-line stanza, that is, in six groups of three (a, a, b), leading up to the final couplet (c, c). There is something rhythmically compelling, almost compulsive, in the effect of Brentano's carefully elaborated metre, rhyme and assonance scheme, the repetition of words and of identical constructions, the mounting metric tension of one single sentence moving steadily across twenty lines to a climax. The rhythmic effectiveness of this poem is perhaps due to what in Coleridge's words might be described as a strikingly successful "interpenetration of passion and will, of spontaneous impulse and voluntary purpose", which alone can create really convincing metre. Brentano has here fulfilled the basic conditions needed for apt rhythmic structuring, the consistently maintained "interfusion of the same throughout the radically different, . . . the different throughout a base radically the same".[32] "Wenn der lahme Weber träumt", another of the poems in the "Tagebuch", has the same extraordinary metrical skill, as Enzensberger's analysis (pp. 43-51) has clearly shown.

The climax "O Stern und Blume" then comes as a coda, as a harmonious relief of preceding tension, mainly because of the variation in rhythm in the last and lengthened line. However inexplicable these groups of juxtaposed and paratactically arranged words may be on the surface, their structure mimes the gesture of answering, explaining, confirming what has gone before. They do this by their rhythmic movement and by an incantatory repetition of sound seeming to point to internal correspondences of meaning. When saying over this haunting invocation ("immer wiederholte ich sie", was Amey's experience of the words of her motto), anyone with ear and mind attuned to invocation and response in Catholic litanies, as was Brentano's, will find himself in a familiar sound-sphere, and indeed on home ground altogether. "Mystical rose", "morning star", "tower of ivory" - such metaphorical invocations in the Litany of Loreto may not make immediate sense to the person praying but are poetically meaningful as an often repeated, summary reminder of known theological truths and of doctrine.

The poem as a whole may be seen in three phases of development. Brentano first describes his motives and moods when writing this story in the simplicity of his heart, a mixture of play and earnest pleading, not meant to cause stress or grief (lines 1-6). He then foresees how poverty will glean the bare fields for the enduring love of Christ, a quest which will take place after the poet himself is dead (lines 7-12) . The three diverse human qualities, "Einfalt", "Schwermut", "Sehnsucht", which went to the making of the poet's work, his harvest, here stand in contrast to the thrice repeated "Lieb", the single divine quality needed for the great harvest of the work of redemption. I think it would be in keeping with Brentano's method to have used this figure of a matching threefold anaphora as a poetic paradigm of the Trinity, of the trinitarian love of the three in one. The rhythmic impulse of the poem as a whole is, in fact, also triadic, leading up to the climax refrain which unites all opposites.[33] The poem continues on the theme of poverty's quest: a man truly poor in spirit will spend the dark night of this life in despised solitude and grateful prayer, trying to sift true values from false, but when the signal comes for dawn, there will be light enough for him to see; he will then be able to read, and also to glean - the pun on "lesen" is, I think, deliberate, and so is the strong initial stress - love's meaning when the cock-crow breaks the spell of darkness.[34] The message to be read aright and harvested at cock-crow will be written on the cross, but not in the sense of being an inscription.[35] The cross is what it stands for, hidden, yet plain to be seen by all who pass it along the way; it incorporates its own meaning in the same way as Brentano's refrain is a poet's model of meaning. In the life now over, this kind of knowledge of the cross and of the Redemption it points to was kept alive by love, and this same love is now also the means of dispelling sorrow (line 17).[36] The cross is here a "Feldkreuz". Brentano used this term throughout the "Tagebuch" for the monument that was to mark the boy's grave. He cannot have been thinking of the squat little tomb-stone shown on the left of the lithograph, all there was room for if the balance of the picture was not to be destroyed. He saw it, rather, as a larger wayside cross of the kind familiar in Southern Germany where he was then living; that is, he saw himself to the end in his favourite guise as "der Pilger", the wanderer without a settled home making his way along the road to eternity. He appears as a pilgrim in "Alhambra" and also in "Segen über diesen Ort", the dedicatory poem of *Das bittere Leiden* and written on the occasion of leaving Regensburg for Munich in 1833. For the pilgrim there is only one resting place:

> Beß're Herberg giebt es nicht,
> Als beim Kreuze draußen an dem Wege.
> Gastfrei ist der Herbergsmann,
> Denn der Dorn, sein Knecht, hält an den Pfaden
> Gern des Pilgers Mantel an,
> Dringend ihn zur Einkehr einzuladen;
> (I, 528-9)

Edward von Steinle's "Gedenkblatt an Clemens Brentano, 1842" depicts the poet dressed as a pilgrim and kneeling by a "Feldkreuz" of the kind he had envisaged in the boy's last entry in the "Tagebuch".

It was Steinle, too, the close friend of Brentano's last years, who provided a conclusive commentary on "O Stern und Blume". The findings of the present enquiry are confirmed by Steinle's interpretation but without this analysis of the poetical and emblematic context his explanation might well not appear convincing.[37] Apart from Steinle's good faith and intelligence, his illustrations to many of Brentano's earlier works prove his understanding of the poet's artistic method and mentality.[38] Moreover, the manner of Steinle's "explanation" in the present instance is in itself significant and may be taken as a strong argument for the reliability of his interpretation. Steinle's son relates that after the publication in 1852 of Brentano's works with the title-page portrait and motto, the poet's sister-in-law said to Steinle that she could not "explain" this motto. He replied "daß er eine ganz einfache Erklärung des Verses zu geben wisse. Als ihn Frau Brentano aufforderte, ihr diese Erklärung mitzuteilen, erwiderte ihr Steinle, er werde das durch eine Zeichnung tun."[39] Steinle gave her his colour and wash drawing (see Plate) as a Christmas present, still, it seems, without any verbal commentary. He did not choose to trust to his own words, which might have been simple enough, as he himself had said; he gave his "explanation" in the form of an emblematic sequence with Brentano's word-groups carefully lettered in conjunction with each scene.

Apart from the first scene, the star and lily, which had a personal connotation for Brentano and Emilie and had been linked by him with the Annunciation, Steinle's sequence shows conventionally accepted designs in the Nazarene mode picturing the earthly life of Christ in the presence of Mary. The three angels linking the main scenes point in turn to the fruits of the Redemption: the church, the possibility of gaining heaven, and the eucharist, which is Christ's eternal presence continued in time. For the main panels the artist has chosen a representative scene from among each of the joyful, sorrowful and glorious mysteries as Brentano meditated them day by day in the contemplative prayer of the rosary. In his *Die Romanzen vom Rosenkranz* which Brentano had wanted Runge to illustrate, he had intended to describe the origin and meaning of this ancient method of meditating on the process and the significance of the Redemption.[40] He saw it as the meeting place of the divine and the human in successive stages of joy, sorrow and glory, each paradoxically synchronized with and present to the other. Brentano never finished his *Romanzen,* he never even approached what was to be the essential theme, but Amey's device, a mystical two-line summary in metaphor instead of the endless earlier epic, is still related to the basic underlying concern of his youthful work.

Each of the mysteries depicted by Steinle represents a paradox and this can only be stated by means of words and symbols which necessarily remain as paradoxical as the facts they stand for. Steinle could have chosen other scenes - Bethlehem instead of Nazareth, Golgotha instead of the tomb, the resurrection instead of the ascension - the idea would have remained unchanged and so would the essential paradox. For he was not aiming at direct allegorical equivalents, "kein Nachmachen, Vorstellenwollen, keine handelnde Abspiegelung" as Brentano put it; what matters to Steinle, and to Brentano in his motto, is the sequence within a process, "eine vor unsern Augen vorgehende Metamorphose in ein Bild ihres Sinns." (II, 1051). In harmony with Brentano's own intentions in his rhyme, Steinle has shown a single unified movement in its progression, related events together constituting the single fact of the Redemption in an emblem. As such, Steinle's drawing may be said to represent and to "explain" Brentano's poetical device,

> O Stern und Blume, Geist und Kleid,
> Lieb, Leid und Zeit und Ewigkeit.

---

[1] "Brentano und seine Märchen", *Aufsätze zur Literatur*, Literarhistorische Schriften I, edited by Wolfram Mauser (Regensburg, 1962), p. 62 and p. 56.

[2] See Jürgen Behrens, Wolfgang Frühwald and Detlev Lüders, "Zum Stand der Arbeiten an der Frankfurter Brentano-Ausgabe", *Jahrbuch des Freien Deutschen Hochstifts* (Tübingen, 1969), pp. 398-426, a report on the new

edition. The present article is based on the interim "Leseausgabe", *Clemens Brentano, Werke*, edited by Friedhelm Kemp, Wolfgang Frühwald and Bernhard Gajek, 4 vols, (Munich, 1963-8), referred to in the body of the article by Roman and arabic numerals for volume and page number. Volume I of this edition contains a comprehensive bibliography of works on Brentano (I, 1249-67) published since the appearance of the *Brentano-Bibliographie* by Otto Mallon (Berlin, 1926; reprint, Hildesheim, 1965); a report by W. Frühwald on recent Brentano research can be found in *DVLG*, 45 (1971), Heft 4.

[3] Emil Staiger, *Die Zeit als Einbildungskraft des Dichters* (Zürich, 1939), pp. 21-98, cited as "Staiger"; Wilhelm Fraenger, *Clemens Brentanos Alhambra. Eine Nachprüfung* (Amsterdam, 1964), cited as "Fraenger"; Wolfgang Frühwald, "Das verlorene Paradies. Zur Deutung von Clemens Brentanos 'Herzliche Zueignung' des Märchens 'Gockel, Hinkel und Gackelaia' (1838)", *Literaturwissenschaftliches Jahrbuch*, N.F., 3 (1962-3), 113-92, cited as "Das verlorene Paradies" and as "*LJb.*"; Hans Magnus Enzensberger, *Brentanos Poetik* (Munich, 1961) (diss. Erlangen, 1955), cited as "Enzensberger".

[4] The lithographs of the first edition, *Gockel, Hinkel und Gakeleja*, Märchen wieder erzählt von Clemens Brentano (Frankfurt, 1838), of which both the Cambridge University Library and the British Museum have a copy, are reproduced in Volume III (*Märchen*) of the "Leseausgabe". For details concerning the lithographs and the artists who carried out Brentano's designs, see Christa Holst and Siegfried Sudhoff "Die Lithographien zur ersten Ausgabe von Brentanos Märchen "Gockel, Hinkel, Gakeleja" (1838)", *LJb.*, N.F., 6 (1965), 140-54. Plate IV in that essay reproduces notes in Brentano's hand with the text of "O Stern und Blume", where the beginning of the second line has the variant order "Leid, Lieb." The typescript dissertation by Wolfgang Schlegelmilch, *Studien zum bildlichen Ausdruck bei Brentano* (Freiburg im Breisgau, 1953), which is reported (*Werke* I, 1180) to contain some discussion of Brentano's motto, has not been available to me.

[5] "Brentanos Lieblingsbilder Rose und Mond, Kerzen und Statuen, Sterne und Blumen, sind niemals bloß sie selbst, sondern zugleich religiöse Geheimzeichen und Kultbilder . . . Seine Wortsymbolik ist nicht bloße Lautmalerei, Schilderung, Allegorie" (Friedrich Gundolf, *Romantiker* (Berlin-Wilmersdorf, 1930), p.325). See too: *Clemens Brentano. Ein Lebensbild* von P. Johannes Baptista Diel, S.J., ergänzt und hrsgb. von Wilhelm Kreiten, S.J., 2 vols (Freiburg im Breisgau, 1877 and 1878), II,

484-9, esp. note 2, p. 488 (author and editor differ in their opinion about the rhyme); Alfons Maria von Steinle, "Ein Spruch Clemens Brentanos, »0 Stern und Blume«", *Historisch-Politische Blätter*, 121, I, (1898), 380-4; Alexander von Bernus and A. M. von Steinle, *Clemens Brentano und Edward von Steinle: Dichtungen und Bilder* (Kempten and Munich, 1909), pp. 213-16.

6 Staiger, p. 96, Enzensberger, p. 94 and p. 104. Claudia Rychner, *Der alte Brentano. Eine Interpretation der »Blätter aus dem Tagebuch der Ahnfrau«* (Winterthur, 1956) (diss. Zürich, 1956), contradicts herself, agreeing categorically with Staiger to begin with but finally admitting that von Steinle's explanation "ist wohl möglich", pp. 104 ff. See too, Werner Hoffmann, *Clemens Brentano. Leben und Werke* (Bern and Munich, 1966), p. 383: "Man hat fast so viel an ihnen [the lines "O Stern und Blume"] herumgedeutet wie an der Grabschrift Rilkes obwohl sie für den, der Brentano kennt, so wenig deutbar sind wie Musik." To this one might add that anyone who knows Rilke and also the context of "O Stern und Blume" would never think of comparing it with "O Rose, reiner Widerspruch".

7 Quoted by Staiger, pp. 96 f., and by Enzensberger, p. 150; Diel-Kreiten, *Lebensbild*, II, 485 f., and A.M. von Steinle, examine this context more fully.

8 Walther Killy, "Gemütserregungskunst. Clemens Brentano" in *Wandlungen des lyrischen Bildes* (Göttingen, 1964), pp. 53-72.

9 See Frühwald, "Das verlorene Paradies", p. 125, and also his edition *Clemens Brentano. Briefe an Emilie Linder* (Bad Homburg, Berlin, Zürich, 1969). Many of these letters have what Frühwald calls "parabolischen Werkcharakter" and, in fact, deliberately conceal the writer's thoughts by means of words; see "Nachwort", pp. 310 ff. For a review of this book, see *MLR*, 66 (1971), 461-3.

10 *Werke* I, 601-4 and note, 1179-80, with full bibliographical references about the refrain; III, 811, 814; III, 826-31; III, 922; III, 929-30.

11 Diel-Kreiten, *Lebensbild*, II, 485;*Werke*, I, 601-4.

12 *Stern und Blume. Untersuchungen zur Sprachauffassung Hölderlins*, by Anke Bennholdt-Thomsen, Abhandlungen zur Kunst-, Musik- und Literaturwissenschaft, 39 (Bonn, 1967), reviewed by M. B. Benn, *MLR*, 64 (1969), 469-70.

[13] See Brentano's allegorical and symbolical drawing for Emilie, the giant "Lebensbaum" (1835/36) at one time owned by E. von Steinle, but destroyed during the last war. Brentano's study for it together with a photograph of the original was recently on exhibition at the Freies Deutsches Hochstift, Frankfurt, see the illustrated catalogue of the Brentano Exhibition, *Clemens Brentano Ausstellung 22. Juni bis 20. September 1970* (Frankfurt am Main 1970), p. 139. The best reproduction of a copy of the drawing, still preserved in the museum at Basel, is in Oskar Walzel's *Gehalt und Gestalt im Kunstwerk des Dichters* (Berlin-Neubabelsberg, 1925), Plate 2. The design is conditioned by baroque emblematic models and also by Runge; see W. Fraenger, "*Alhambra*", p. 9 and p. 82.

[14] For an analysis of this work, see C. Rychner, *Der alte Brentano*, and for a bibliography on this Märchen in general, see III, 1063 f.

[15] *Clemens Brentano, Briefe,* edited by Friedrich Seebaß, 2 vols (Nürnberg 1951), letter of 21 January 1810, Vol. II, p. 10 (cited as "Seebaß"). The idea of the arabesque structure of the "Gockelmärchen" was first put forward by R.A. Schröder in his essay on Brentano, *Gesammelte Werke* (Frankfurt am Main, 1952), Vol. II, pp. 717 ff., and developed by W. Frühwald, "Das verlorene Paradies", pp. 129 ff.

[16] While none of the fourteen lithographs have captions in Brentano's 1838 edition of the "Gockelmärchen", he himself referred to the last lithograph as "Das Kinderstühlchen vor St. Eduards Stuhl", while his correspondent on this occasion, J.F. Böhmer, called it "O Stern o Blume nach Runge mit St. Edwardsstuhl u. dem Schnitter", quoted by Holst-Sudhoff, *LJb.* N.F., 6 (1965), 147 and 149; see Plate.

[17] See the catalogue of the Frankfurt Brentano exhibition, pp. 138 ff. and plate 16 for L. E. Grimm's 1837 portrait of Brentano against a background showing this picture of St Catherine and scenes from the "Gockelmärchen". The frontispiece of the ninth edition (1852) of Brentano's *Das bittere Leiden unsers Herrn Jesu Christi* (1833) is an engraving by E. von Steinle, "Passionsmitleiden der H. Catharina von Siena" which shows St Catherine putting a crown of thorns on her own head as she kneels before the risen Christ.

[18] Psalm 126, verses 5 and 6.

[19] The refrain is used as an evocative leitmotif at other points of the

"Gockelmärchen", foreshadowing, sometimes in a more trivial context (III, 671, 694, 809) sometimes seriously (797, 809, 811, 814, 815), its full signifcance in the "Tagebuch". Compare too its use in the "Schnitterlied" and in Amey's wedding song where the mysteries of the Redemption help thesoul at death and are the substance of its song of praise in eternity (III, 922 and 926).

20 Hermann Hugo's *Pia Desideria Animae*, one of the most popular devotional books of its time, was published in 1624 and thereafter in many editions. The English edition in my possession was printed by E. and R. Pawlet, "at the signe of the Bible in Chancery-lane, neer Fleet-street" London 1703. Francis Quarles, *The School of the Heart (of itself gone way from God) Brought back again to him and instructed by him, in 47 emblems*, 1635. In my edition (Bristol, 1808), each emblem has a two-line motto in Latin with an English translation. "The Ladder of the Heart" (no. 37) shows the heart with a miniature ladder in it, and has the motto: "Would you scale Heav'n, and use a Ladder's aid, / Then in thy Heart let the first Step be made." The emblem is expounded in an ode where the stanzas are printed in the shape of the steps of a ladder, pp. 116-18.

21 See William A. Coupe, *The German Illustrated Broadsheet in the Seventeenth Century. Historical and Iconographical Studies*, Two Parts (Baden-Baden, 1967), Part I, pp. 169-72 (The Ladder), and Part II, Plates 93 and 94.

22 There is a copy of this broadsheet in Cod. Guelf. 31.8, Aug.2°, at the Herzog August Bibliothek, Wolfenbüttel, by whose kind permission the plate is here reproduced. See also p. 136, No. 25 in Josef Benzing, "Der Kupferstecher, Kunstdrucker und Verleger Johann Bussemacher zu Köln (1580? bis 1616?)" in *Aus der Welt des Bibliothekars. Festschrift für Rudolf Juchoff zum 65. Geburtstage*, edited by Kurt Ohly and Werner Krieg (Cologne, 1961). - I would like to thank F.J.S. for his help with emblems and for producing apposite material from his collections.

23 SCALA VITAE AETERNAE. Das ist / Die Leiter ins ewige Leben / der heiligen Schrifft gemeß / gestellt und in Deutsche Rhytmos gebracht / Zu sonderlichen Ehren und Wolgefallen / dem Christlicher Läser Unterthenigst *Dedicirt* und in Druck gegeben: Durch Christianum Plack von Braunschweigk, Cod. Guelf. 38.25, Aug. 2° fo. 82, Wolfenbüttel.

24 The cock, whom Brentano in his Märchen called by his Greek name, Alektryo, was an emblem of vigilance. He was often pictured together with

other emblems of the Passion (the crown of thorns, dice, scourge) as a warning conscience figure and perched on top of the column of the flagellation. For the appellation "Alektryo" compare Johannes Praetorius, *Alektryomantia*, 1680; see von Faber du Faur, *German Baroque Literature*, No. 774.

25 "Erklärung der Sinnbilder auf dem Umschlage dieser Zeitschrift" in: *Hesperus, ein Nationalblatt für gebildete Leser*, Hsg. von Christian Carl André in Brünn, Vol. I (Prague, 1812), pp. III-VII. (Mallon Bibliography, No. 48); *Werke*, II 1046-54.

26 Letter of 3 September 1802, *Hinterlassene Schriften von Philiipp Otto Runge, Mahler*, hrsgb. von dessen ältestem Bruder (Hamburg 1840 and 1842), 2 vols, Deutsche Neudrucke (Göttingen, 1965), II, 149 and 148 (cited as *Schriften*).

27 Brentano's three letters to Runge all date from 1810: 21 January, *Schriften* pp. 393-406, 18 March, pp. 407-9, June, pp. 413-6. The first two appeared in Seebaß's selection, Vol. II, pp. 3-24. Brentano also wrote a memorial notice of Runge and a poem about him, which appeared in the *Berliner Abendblätter* of 19 December 1810, "Andenken eines trefflichen Deutschen Mannes und tiefsinnigen Künstlers", *Schriften, II, 551-4.* For the general connexions between Brentano and Runge, see Frühwald, *Das verlorene Paradies* and also his bibliography; Robert Diehl, "Ph.Otto Runge und Clemens Brentano. Ein Beitrag zur Buchillustration der Romantik", in *Imprimatur*, Vol. IV (Hamburg, 1935), pp. 53-74; and Wilhelm Schellberg, "Clemens Brentano and Ph. Otto Runge", *Literaturwissenschaftliches Jahrbuch der Görres-Gesellschaft*, 8 (1936), 166-215. See also W. Robson-Scott's illuminating comments on Runge, and further bibliography in his essay, "German Romanticism and the Visual Arts" in *The Romantic Period in Germany; Essays by Members of the Germanic Institute*, edited by Siegbert Prawer (London, 1970).

28 Runge elsewhere gives a more detailed description of "Die Nacht", *Schriften*, I, 32-3: the grotesque plants, "allerley wunderliche Gestalten", above the sleepers, represent their unquiet dreams, but the angels emerging from night's poppy-flower bring peace and protection.

29 This description of night is one of Runge's "Rubriken zu den vier Tageszeiten" in which he attempts to define the times of day in terms of changing light in its relationship to man, and in connexion with the four dimensions of God's love as St Paul saw them in Ephesians, III, 18: breadth,

length, height, depth. Night and death correspond to "Tiefe".

30 As is clear from "Wenig wohl um uns bekümmert", and from his letters to Runge, Brentano associated his ideas about night and the heavenly constellations not only with Runge but with the opening stanza of Hölderlin's "Brot und Wein": "Besonders ist 'die Nacht' klar und sternhell und einsam, und eine rück- und vorwärtstönende Glocke aller Erinnerung" (Seebaß, II, 7).

31 The poem for Luise Hensel, "Zweimal hab' ich dich gesehn" (1821), I, 449-55, has the same image of the mown cornfield, the gleaner, her prayer by the poet's grave; compare Enzensberger, pp. 97 f.

32 Samuel Taylor Coleridge, *Biographia Literaria,* "Language of metrical composition", chap. 18.

33 Structural patterning of this kind was also favoured by Runge: In studies for "Der Morgen", the three children standing on the stamens of the lily "haben, wie sie gestellt sind, Beziehung auf die Dreyeinigkeit" *(Schriften,* I, 31) and Brentano copied this model in his "Der Lebensbaum". St Paul used a striking threefold anaphora to both explain and represent the Trinity in I Corinthians 12, 4-6.

34 Brentano often uses this idea. In *Die Gründung Prags,* Act 1, the witch Zwrakta realizes that her evil spells will be powerless as soon as the cock crows to herald dawn: "Bald reißt der Hahn mit sichelförmgem Schrei / Ins Herz der Nacht, und bricht die Zauberei.' (IV, 589).

35 The first editors of Brentano's works put a colon before the final refrain in this poem and inverted commas round it. This has been copied in most editions ever since, including III, 930, but it was not Brentano's original intention, as is evident from his own edition of the "Gockelmärchen" in 1838 (pp. 345-6). Some of Maria Schmidt-Ihm's otherwise interesting comments in "Anmerkungen zu Brentano's 'Eingang'", *Acta Germanica,* 3 (1968), 153-65, which only came to my notice when the present article was in proof, are invalidated by her use of a faultily punctuated text of the poem.

36 Grammatically, line 17 could also be rendered "what love obtained, what sorrow dispelled" i.e. making "Lieb" and "Leid" nominative instead of accusative, or else "Lieb" could be accusative and "Leid" nominative. Although a reasonable case could be made for either of these alternatives, the rhythmical stress seems to point to the accusative case for both "Lieb" and

"Leid".

[37] Staiger, p. 96.

[38] Many of Steinle's illustrations, and also his "Gedenkblatt, 1842" are reproduced in *Clemens Brentano und Edward von Steinle. Dichtungen und Bilder* edited by Alexander von Bernus and Alfons M. von Steinle (Kempten and Munich, 1909); thanks are due to the Kösel Verlag for permission to reproduce the relevant plate. Some of Steinle's illustrations for Brentano's *Chronika* are reproduced in "Brentano's *Chronika* and its Revision" by the present writer, *LJb.*, Sonderband (1971), pp. 160-84.

[39] *Clemens Brentano und Edward von Steinle*, pp. 213-14.

[40] On the origin and symbolism of the rosary, see Eithne Wilkins' study, *The Rose-Garden Game. The Symbolic Background to the European Prayer-Beads* (London, 1969).

Eichendorff und Shakespeare

Festvortrag zur Jahresversammlung der Eichendorff-Gesellschaft, 7. April 1972

Hugo von Hofmannsthal sagte einmal, »es seien dies die wahren Leser Shakespeares, und in ihnen Shakespeare auch einzig lebendig, die eine Bühne in sich trügen«; und bei Ludwig Tieck heißt es im *Phantasus,* daß »die Bühne *in* der Phantasie *für* die Phantasie erbaut« dem romantischen Dichter im allgemeinen ein unabsehbar weites Feld eröffnet habe: er müsse aber dabei ganz bewußt das Dramatische und das Theatralische voneinander unterscheiden, denn bei der unsichtbaren Bühne in der Phantasie handle es sich um das Theatralische.

Dramatiker war Eichendorff natürlich nicht; sein Sinn für das Theatralische dagegen war ausgesprochen stark entwickelt, und ohne Zweifel trug er als Erzähler und auch, wie das seine kritischen Schriften beweisen, als schöpferischer Leser der großen Dramen der Weltliteratur Hofmannsthals unsichtbare Bühne der Phantasie in sich. Vieles in seinen Erzählungen erinnert unmittelbar an das Theater, an die Voraussetzungen und sogar an die Technik der Bühne, nicht aber an das eigentlich dramatische Widerspiel der Mächte selbst. Die Erzählwerke sind, wenn nicht versetzte Dramen, doch jedenfalls theatralisch angehaucht, ja manchmal sogar auch dem Inhalt nach ganz mit der Theateratmosphäre gesättigt, zumal wenn es, wie in den *Glücksrittern* und in *Dichter und ihre Gesellen,* um Akteure und um das Schauspielerwesen selbst geht. Den *Taugenichts* hat man, wie *die Glücksritter,* ein Lustspiel in Prosa, eine erzählte Komödie genannt, und hier wie in den beiden Romanen, *Ahnung und Gegenwart* und *Dichter und ihre Gesellen,* hat man beständig den Eindruck, Eichendorff regiere wie ein Theaterintendant von der Kulisse aus das Geschehen und das Ganze spiele auf einer imaginären Bühne. Vieles trägt zu diesem Eindruck bei: als Erzähler wirft sich Eichendorff auffallend gern in Szene, so daß der Leser malerische Menschengruppen als belebte Tableaux erblickt gegen den nur flüchtig entworfenen Hintergrund der etwas wesenlosen, attrappenhaften, sich stets gleichbleibenden Landschaft von Garten, Wald, Strom, Schloß und Residenz, alles zusammengenommen, die unverkennbar Eichendorffsche Welt, nämlich die Welt als Bühne, als Vorspiel auf das eigentliche Sein in der Heimat »über'n Strom der Zeit«. Denkt man rückblickend ans Erzählwerk, so schweben einem eher vereinzelte Bilder und Gruppen, Situationen und Stimmungen vor, weniger eine Handlung als ein Geschehen. Ist der Faden der jeweiligen Erzählung oft verworren, so bleiben einem dafür einzelne, im wahren Sinne theatralisch zu nennende Höhepunkte, ob komischer oder tragischer Art, in der Erinnerung: die ergötzliche Situation des Taugenichts im italienischen Gebirgsschloß, wo man ihn für ein verkleidetes Mädchen hält; der Selbstmord der Gräfin Romana im brennenden Schloß ihrer Ahnen; der Maskenball mit dem als Totengerippe verkleideten Fremden; Prinz Romano, der inmitten der festlichen Feuerwerke wie auf einem tollgewordenen Schaukelpferde vor dem Palast der Gräfin Aurora anlangt.

Eichendorffs enge Beziehungen zur sichtbaren Bühne der südlichen Barocktradition sind ausreichend bekannt. Aus seinen Tagebucheintragungen weiß man, daß er und sein Bruder von Jugend auf ausgesprochene Theaternarren waren, die fast tagtäglich in die »Comedie« liefen, mitnahmen, was es eben gab, meist mittelmäßige, jetzt längst vergessene Trivialstücke, ab und zu etwas Gutes. Shakespeare-Aufführungen hat er, soviel man weiß, überhaupt sehr selten gesehen, da es auf der damaligen deutschen Bühne wenige gab, und auch dann nur in entstellender Bearbeitung oder Inszenierung. Aus dem Dialog zwischen zwei Intendanten in E. T. A. Hoffmanns *Seltsame Leiden eines Theaterdirektors,* zuerst 1817 erschienen, also in Eichendorffs Breslauer Jahren, geht hervor, daß die Schauspieler von damals zu keiner Shakespeare-Aufführung zu bringen waren, außer in den althergebrachten Bearbeitungen der großen Schauspieler (z. B. Ifflands); und Shakespeares Lustspiele gab es zu diesem Zeitpunkt auf der deutschen Bühne überhaupt nicht, im Gegensatz zu England, wo die drei romantischen Komödien, *As You Like It, Twelfth Night* und

Much Ado About Nothing, damals die beliebtesten Shakespeare-Stücke überhaupt waren. In dem genannten Werk beschreibt Hoffmann eine sehr erfolgreiche, aber leider nur imaginäre Einübung und Aufführung von »jenem herrlichen Lustspiel«, *Twelfth Night (Was Ihr wollt),* in textgetreuer Gestalt. Eichendorff aber hat in jungen Jahren nur den *Macbeth* in Schillers Bearbeitung gesehen, und zu diesem Zeitpunkt — Berlin, 11. Dezember 1809 — war es ihm hauptsächlich um die Hexen zu tun und nicht, wie später, um das metaphysische Rätsel des Bösen in der Welt. Es war im Berliner Schauspielhaus, und Iffland selbst spielte König Duncan. Eichendorff notiert wie folgt: »Bis ins innerste Mark grausenhafter Anblick der drei Hexen mit ihren grauen Kitteln, langen, dürren Fingern, gespenstischen Stellungen und wildverworrenen Haaren, durch die die Blitze leuchten. Fürchterliche Scene und Chorus, wo die drei Hexen um den Zauberkessel tanzen (Judenleber), wunderbar-schneidender Klang, wenn die mit Pfauenfedern geschmückte Fee aus dem Kessel steigt«. Ein aufregendes Opernballett, aber kaum Shakespeares Höllengeister auf der schottischen Gebirgsheide. Von der Macbeth-Vorstellung im Wiener Burgtheater, zwei Jahre später (1811), heißt es lakonischer: »Unerträglich verpfuscht. Hexenscenen ohne allen Gusto.« In späteren Jahren aber zitiert Eichendorff, als Shakespeareleser, gerade diese Tragödie als Exempel der ausgesprochen christlichen Weltauffassung seines Dichters: »Im Macbeth *scheint* durchaus ein heidnisches Fatum zu walten. Die Orakelsprüche der Hexen reißen den Helden von Frevel zu Frevel bis zum endlichen Siege fort. Aber droben ist es anders bestimmt. Macbeths irdischer Glanz wendet sich für ihn zum Fluche, und dieser Fluch wird zum Segen der Unterdrückten«.

Im großen ganzen also war der Ort von Eichendorffs Begegnung mit Shakespeare die unsichtbare Bühne seiner Leserphantasie, und gerade für die Vorzüge dieser inneren Bühne erhoben sich damals in Deutschland, wie auch in Englands romantischen Kreisen, mächtige Stimmen. In England vertrat diese Ansicht der romantische Essayist Charles Lamb, der die schönen Nacherzählungen *Tales from Shakespeare* geschaffen hat: »Es klingt zwar paradox, aber ich kann mir nicht helfen: Shakespeares Stücke eignen sich weniger für die Bühne als die beinahe jedes anderen Dramatikers«. Und in Deutschland behauptet Goethe 1813, ein Jahr also nach seiner eigenen, für unsere Begriffe vollkommen verfehlten Bearbeitung von *Romeo und Julie* für sein Weimarer Theater: »Shakespeares Werke sind nicht für die Augen des Leibes... sie enthalten viel weniger sinnliche Tat als geistiges Wort... So gehört Shakespeare notwendig in die Geschichte der Poesie; in der Geschichte des Theaters tritt er nur zufällig auf« *(Shakespeare und kein Ende,* 1813 und 1826). Was man nun auch zu diesen erstaunlichen Behauptungen meint, Eichendorffs lebenslängliches Verhältnis zu Shakespeare beweist, daß er sich durchaus nicht nur im wirklichen Theater dichterisch erleben läßt. Vielleicht aber verstärkte dieses von der wirklichen Bühne isolierte, rein poetische Erleben eines überwältigend großen Dramatikers Eichendorffs lyrische, oft ungenau wesenlose, zweidimensionale Darstellung seiner epischen Stoffe, wo eher straffe Erzählung und dynamisch lebendige Charakterschilderung herrschen sollten. Denn der eigentlich dramatische Eindruck und eine lebendige Theatralik im allgemeinen sind nun einmal vom lebendigen Schauspieler abhängig, vom dreidimensionalen, leibhaftigen Menschen, seiner Stimme, den Gesten, dem ganzen Auftreten. Bleibt das alles weg, so hat man schließlich nur noch die Struktur des erzählten Theaters, die Stimmung der Bühne, das lyrisch-theatralische Spiel mit Gefühl und Gedanken, aber weder die Wirklichkeit des lebendig dargestellten Dramas noch die eigentlich epische Entwicklung des Romans. Aber auch Dramen lassen sich in dieser Weise schreiben, und Eichendorff hat es getan, besonders in seinen beiden Tragödien, nicht aber in den Satiren und im Lustspiel. Mit Spiel, Scherz und Lustigkeit jedoch will ich mich heute abend vornehmlich befassen; denn hier sehe ich den eigentlichen Zusammenhang zwischen Eichendorff und Shakespeare.

Im Gegensatz zu anderen deutschen Dichtern der Generation vor ihm, z. B. Lessing, Herder oder Goethe, hat Eichendorff aber anscheinend kein einmalig überwältigendes Shakespeare-Erlebnis durchgemacht, und nur selten hat er, wie das schon seine zurückhaltende Art war, über sein Verhältnis zu diesem Dichter etwas Bekenntnishaftes schriftlich festgelegt. Er hat wohl im Alter in seiner bewußt ethisch gehaltenen *Geschichte des Dramas* (1854) einiges Schöne über ihn als christlichen Dichter geschrieben, aber mit der bahnbrechenden Shakespeare-Kritik der beiden Schlegels, Adam Müllers und Ludwig Tiecks kann man das kaum vergleichen. Trotzdem aber scheint mir Shakespeares Geist gewissermaßen über Eichendorff als Erzähler zu walten, so überraschend diese Behauptung auch anfangs scheinen mag. Der englische Leser Eichendorffs, von Shakespeare kommend — und bewußt oder unbewußt kommen auch englische Germanisten von dieser geheimnisvollen dichterischen Welt her — fühlt sich von Anfang an, nicht nur in den wenigen Dramen, sondern im gesamten Erzählwerk, ganz unmißverständlich an Shakespeare erinnert, und zwar besonders an die Atmosphäre der »romantic comedies«, der romantischen Lustspiele. Auf jeden Fall fühlt sich der Engländer — aber er muß Deutsch können, denn Übersetzungen gibt es kaum — auffallend rasch bei Eichendorff beheimatet. Meine Ausführungen wollen nun dieses Gefühl der Ähnlichkeit und Analogie mit Shakespeare von verschiedenen Richtungen aus beleuchten und hoffentlich auch begründen.

Eichendorff gehörte zur ersten Dichtergeneration in Deutschland, die Shakespeare von Anfang an gewissermaßen unmittelbar als Leser erlebte, nämlich mittels der A. W. Schlegelschen Übersetzung der siebzehn Stücke, die in den für Eichendorff wichtigen Entwicklungsjahren, 1797—1810, erschienen sind. Die Übersetzung wurde dann durch Tieck und seine Gehilfen weitergeführt und zwischen 1825 und 1833, wiederum schöpferische Jahre für Eichendorffs Dichten, vollendet. Auch für die ältere Generation des ausgehenden 18. Jahrhunderts war Shakespeare schon das größte, vom Ausland stammende Bildungserlebnis gewesen, aber für den Goethe des *Götz* oder den Schiller der *Räuber* war er in der Prosa-Übersetzung von Wieland und Eschenburg noch keineswegs ein selbstverständlicher, integrierender Bestandteil der geistigen Welt und Literaturlandschaft Deutschlands geworden, wie das dann ab Anfang des neuen Jahrhunderts durch die geniale romantische Übersetzung in Shakespeares eigenem Versmaß der Fall war. Denn erst Goethe und Schiller in ihrer klassischen Entwicklung haben die sprachliche und rhythmische

Ausdrucksmöglichkeit für die deutsche Sprache geschaffen, die diese—übrigens in der Welt ganz einmalige—Einbürgerung Shakespeares überhaupt erst möglich gemacht hat. Die jüngeren, hier in Frage kommenden Dichter, wie Eichendorff und Arnim, später dann auch Grabbe, Büchner und Otto Ludwig, insofern sie Shakespeare nicht auf Englisch lesen konnten (Eichendorff konnte das, soviel man feststellen kann, *nicht),* wurden damals instand gesetzt, Shakespeare viel tiefgreifender in sich aufzunehmen und daher auch viel allgemeiner und unauffälliger im Einklang mit ihrem eigenen dichterischen Wesen zu verwerten. Auch durch ihr nationales Empfinden konnten diese jüngeren Dichter sich mit Shakespeare irgendwie wesensverwandt fühlen. Der geistige Kontakt mit dem größten Dichter jenes Landes, das Eichendorff »das frommernste halbdeutsche England« nennen konnte, war für ihn dichterisch wirksam, noch ehe er die Spanier — die er auch in Schlegelscher Übertragung lesen konnte und später selbst übersetzte — besser kennen lernte. Bei Eichendorff heißt es: »Shakespeare ist durch den germanischen Geist Altenglands, der durch seine Dramen weht, fast unser Landsmann geworden«. Durch die romantische Übersetzung und bahnbrechende, ganz neuartige Kritik, besonders der bis dahin wenig beachteten Lustspiele, wurde Shakespeare also endgültig für den deutschen Kulturkreis gewonnen, d. h. für den Leser, damit auch für den genialen Vorleser — ich erinnere an Ludwig Tiecks glänzende Shakespeare-Vorlesungen in Dresden, die auch Eichendorff gehört hat. Tieck las mit Vorliebe Lustspiele.

Da Eichendorff in seinen theaterfreudigen Wiener Jahren an *Ahnung und Gegenwart* arbeitete und im Hause Friedrich und Dorothea Schlegels verkehrte, kannte er die Lustspiele Shakespeares schon recht gut: Er konnte sogar annehmen, wie Tieck in den Rahmengesprächen des *Phantasus,* daß der gebildete und künstlerisch interessierte Mensch in der Residenz diese oder jene Shakespeare-Komödie damals so gut wie auswendig kannte. Das geht aus einer sehr gelungenen Episode in Eichendorffs Roman hervor, die auf ein wirkliches Erlebnis des Bruders, Wilhelm, zurückgehen soll. In einer aesthetischen Teegesellschaft trifft der Graf Leontin des Romans mit einem Modedichter zusammen, der, wie Malvolio in *Twelfth Night,* vom Teufel des Hochmuts besessen ist. Als einzige Antwort auf die hochnäsigen, alles besser wissenden Fragen dieses Dichters zitiert Leontin unentwegt und mit ernstem Gesicht den ganzen höheren Unsinn, mit dem Malvolio von den Spaßmachern des Stücks, Sir Toby und seiner Nichte, Maria, und Feste, dem Narren, unbarmherzig gehänselt wird. Gräfin Romana, die dabeisteht, weiß sofort, um was es sich handelt, und übernimmt die lustige Rolle der Maria. Durch diese Shakespeare-Montage erteilt also Eichendorff den ihm verhaßten, eingebildeten Modedichtern der Wiener und Berliner Salons eine scharfe Lektion, denn keiner sieht sich gerne als Malvolio hingestellt, als der puritanische, dumm-eitle Spielverderber, Haushofmeister des Fräuleins Olivia in *Twelfth Night.*

Man könnte noch weitere, ganz unauffällige Shakespeare-Allusionen in beiden Romanen anführen, an die Lustspiele, an *Heinrich IV. (1. u. 2.),* die es Eichendorff besonders angetan hatten, Falstaffs wegen, ja sogar an wichtiger Stelle an *Hamlet;* aber Weiteres erübrigt sich, denn es sollte nur dargelegt werden, daß Eichendorff zur ersten Generation in Deutschland gehörte, die sich, wie Leontin und Romana, auf ganz selbstverständliche Weise Shakespearisch unterhalten konnte. Gleichzeitig wurde auch in England die Anspielung auf Shakespearefiguren und -situationen die Mode im Roman, besonders bei Walter Scott, der von seinem ersten anonym erschienenen Roman ab, *Waverley,* 1814 *(Ahnung und Gegenwart* erschien 1815, einige Jahre nach der Niederschrift), dauernd auf Shakespearsche Parallelen zurückgreift. Mit besonderer Vorliebe und aus ähnlicher Gemütsverfassung — Eichendorff schätzte Scott — zitiert er Falstaff, Sir Toby und die Narren. Der Waverley-Roman trägt noch außerdem ein Motto aus Shakespeare, wie das später auch bei Eichendorff der Fall war: das Motto zu der Novelle *Viel Lärmen um Nichts,* ein Shakespeare-Titel, stammt aus dem Epilog zum *Sommernachtstraum* und deutet damit auf die imaginäre Bühne, auf der sich jene an Maskerade und Verkleidungen reiche Novelle abspielt:

> If we shadows have offended
> Think but this, and all is mended,
> That you have but slumbered here

While these visions did appear.

Wenn wir Schatten euch beleidigt,
O so glaubt—und wohl verteidigt
Sind wir dann!—ihr alle schier
Habet nur geschlummert hier
Und geschaut in Nachtgesichten
Eures eignen Hirnes Dichten.

Nirgends bei Scott oder bei Eichendorff handelt es sich übrigens um Shakespeare-Parallelen in der Handlung, sondern allein um eine Analogie in der freudigen Lustspielstimmung und sozusagen um eine Erweiterung des dichterischen Horizonts.

Anders stand es in dieser Hinsicht mit Eichendorffs Komödie *Wider Willen,* mit der er sich schon im Jahre nach dem Erscheinen des ersten Romans und der Rückkehr aus den Freiheitskriegen beschäftigte. Sie erschien 1822 in einer Danziger Zeitschrift als Fragment, und erst elf Jahre später kam die vollständig umgearbeitete Fassung unter dem Titel *Die Freier* heraus. Gerade in diesen Zwischenjahren (1825—1833) erschienen in allmählicher Folge die neun Teile der nun vervollständigten Schlegel-Tieckschen Shakespeare-Übersetzung und führten, wie man annehmen darf, zu erneuter und reiferer Shakespeare-Lektüre seitens Eichendorffs. Vergleicht man nun das technisch unbeholfene Fragment *Wider Willen* und seine direkten Shakespeare-Übernahmen (jedoch im spanischen Versmaß) mit den *Freiern,* dem durchaus selbständigen Endprodukt von 1833, so versteht man erst, was es heißt, Shakespeare schöpferisch und dem eigenen Wesen gemäß zu erleben, ohne sich von ihm überwältigen zu lassen. Wieder schwebte Eichendorff das ihm so durch und durch sympathische *Twelfth Night* vor, aber während er im Fragment immer noch die Malvolio-Spaßszenen, sowie auch den alten Roué, Sir Toby, im Sinn hatte, so hat sich in den *Freiern* die Einwirkung Shakespeares, bis auf einige Motive, die man eher als Allgemeingut der Lustspieltradition betrachten sollte, in etwas immer noch sehr Spürbares, doch bereits rein Atmosphärisches verwandelt, ganz der eigenen dichterischen Art Eichendorffs angepaßt. Die frühen Shakespeare-Komödien überhaupt, vor allem auch *As You Like It (Wie es Euch gefällt)*, kommen hier in Betracht.

Die beiden für Eichendorff wichtigsten Stücke sind, dem Titel nach, in ihrer deutschen Übersetzung nicht leicht auseinanderzuhalten und werden auch oft von Kritikern in diesem Eichendorff-Kontext verwechselt. Ich darf daher eine Erklärung vorausschicken und Sie auch kurz an den Inhalt wenigstens der einen Komödie erinnern. *Twelfth Night or What You Will*, ist von Schlegel aus nur durch den Untertitel, *Was Ihr wollt*, bekannt, in England aber nur durch den Haupttitel, *Dreikönigsabend*, denn es handelt sich um die zwölfte Nacht nach Weihnachten, also um das Fest der Epiphanie. Das zweite für Eichendorff hauptsächlich in Frage kommende Stück heißt überhaupt nur *As You Like It, Wie es Euch gefällt*, die Geschichte von vier Liebespaaren, besonders von Rosalind und Orlando, im Wald von Arden. Mit diesen beiden Titelformulierungen wollte Shakespeare andeuten, daß es sich in diesen jetzt »romantisch« oder »festlich« genannten Komödien um keine damals anerkannte, regelrechte Gattung des Lustspiels handelte; die Zuschauer wurden also eingeladen, die Stücke nach Belieben aufzufassen, als was immer sie wollten oder wie es ihnen eben gefiel. Für englische Begriffe hat aber der Titel, *Twelfth Night*, schon vom Anfang an ganz deutlichen Anklang an lustig verlebte Festtage. Ob das Stück am Hof der Königin Elizabeth am richtigen Tage erstaufgeführt wurde oder, wie dann wiederholt später, in Grays Inn, den Juristeninnungen in der City — der nämliche von Shakespeare als Theater benutzte Raum existiert übrigens noch heute im Herzen Londons—,weiß man nicht genau; auf jeden Fall war das Stück der Stimmung nach von Shakespeare als Teil der Winterfestlichkeiten des Jahres 1601 oder 1602 geplant. Ähnlich wie bei der Fastnacht in Deutschland handelte es sich im Zeitalter Shakespeares um den Exorzismus der winterlichen Düsterkeit durch Scherz und Glück der Liebenden, die aber auch ihrerseits manche trübe Illusion auszutreiben hatten, ehe sie ihr Glück richtig genießen konnten. Dazu halfen ihnen die Spaßmacher und die Narren, vor allem der »Lord of Misrule«, das Oberhaupt der Mißregierung, eine Art von Fastnachtskönig, der während der zwölf Tage der winterlichen Feste zwischen Weihnachten und Dreikönigsfest die Macht ergreifen durfte und allgewaltig seine Untertanen regierte, beschimpfte, auslachte, aber auch bekehrte durch seine Narrenfreiheit. Mit seiner Begleitfigur, dem eigentlichen Narren, spielte er, besonders den Verliebten oder den Spielverderbern jeden Alters, die tollsten Streiche.

In *Twelfth Night* handelt es sich um den Fürsten Orsino, dem eine exaltierte übermäßig empfindsam-romantische Auffassung von der Liebe ausgetrieben werden soll. Er seufzt hoffnungslos für Olivia, die sich ihrerseits aus maßloser Trauer über den Tod von Vater und Bruder vor der Liebe verschließt. Doch das unterdrückte Gefühl überrumpelt sie bald: sie verliebt sich in die als Page verkleidete Viola, die dem Fürsten Orsino dient und ihn ihrerseits heimlich liebt. Violas Zwillingsbruder, wie sie selbst aus einem Schiffbruch errettet, heiratet am Ende Olivia, die ihn schon durch seine Zwillingsschwester liebt, während Orsino vernünftigerweise seinen ehemaligen Pagen, Viola, heimführt, so daß sich alles in Wohlgefallen und Liebesglück auflöst. Mit Hilfe des Narren, Feste, treibt Olivias versoffener, aber unverwüstlich heiterer Onkel, Sir Toby, der die Rolle des »Lord of Misrule« in dieser Festkomödie spielt, dem puritanischen Malvolio in der schon erwähnten Episode den Hochmutsteufel aus. In einer berühmt gewordenen Frage ruft er ihm zu: »Dost thou think, because thou art virtuous, there shall be no more cakes and ale? —»Meinst du, weil du ein Tugendbold bist, es soll weiterhin keinen Kuchen und kein gutes Bier mehr geben?« (Akt II,3). Übrigens übersetzt hier Schlegel, für englische Begriffe vollkommen unmöglich: ». . . daß es deshalb in der Welt keine Torten und keinen Wein mehr geben (solle).«

Für Eichendorff-Kenner braucht man gar nicht im einzelnen auszuführen, daß es sich in *Twelfth Night* um eine Lustspielintrige genau nach Eichendorffs Herzen handelt, und zwar so ganz in der echten Lubowitzer Art, den tollen Streichen in den schlesischen Adelsschlössern mit ihren köstlichen alten Originalen. Wie Eichendorff in seinem Aufsatz *Deutsches Adelsleben am Schlusse des achtzehnten Jahrhunderts* meint, »da fehlte es nicht an manchem ergötzlichen Junker Tobias oder Junker Christoph von Bleichenwang«, d. i. Sir Andrew Aguecheek, der Freund Sir Tobys. Über Shakespeares Lustspiele sagte Eichendorff in seiner Literaturgeschichte, daß sie uns wohl wahrheitsgetreu mitten in das nationale Leben seiner eigenen Zeit versetzen, »aber in dieses Alltagsleben, wo er es nicht geradezu auf märchenhaften Boden stellt, blitzt und leuchtet unversehens durch irgendeine offengelassene Thür oder Dachluke der Glanz eines fernen Wunderlandes herein. So geht in *Was Ihr wollt* eine Liebesgeschichte melodisch durch den tollen Rumor der Narren.« Diese schöne Charakterisierung könnte man unverändert auf sein eigenes Lustspiel, *Die Freier*, übertragen, desgleichen auch seine Bemerkung, Shakespeare hätte keineswegs nur das Satirisch-Komische verstanden, sondern vor allem auch das wirklich Lustige, den reinen Scherz, das frohe Spiel des wahrhaft kindlichen Herzens, so daß es bei Shakespeare Stücke gibt »wo die Menschen wie freie Waldvögel sich in unverwüstlicher Heiterkeit unter einem ewigblauen Himmel bewegen«.

In *Twelfth Night* sind die meisten Figuren in irgendeinem wichtigen Sinne nicht nur voreinander verkleidet oder verstellt, sondern auch—und das ist der tiefere Sinn der äußerlichen Verkleidung—vor sich selbst: keiner ist eigentlich ganz was er scheint oder das, für was er sich selbst hält. Jeder muß durch die Ereignisse umlernen, den Schein in Sein verwandeln. Die Maske hilft sowohl Viola als auch Olivia, das wahre Wesen der eigenen Liebe wie der Liebe überhaupt instinktiv zu erfassen: »I am not what I am«, sagt sie in ihrer Pagenverkleidung über sich selbst, »ich bin nicht das, was ich bin«; »nothing that is so, is so«, heißt es dann weiter, da ihr und auch Orsino und Olivia bisher Unbewußtes auf einmal klar wird. Ja selbst Feste, der weise, melancholische, aber liebenswerteste aller Narren Shakespeares, geht in der Verkleidung des Priestermantels zu dem als verrückt eingekerkerten Malvolio. Auch singt der Clown, von seiner überlegenen Position aus, die wunderbaren, stimmungstragenden Lieder des Stücks, z. B. »O mistress mine, where are you roaming?« und das Schlußlied, das mit seinem zauberischen Refrain das ganze Menschenleben zusammenfaßt und schildert:

> When that I was and a little tiny boy,
> With hey, ho, the wind and the rain;
> A foolish thing was but a toy,

For the rain it raineth every day...

A great while ago the world begun,
With hey, ho, the wind and the rain;
But that's all one, our play is done,
And we'll strive to please you every day.

Hier, und oft, scheint die leise Wehmut, eine geheime Trauer, die Heiterkeit des Ganzen in Frage zu stellen. Die variationsreiche Sprache, teils Prosa, teils reinste Lyrik, trägt zum Eindruck des »bittersweet« bei. Kennt man Eichendorff, so braucht man kaum den Hinweis, daß er sich oft in einer der Stimmung nach ganz ähnlichen Welt bewegt.

In *As You Like It* verkleidet sich Rosalind als Schäfer Ganymed und trägt ihrem Geliebten, Orlando, auf, er soll ihn, Ganymed, zur Stillung der Sehnsucht und auch zur allgemeinen Übung in der Liebe, als »Rosalind« anreden und behandeln, was auch geschieht. Der Reiz dieser sozusagen doppelten Verkleidungsmaskerade, durch die Rosalind dem Schmerz und der Liebe freien Lauf lassen kann, ohne Sitte und Zartheit im geringsten zu verletzen, während die Zuschauer das schöne Gefühl des Besserwissens genießen, übertrifft alles, was sogar Shakespeare selbst in dieser Hinsicht geleistet hat, mit vielleicht der einzigen Ausnahme der als Page verkleideten Imogen in *Cymbeline*.

Wie in den Komödien Shakespeares und des Barocks überhaupt, geht das Motiv der Verkleidung, der Maskerade, mit aufälliger Beständigkeit durch das gesamte erzählerische und dramatische Werk Eichendorffs hindurch und erreicht in den Werken, die unter der erneuten Shakespearelesung in den zwanziger und dreißiger Jahren entstanden sind, einen Höhepunkt. Vielleicht betrachtete er—wie auch Shakespeare—die Maskierung des eigentlichen Selbst als etwas Ähnliches wie die Maske der Illusion im Theater überhaupt, die dem Zuschauer hilft, die Wahrheit über dieses Selbst und über seine Mitmenschen zu erkennen, die Zweiheit, die Doppelheit des menschlichen Geistes, den wunderbaren Widerspruch in uns. In *Twelfth Night* sowie in den *Freiern* drängt die Maskierung das als Mann verkleidete Mädchen in die Enge: zum Duell herausgefordert, gelangen Viola und Flora (III.4 und III.2) zu einer ganz radikalen Selbsterkenntnis der fingierten Position, die für das Elisabethanische Publikum noch pikanter war, da Shakespeares weibliche Rollen ohnehin von hübschen Knaben gespielt wurden. Solche Situationen aber, wie die Verkleidung im allgemeinen, waren weder von dem einen Dichter noch von dem anderen als bloßer Lachreiz zu verstehen; diese Technik zieht vielmehr auch den Zuschauer in ein geheimes Vertrauen: indem die in Frage kommende Figur zweierlei Schichten ihrer Persönlichkeit auf einmal in Bewegung setzt, während der Gesprächspartner auf der Bühne nur eine durchschaut, kommt ein reizvolles Spiel des Inkognito zustande. Man wird dadurch noch unmittelbarer in das allgemeine Rollenspiel verwickelt, sieht die gesamte Welt als Bühne an. In *As You Like It* trägt das der Ironiker, Jaques, vor: »All the world's a stage, / And all the men and women merely players: / They have their exits and their entrances; / And one man in his time plays many parts.« / . . . »sein Leben lang spielt einer manche Rollen.« Die Menschen in den *Freiern* tragen bewußt einen Komödienmantel und nennen ihre Verkleidung auch bei diesem Namen; legen sie ihn dann schließlich am Ende ab, so sind sie wieder sie selbst, nur haben sie sich unter dem Schutz des Komödienmantels irgendwie gewandelt, sind zu einer neuen Be-sinnung gekommen über ihre eigentliche Rolle im Leben. In Shakespeares Altersstück, dem *Tempest,* verzichtet Prospero auf seiner Insel im Weltenmeer zum Schluß freiwillig auf Zaubermantel und Zauberstab und wird wieder der Fürst von Mailand, hat er doch sein Vertrauen in die Menschheit und in die eigenen rein menschlichen Kräfte ohne Hilfe der Zauberei wiedergewonnen. Der Komödienmantel der Verkleidung ist also auch eine Art Zaubermantel, der dem, der darunter steckt, neue Schichten der eigenen Persönlichkeit offenbaren kann und ihm hilft, die neuentdeckte Einsicht zu integrieren, den Kräften der Ordnung im allgemeinen zum endgültigen Sieg zu verhelfen. Hinter diesem schlichten, geradezu abgedroschenen Motiv, vor dem weder Shakespeare noch Eichendorff je zurückscheuten, lag die lebenslängliche Beschäftigung dieser Dichter mit dem »gnothi seauton«, dem »erkenne dich selbst«, wofür das veränderte Kostüm der jeweils gespielten Rolle geradezu das Symbol zu nennen ist.

Eichendorffs Stück, *Die Freier,* stellt ein *ne plus ultra* an Verkleidungen dar, wie das auch z. B. in Shakespeares *The Comedy of Errors* der Fall ist: man hält sich geradezu den Kopf vor Verwirrung, aber das schadet nichts, denn das ganze Stück spielt in einer unvergleichlich heiteren Atmosphäre von Scherz, Frohsinn und Frühlingsglanz. »Die lustige Rakete steigt!« ruft Flora mit übermütiger Heiterkeit; die Explosion der Komik, wie bei Shakespeare, in geschickt und stimmungsvoll zwischen Vers und Prosa wechselnder Sprache und auch mit reizvoll witzigem Wortspiel, läßt keinen unversehrt, wenn auch nicht jeder eine schöpferische Wandlung erfährt. Verkleidung über Verkleidung weist den Weg zum besseren Verständnis des eigenen Narren. Später heißt es bei Eichendorff: »Das Komische geht... überall dem verborgenen und sorgfältig gehüteten Narren der vernünftigen Leute zu Leibe, der sich einst in unserem Hanswurst verkörpert hatte«. Bei Shakespeare ist da immer noch der Narr in eigener Person, der die Rolle des witzigen Analytikers, des Bewußtmachers spielt, die bei Eichendorff jeweils von den Hauptpersonen selbst, für sich und andere, übernommen wird.

Die Hauptpersonen in Eichendorffs Lustspiel, Graf Leonard und Gräfin Adele, sind keineswegs ohne Humor, dabei aber doch der romantischen Sehnsucht verfallen und der Scheu vor der praktischen Gegenwart, der festen Position. Verkleidet gehen sie einander entgegen, denn keiner von beiden will sich der endgültigen Entscheidung, dem Prüfstein der Ehe, überantworten. Rückwärtsblickend erinnert diese Kompliziertheit an Shakespeares originellstes Liebespaar, Benedict und Beatrice in *Much Ado About Nothing,* und voraus deutet sie auf H. v. Hofmannthals Graf Kari und Gräfin Helene in *Der Schwierige,* der Wiener Komödie der chronischen Mißverständnisse. Hier aber hat sich die eher äußerliche Technik der Verkleidung auf ein subtiles Wortgefecht reduziert; aber auch das so gelungene und nicht aufhörende Wortspiel bei Eichendorff, wie bei Shakespeare, ist ja selbst eine Abwandlung der wirklichen Verkleidung: man spielt Verstecken mit den Worten, die sich anders geben als sie sind und dabei in doppelter Rolle funktionieren. Ich darf hier bemerken, daß das von Shakespeare und von den Engländern überhaupt so beliebte

Wortspiel, oder »pun«, im Deutschen im Vergleich weit weniger entwickelt ist, aber ganz besonders von Eichendorff, und auch von Brentano, mit glänzender Komik gehandhabt wurde. —Auf mehr offensichtlich komischer Ebene wird Adele auch von anderen Freiern umworben, alle verkleidet. Der Anstifter der allgemeinen Konfusion auf dieser Ebene, der »Lord of Misrule«, der sich in dieser festlichen Komödie das Recht der Narrenfreiheit herausnimmt, ist der Jäger Victor, Geliebter der Zofe Adelens. Seinem Namen gemäß triumphiert er schließlich über alle: »Ich will kein Jäger sein«, ruft er, »wenn ich nicht alle diese mausigen Stoßvögel von Freiern an *einen* Narrenspieß stecke, um sie langsam am Feuer der Liebe zu braten.« Überall wird der verborgene, sorgfältig gehütete Narr vernünftiger Leute durch jede Verkleidung hindurch herausgefordert.

Den gleichen Zweck — solch bewußte Einsicht — erreicht Eichendorff, wie auch Shakespeare, im Lustspiel, wenn er fast ausnahmslos jede Stellung seiner Figuren ganz leise und immer liebevoll parodiert. Durch Leonards Monolog im Walde, bei seinem ersten Auftreten, ». . . in etwas phantastischer Reisekleidung . . . man hört in der Ferne Waldhörner«, parodiert er selbst die eigenen romantischen Einfälle, auch sogar im Rhythmus der Sprache, der gewisse Modelle aus Eichendorffs Werk in nicht überhörbarer Weise ironisiert; und die übrigen »mausigen Stoßvögel« von Freiern im Stück sind gewissermaßen ein ironischer Kommentar auf Leonard selbst. Das gleiche Verfahren findet sich in *As You Like It.* Nicht nur parodiert Shakespeare seine eigene Liebeslyrik, sondern keine einzige Position — das Hofleben in der Stadt, die pastorale Idylle im Wald, die einfachen Liebhaber, die komplizierten, die lustigen Menschen, die Melancholiker, die Treuherzigen, die Zyniker —bleibt unangetastet, ausgenommen allein die des frommen Einsiedlers im Wald, der übrigens auch für den englischen Dichter gelegentlich eine Perspektivenfigur sein kann. Shakespeare stellt alle diese Gegensätze ganz einfach nebeneinander und überläßt ihnen auch, ohne jegliches Moralisieren, den gegenseitigen Kommentar, während der Narr, sehr schön Touchstone (deutsch: Prüfstein) genannt, allmählich allen die Binde von den Augen nimmt. Sogar die bezaubernde Rosalind, sowie bei Eichendorff die jeweilige Gräfin Aurora, wird leise ausgelacht. Doch führt das alles nie zu Ernüchterung oder Ratlosigkeit, sondern zu neuer Einsicht und deshalb zu neuer Lebensweisheit. Alles gelind Umgeworfene ersteht dauernd wieder neu, d. h. alles, nur nicht die falschen Illusionen im redlichen Herzen: die im Grunde guten Menschen werden nie wie Malvolio, der Schlechtgewillte, beschämt, sondern nur wie *en famille* aufgezogen — so, in den *Freiern,* der köstlich philisterhafte Beamte, Fleder, und die beiden heruntergekommenen Artisten, Flitt und Schlender, wo, wie so oft bei beiden Dichtern, die Komik schon mit dem Namen anfängt: so heißen die Arbeiter im *Sommernachtstraum* Snug, Bottom, Snout und Starveling.

»Pyramus und Thisbe«, das Hochzeitsfestspiel der Arbeiter im *Sommernachtstraum,* war ganz offensichtlich Shakespeares fröhlich spaßhafter Kommentar zu seiner eigenen jugendlichen Liebestragödie *Romeo und Julia.* Er wollte sich über sie nicht eigentlich lustig machen, sondern vielmehr einen Ausgleich der gestörten Ordnung schaffen, indem er durch gutmütiges Gelächter und durch das Spiel die Spannung löste. Bei Shakespeare, wie auch bei Eichendorff, lagen das Komische und das Tragische nie weit auseinander; wie die Romantiker im allgemeinen, so hat Eichendorff in seiner Kritik das Nebeneinander der komischen und tragischen Stimmung bei Shakespeare psychologisch und auch künstlerisch durchaus verstanden und gerechtfertigt. Schiller konnte diese Stimmungsmischung bekanntlich nicht vertragen. Nach dem Königsmord im *Macbeth* kommt als erlösender Gegensatz zu der schrecklichen Spannung die berühmte Szene, wo der Pförtner sich, wie am Tor der Hölle selbst, in derb zweideutiger, ja unanständig-witziger Schimpferei ergeht. In Schillers schon erwähnten *Macbeth* Bearbeitung singt dieser gemeine Kerl statt dessen ein frommes Morgengebet: »Verschwunden ist die finstre Nacht, / Die Lerche schlägt, der Tag erwacht...«. Auch die Hexen waren Schiller nicht erhaben genug, so daß A. W. Schlegel den Spottvers ergehen ließ:

> Du willst in Furien die Hexen travestieren.
> Meinst du, das sei die Art mit Hexen umzugehen?
> Da werden beiderseits die Damen protestieren.

Für Eichendorff war der Humor im Grunde genommen der Zusammenprall des Komischen und des Tragischen, den Shakespeare in seinen »tiefsinnigen« Narren (so nennt sie Eichendorff immer) auf die Bühne stellte.

Unbedingt hätte Eichendorff gegen Schiller und auch gegen Goethe E. T. A. Hoffmann recht gegeben, der in dem oben genannten Werk behauptete, daß »nur der vom tiefsten Humor beseelte Schauspieler« den Hamlet darstellen könne. Doch warnte Eichendorff ausdrücklich vor leichtsinniger Nachahmung Shakespeares in dieser Hinsicht: »Das Komische«, sagt er, »ist überall nur da von Bedeutung [in der Tragödie], wo es auf einer großen, sittlichen Grundlage ruht, der es zur Folie dient«, wie eben bei Shakespeare und auch bei dem »wesentlich tragischen Don Quixote«. In seiner Hohenstaufentragödie, *Ezelin von Romano,* hat Eichendorff versucht, ein reines Gleichgewicht der Stimmungen künstlerisch zu gestalten. In der Atmosphäre vorbildlich waren ihm hier die beiden Teile von Shakespeares *Heinrich IV.,* für die er schon durch Adam Müllers bahnbrechende Kritik in diesem Kontext des Komisch-Tragischen eine besondere Vorliebe hatte, wohl auch wegen der Gestalt des Falstaff.

Man hat Eichendorff seine sogenannte Nachahmung des »eigentümlichen *clair-obscur* der Shakespearschen Stimmungsmischung« wenig gelinde vorgeworfen; mir scheint es, im Gegenteil, daß gerade die Stimmungsmischung, und namentlich das Komische in dieser Tragödie, das wirklich Geglückte ist, nicht, weil es sich um eine geschickte Shakespeare-Nacheiferung handelt (auch hier war Eichendorff nicht Epigone), sondern weil Eichendorffs komische Muse ihm eben wesensnaher und vertrauter war als die tragische. Denkt man sich dieses Stück eher als die pikareske Kriegskomödie des Grafen Carrara und des Fräuleins Zilie, zusammen mit den schurkenhaften Dienern, Mercutio und Jakob, und dagegen Ezelins frevelhafte Hybris der Macht und Violantes sehnsuchtsvolle Wald- und Schloßwelt nur als Hintergrund, so wird das ganze Stück auf einmal viel überzeugender. Genau so betrachtet man ja gewöhnlich Shakespeares Historie um den Thronfolger, Prince Hal, wo das wirklich Eindrucksvolle die pikareske Handlung um Falstaff und die Schweinskopfschenke in Eastcheap ist, und viel weniger die tragische Hintergrundshandlung um den reuevollen Königsmörder und König des Titels, Heinrich IV. Freilich fehlt es Eichendorff, wie jedem anderen Dichter, an einem Falstaff, der gesetzlos mit unbändigem Gelächter die Welt auf den Kopf stellt, und auch an der Verbindungsfigur des Prinzen, der die beiden Welten zusammenhält: im *Ezelin* werden die pikareske und die tragische Welt eben nur gegeneinander gestellt, nicht aber künstlerisch integriert — was aber nicht beweist, daß Shakespeare Eichendorff ganz verdorben hat, sondern nur, daß Eichendorff der tragische Stoff im Grunde nicht lag. Die komischen Figuren im *Ezelin* haben wahres Eigenleben, vielleicht auch gerade deshalb, weil sie einen parodistischen Kommentar auf die eigentlich tragischen darstellen, deren romantische Haltung und Aktion sie gewissermaßen ironisch wiederspiegeln. Diese Technik ist bei Eichendorff so offensichtlich, daß man an ein bewußtes Verfahren glauben muß, und als Beweis könnte man bemerken, daß er im gleichen Jahr mit dem *Ezelin* (1828) die Literatursatire *Meierbeths Glück und Ende* herausgab, unter anderem eine äußerst amüsante Ehrenrettung Shakespeares gegen Josef Meyers schauderhafte *Macbeth*-Übersetzung oder Travestie (1824). Unzweifelhaft ist aber diese Satire auch in mancher Hinsicht eine Glosse des eigenen Trauerspiels, was man im Detail ausführen könnte. — Shakespeares *Hamlet* fällt ins gleiche Jahr wie seine glänzendste Komödie, *Twelfth Night* (1601 bis 02).

Das Verkleidungsmotiv und die Selbstparodie durch Parallelhandlung oder entsprechende Komik sind also beiden Dichtern eigen und dienen letzten Endes der Förderung der heiter-scherzhaften Selbsterkenntnis. Ort dieser inneren Selbstbegegnung der Menschen ist bei Shakespeare oft, und bei Eichendorff fast immer, der Wald. Interessant ist es nun, daß Eichendorff in seinen kritischen Schriften Shakespeares gesamtes Werk oft mit einer Landschaft, genauer, dem Wald selbst, metaphorisch wiedergibt. Der germanische Geist Altenglands *weht* durch seine Dramen, heißt es da, sein Werk ist ein tiefer Zaubergrund, ein Zauberwald, wo sich leichtsinnige Nachahmer »ohne die ihm eigentümliche Andacht des Gefühls«, ohne »seinen Ernst und seine tiefsinnige Orientierungsgabe« hineingewagt und kläglich verirrt haben. Eichendorff verteidigt den häufigen Szenenwechsel bei Shakespeare und meint: »Uns wenigstens ist immer ein freier Wald mit seinen wildverschlungenen Ästen und tausend verworrenen Vogelstimmen schöner vorgekommen, als die symmetrischen Zier- und Hofgärten mit ihren Novantiken und Schiller'schen Redeblumen«. Auch zu Shakespeare ist Eichendorff durch das Medium des Bildes gekommen, denn der ganze Begriff wurde in ein dichterisches Bild verwandelt. Der englische Dichter war also für Eichendorff ganz einfach ein Naturphänomen und vielleicht läßt sich das Bild des Waldes in diesem Zusammenhang durch Ähnliches in der Shakespearekritik des mit Eichendorff (in Berlin und besonders in Wien) befreundeten Adam Müller erhellen. Müllers Dresdener Vorlesungen über das Drama stammen aus dem Jahre 1806, und Eichendorff las sie begeistert in Müllers und Kleists *Phöbus* des Jahres 1808. Es ist anzunehmen, daß Müllers *Fragmente über William Shakespeare,* zwei Jahre früher also als die weit berühmtere 12. Vorlesung A. W. Schlegels über Shakespeare, in mancher Hinsicht für Eichendorffs Shakespearebild ausschlaggebend wurden; das gilt besonders auch von Müllers sehr charakteristischen Ausführungen über die oben erwähnte Symbiose des Tragischen und Komischen bei Shakespeare, seinen grundlegenden Begriff des Ausgleichs durch die Polarität. Im Zusammenhang mit Shakespeares romantischen Komödien macht Müller einige Bemerkungen über den Wald als deren Hintergrund und fährt dann fort: »Die germanisch [romantische] Zeit war aus den Wäldern gekommen: Eichenhaine waren ihre ursprünglichen Tempel... Was von der griechischen und römischen Heiden Gottesdienst und Mythologie zur Wissenschaft germanischer Völker kam, erhielt unter den Händen dieser Völker gewissermaßen einen Blumen-, einen Waldgeruch. Immer ist es, als würde es betrachtet durch einen dichten Vorgrund von Wald und Grüne... bei Nacht, wenn die Tierwelt untergegangen und das Leben der Pflanzen üppiger und duftiger hervortritt.. . Daher der träumerische Charakter ihrer Fabeln, der besonders hervorschimmert aus den beiden vornehmlichsten Gattungen der modernen Poesie, der Romanze und dem Märchen.« Ich sehe den Wald hier natürlich nicht als abgedroschenes Stimmungsklischee, sondern als ein durchaus nicht eindeutiges, psychologisches wie dichterisches Bild. In Eichendorffs Romanen, in jeder Novelle, jedem Drama, den Gedichten, bleibt der Wald der beständige Hintergrund seiner Phantasie, die Kulisse, vor welcher der Mensch seine Rolle spielt. Im Walde verlieren, suchen und finden sich Eichendorffs Menschen selbst und einander, ebenso wie jene Shakespeares; *Dichter und ihre Gesellen* gipfelt in einem leise ironischen Waldtableau hoch oben in den Bergen bei einer verfallenen Klosterruine: »Ich spiele den letzten Akt«, ruft »das geistliche Soldatenherz«, Viktor-Lothario, aus, »Gräber, Hochzeit, Gottes grüne Zinnen und die aufgehende Sonne als Schlußdekoration.« Verwirrung und Verkleidung in den *Freiern* erreicht in einem einsamen Grund des gräflichen Schloßwaldes den Höhepunkt. In Shakespeares romantischen Komödien ist der Wald der Ort, wo Freiheit von alltäglichen Bindungen besteht, und wo die Liebenden sich in Traum, Gefahr, Schmerz, Spiel und Freude neu erkennen, verwandeln und finden. So der Wald von Arden in As You *Like It,* wo es alles auf einmal gibt, barocke Schäfer, Höflinge und Narren, fromme Einsiedler, Palmen und Eichen, wilde Löwen; der Wald in *Winter's Tale,* der, wie selbst Böhmen für Shakespeares Zwecke, dicht am Meeresstrand liegt; der sommerlich-nächtige Wald bei Athen im *Midsummer Night's Dream,* wo die Liebe der Menschen und der Waldelfen durch mutwillig inszenierte Verwechslung und Verwirrung geläutert wird; der Schloßwald des Fürsten von Navarre in *Love's Labour's Lost,* wo die Liebenden wie im Reigentanz die Partner wechseln bis sie schließlich den richtigen finden; und, mehr schauerlich, Wald und Heide in *Macbeth, King Lear* und *Cymbeline,* wo die Menschen, wie auch in Eichendorffs beiden Tragödien, ein besonders enges Verhältnis zu den kosmischen Naturmächten haben, zu Sturm, Himmel, Mond und Sternen. Auf der modernen Bühne ist der romantische Wald Shakespeares oder Eichendorffs auf einen einzigen kahlen Baumstrunk zusammengeschrumpft wie in Samuel Becketts *Waiting for Godot.*

Um das Gefühl der Stimmungsähnlichkeit zwischen Eichendorff und Shakespeare in seinen romantischen Komödien könnte man auch noch weitere Analogien aufstellen. Wie Shakespeare, der aus italienischen Novellen schöpfte, begnügt sich Eichendorff in seinem erzählerischen Werk mit einfacher, althergebrachter Intrige und Handlung, sogar mit märchenähnlichen Stoffen, und wiederholt diese schon an sich nicht neuen Geschichten in dauernder, leichter Variation: Fortuna, der Zufall, regiert das Geschehen. Schon die verwirrende Wiederholung und Ähnlichkeit der Eichendorffschen Namen — Aurora, Julie, Florens, Florentin, Fortunat, Fortunatus, Leonard, Leonardo, Romana, Romano, usw. — deutet auf diese unerschrockene Variationstechnik; es geht hier um etwas ganz Bewußtes und weist nicht auf Mangel an Erfindungskraft, sondern auf eine ganz bestimmte, traditionelle Annahme über das, worum es sich in der Dichtung überhaupt handelt. Auch in den novellenartigen, ja von Friedrich Schlegel kurzweg als *»Novellen«* bezeichneten Komödien Shakespeares, fällt es schwer, die verschiedenen Julien, Heros, Claudios, Antonios und Angelos auseinanderzuhalten. Die Handlung dieser Stücke fällt durchaus unter die hergebrachten Regeln der Literaturherstellung oder Poesis der Renaissancezeit, wo man nicht an erster Stelle originelles Material oder neue Geschichten suchte, sondern eben nur eine neue *Be*handlung der schon seit immer bekannten Handlung. Das war also Ende des 16. Jahrhunderts eine allgemein europäische Erscheinung, nicht aber zu Eichendorffs Zeit, zumal nicht im epischen Bereich, wo solche beständige Selbstwiederholung und Variation, außer im reinen Märchen, überhaupt etwas Seltenes ist. In seinem Erzählwerk bedient sich Eichendorff der schon damals im Verschwinden begriffenen Tradition der barocken Lustspielbühne, wie er sie in Wien vorfand, aber ganz besonders auch bei Shakespeare: hier wirkte eine bereits geschaffene, an sich schon ganz Eichendorffsche Welt als atmosphärische und künstlerische Anregung, wenn nicht als direktes Modell. Eben weil dieses Strukturprinzip an der Oberfläche versteckt liegt, wie so manches bei Eichendorff, hat man es vielleicht nicht genug in Betracht gezogen für sein gesamtes erzählerisches Werk und auch wirklich die Folgen daraus gezogen. In der Art der Romantiker, die sich eher als vom Leben selbst von schon gestalteten künstlerischen

Vorbildern anregen ließen, also vom Buch her schafften, vom schon Aufgeschriebenen oder Gemalten, wie Brentano und Novalis von der Chronik, Wackenroder von der Künstlerbiographie, Tieck vom Volksbuch und Märchen, die Nazarener von Raffael her, schöpfte Eichendorff vieles aus der Welt von Shakespeares romantischen Lustspielen und fühlte sich dort auch künstlerisch beheimatet.

Gerade hier fand er auch die ihm temperamenthaft entsprechende Mischung von Scherz und Wehmut, Spott und Mitleid, Spaß und Sitte, und was er selbst Shakespeares »melancholischen Witz und kriegerischen Scharfsinn« nannte. Vor allem fühlte er auch in diesen Stücken, und bei Shakespeare überhaupt, als an dem an der Wetterscheide zwischen Alt und Neu Stehenden, »die geheimnisvolle Trauer über den Untergang einer schöneren Welt«, wie er es bezeichnet. Es war die Trauer über den Untergang des christlichen Rittertums. Eichendorff hat sich durch einige Bemerkungen in seiner *Geschichte des Dramas* über das Katholisch-Religiöse bei Shakespeare den Tadel Gustav Freytags zugezogen, denn Shakespeare repräsentierte für Eichendorff »jene Naturseite des Christentums, die in der alten Kirche von jeher in ihren Traditionen, Legenden und Bildern vertreten war«. Die neuere Kritik hat aber Eichendorff hier durchaus recht gegeben, denn es handelt sich ja, mit einer Ausnahme, bei allen Stücken um Themen aus der vorreformatorischen Epoche, und Shakespeare, als Sohn eines Katholiken (wie man jetzt weiß), enthielt sich ganz bewußt jeder religiösen Polemik. Vor einigen Wochen hielt der Stratford-Shakespeare-Intendant, Terry Hands, in Cambridge einen Vortrag, in dem er unter anderem die Schwierigkeiten einer Shakespeare-Produktion von *Richard III.* mit der Comédie Française in Paris (wo er eben herkam) darstellte. Er sagte, es sei ihm erst mit den Pariser Schauspielern eigentlich klar geworden, daß bei uns in England die mittelalterlich-christliche Tradition—und nicht nur auf der Bühne, sondern im Volk selbst, aus dem die Schauspieler ja meistens stammen—noch unbedingt lebendig sei, und zwar gerade auch durch Shakespeares Ethos und Weltbild. In Frankreich dagegen sei durch den schroffen Bruch des siebzehnten Jahrhunderts diese mittelalterliche Tradition, trotz der Kirche, ganz verloren gegangen. Eichendorff, der selbst in ungebrochener Tradition stand, hat also ganz richtig Gervinus gegenüber dieses wichtige Moment bei Shakespeare erfühlt und erfaßt. Eichendorff forderte vom Lustspiel und vom Drama überhaupt eine christliche Atmosphäre, nicht das »überblümte und geschminkte Christentum«, wie er es nennt, »kein Dogma, keine Moraltheorie wie in Tendenzstücken,« sondern »das religiöse und zwar spezifisch *christliche* Gefühl, wie es (z. B.) in Shakespeares Schauspielen unsichtbar und doch unverkennbar waltet . . . eine christliche Atmosphäre, die wir unbewußt atmen, und die in ihrer Reinheit die verborgene höhere Bedeutsamkeit der irdischen Dinge von selbst hindurchscheinen läßt... Wer fragt im Frühling, was der Frühling sei? Wir sehen die Luft nicht, die uns erfrischt, und sehen das Licht nicht, das doch ringsum Laub und Blumen färbt«. (Bezeichnend für Eichendorffs kritische Methode ist, daß Shakespeare hier wieder als Natur, als der Wald selbst erscheint). Wieder gibt die neuere Kritik Eichendorff hier recht. *As You Like It* ist sogar als Lustspiel dafür bekannt, daß hier in hervorragendem Maße die spezifisch christlichen Ideale und Tugenden der Demut, des Mitleids, des Verzeihens, der barmherzigen Nächstenliebe und Treue ganz unauffällig und *implicite* dargestellt werden; das Stück ist fröhlich und fromm im angenehmsten Sinne dieser beiden Worte, sowie vieles von Eichendorff.

Am Ende von *As You Like It,* da die vier glücklichen Liebespaare zum Hochzeitstanz antreten, rezitiert Hymen die Begleitstrophen, darunter die Zeilen: »Im Himmel ist heiterer Frohsinn, wenn Irdisches sich eint und schlichtet«, »Then is there mirth in heaven / When earthly things made even / Atone together«. Am mitternächtigen Schluß von Eichendorffs *Freiern* ruft der einst so griesgrämige alte Gärtner Adelens ein frohes »Vivat! und Feuerwerk und Hochzeitscarmen« aus, und Leonard befiehlt: »Voran die Fackeln, daß die Ström' im Grunde / Und alle Fenster in dem stillen Schloß / Aufblitzen in dem lust'gen Widerscheine! / Tag soll es sein — mir ist so licht im Herzen! (Er führt die Gräfin schnell fort. Hörnerklang, nach und nach immer leiser).« Hier leuchtet die innig versöhnte Freude in den dunklen Wald, die dunkle Welt, ins jeweilige Gehäuse der Menschen, und das ist die richtige Stimmung am Ende einer romantischen Komödie: die Heiterkeit, weil sich alles nun gelöst und geeint hat, »Mirth in heaven, when earthly things made even atone together«, und wenn, wie auf der letzten Seite des *Taugenichts,* wenigstens im Spiel der Dichtung die Mächte der Ordnung siegreich sind und man sagen kann, es ist *»alles, alles gut«*. Über Vielem im Leben Eichendorffs waltete in der Tat ein Unstern; seine Ehe aber brachte ihm ein tiefes Glück; hier war »alles, alles gut«, Für diesen Vortrag trifft es sich schön, daß gerade heute, der 7. April, der Jahrestag von Eichendorffs Hochzeitstag ist: An diesem Tage, also heute genau vor 157 Jahren, wurde er mit Luise von Larisch in der Sankt Vinzenz-Kirche in Breslau getraut.

Die Oxforder Anglistin, Dame Helen Gardner, schreibt in einem Shakespeare-Aufsatz folgendes über die Komik im Allgemeinen: »Die Komödie zeigt im Bilde den Triumph des Lebens über Zufall und Zeit; in symbolischer Form verkörpert das Lustspiel unser freudiges Glück darüber, daß wir Wandel und Zufall des Lebens diesmal stellen und meistern konnten.« Das Lustspiel strebt ganz selbstverständlich, wie das Märchen, der Hochzeit zu, die das Leben erhält und erneut und den »vollen Strom der Zeit«, wie es Rosalind nennt, weiterführt, neue Chancen, Abenteuer, Veränderungen, mit sich bringt. Eichendorffs *Freier* ist vom Geist der Komödie in diesem Sinne beseelt, und eben weil die Komödie, dies eine Mal, symbolisch über Zeit und Zufall den Sieg davonträgt, gibt es in dieser Literaturgattung, wie so oft im Erzählwerk Eichendorffs, wenig Ereignisse, sondern nur ein leicht verbundenes Geschehen (happenings), Begegnungen, Verwechslung, Verkleidung, die dem Zufall unterliegen und wo der Ort sich immer gleichbleiben kann, ob Wald, Garten oder Schloß. Auch zeitlos ist diese Welt, weil eben die Zeit durchaus unwichtig ist und nie ausläuft, wie in der Tragödie, wo Schreckliches sich in streng gemessener Zeit ereignet, die zum Endgültigen in der Zeitspanne alles menschlichen Lebens führt, zum Tod, dem entsprechenden Sinnbild für die tragische Handlung, wie der Hochzeitstanz für das Lustspiel.

Das Komische muß aber, nach Eichendorff, unbedingt auf einer großen sittlichen Grundlage ruhen, der es zur Folie dient, wie bei Shakespeare und den Spaniern des Goldenen Zeitalters.

Shakespeare und Calderón waren für Eichendorff Inbegriff des christlichen Dichters schlechthin, mit dessen Dichterberuf er seinen eigenen mit aller Bescheidenheit als wesensverwandt auffassen durfte. Ständig nennt er diese beiden zusammen, und gebraucht für beide das Gleichnis vom Magier, vom Zauberer, der das Zauberwort trifft, wodurch jenes schlummernde Lied, das unergründlich in allen Dingen schläft — in der Natur, in den Träumen der Waldeinsamkeit, wie im Labyrinth der Menschenbrust — wieder geweckt wird, so daß die Welt anhebt zu singen. Das ist für Eichendorff die eigentliche Tat des Dichters, Shakespeares, Calderóns, seine eigene Tat.

Als Eichendorff dem Alter entgegenging, las er Shakespeare als Buch des Lebens, als »theatrum mundi«, das ihm über manches Schwere im Weltendrama seiner eigenen Epoche hinweghalf; denn wie Shakespeare im wunderbar-versöhnten Alterswerk, *The Tempest,* sah er die Welt bis zum Schluß als Bühne. Als Antwort auf die Bitte eines Freundes (es war sein ehemaliger Vorgesetzter, Theodor von Schön), er möge ihm »ein Buch für Geisteserfrischung« empfehlen, schrieb Eichendorff 1839 aus Berlin, ein modernes Buch wisse er leider nicht zu nennen, Shakespeare dagegen »ist und bleibt doch der Meister, erfrischend für alle Zeiten«. Aus dem »hohlen Floskelwesen, dem unnützen Geschwätz« auf der Bühne seiner Zeit, wo er zuschauen mußte »ohne Hoffnung den 5ten Akt zu erleben«, wie er sagt, flüchtete er sich in die Welt Shakespeares und seiner geliebten Spanier, und dort fand er die für die Gegenwart verlorene Welt der Schönheit, des Frohsinns und des Adels der Gesinnung durch des Dichters »geheimnisvolle Wünschelrute« wie durch einen Zauberschlag neugeschaffen wieder. Sie half ihm das zu überwinden, was er in dem von Dietmar Kunisch in *Sprache und Bekenntnis* veröffentlichten Memoirenfragment das tragische Gefühl »von der Nichtigkeit, Vergänglichkeit des Weltglanzes und Lebens« nannte und als solches sein Leben lang empfand. Dabei ließ er sich aber nie wie Shakespeares Menschenhasser, Timon von Athen, den er oft anführt, durch die Misere und die Jämmerlichkeit der Welt überwältigen; immer wieder, sogar auch in seiner Lieblingsrolle als Einsiedler, warf er sich aktiv ins Gefecht. »Vor dem Neuen schützt keine Chinesische Mauer«, sagte er einmal, das Neue vielmehr, sei es noch so entmutigend, sei trotzdem scharf und unverzagt ins Auge zu fassen.

Zur Zeit, da der junge Eichendorff in Wien an seinem ersten Roman arbeitete, hielt Coleridge, der größte Shakespearekritiker der englischen Romantik, in Bristol (1810) eine Vorlesung, in der er zum Schluß folgendes sagte: »In den Dramen Shakespeares sieht jeder sich selbst und die eigene Gesinnung, wird sich aber dessen nicht eigentlich klar bewußt. So ergeht es dem Reisenden bei einem gewissen Naturphänomen im Morgennebel der Gebirgswelt: er sieht dort die Wiederspiegelung seiner eigenen Gestalt, aber durch die Glorie um das Haupt und durch das Riesenhafte des Ausmaßes wirkt es nicht wie das eigene Abbild.«

In diesem Gleichnis bringt Coleridge das Erlebnis Shakespeares bei jedem künstlerisch aufnahmefähigen Menschen mit dem bekannten Phänomen in Verbindung, das er während einer Deutschlandreise bei Sonnenaufgang auf dem Brocken im Harzgebirge erlebt hatte. Ich möchte vorschlagen, daß sich dieses Gleichnis des englischen Romantikers auch auf Eichendorffs Verhältnis zu Shakespeare anwenden ließe; bezeichnenderweise sagte Eichendorff einmal über Shakespeare, den Menschen und den Dichter: »Überhaupt liegt Shakespeares Bedeutung zum großen Teil in seiner eigenen Charakterschönheit, in der ethischen Gabe, überall nur mit dem Hohen, wo und wie es sich äußere, zu sympathisieren und das Gemeine zu hassen... Weil er selbst so ohne Falsch, so hat sich ihm auch die Welt vertraulich gezeigt in ihrer ursprünglichen Schönheit, und mit allen Schauern und Abgründen, die auf die arme Schönheit lauern. Er idealisiert nirgend willkürlich... er *deutet* nur die geheimnisvolle Hieroglyphenschrift, in der der Herr die Weltgeschichte dichtet.«

"Übergang vom Roman zur Mythologie"

Formal Aspects of the Opening Chapter of Hardenberg's *Heinrich von Ofterdingen, Part II*

The unfinished opening chapter of the second part of *Heinrich von Ofterdingen* has, in general, been regarded either as an appendage to Part I, "Die Erwartung," or else mainly related to the planned continuation as a whole, "Die Erfüllung." The second part, however, consists in the main of the plans and disjointed notes out of which Tieck constructed a sequent narrative to indicate the nature of the continuation Hardenberg did not live to write. Neither of these approaches to the opening chapter, or even a judicious mixture of the two, is quite satisfactory: "Die Erwartung" is complete in itself whereas "Die Erfüllung" as a whole is a mere hypothesis to which Tieck's accomplished fluency has given a somewhat spuriously finished look bearing little resemblance to the form of Hardenberg's own tentative jottings. He did, however, produce this one carefully structured, even though unfinished opening chapter in the course of the last summer and autumn of his life (1800), and these few pages, seventeen in the first volume of the new Kluckhohn-Samuel edition, represent, as far as is known, a fully shaped literary entity, quite different in kind from the remaining fragmentary notes. It was at any rate published as such by Tieck and Friedrich Schlegel in their first edition of Hardenberg's works in 1802, the year after his death.

There is the further point that whereas no manuscript of Part I now exists, and the work we know is that of the first printed text as edited by the poet's friends, the original of the opening chapter of Part II, and even a draft of the first page of it, have survived in Hardenberg's own manuscript.[1] The editors of the new critical edition of Novalis's works have not as yet published this chapter in the poet's own spelling, but they have at least been able to check and reproduce Hardenberg's quite idiosyncratic punctuation and have also provided variant readings, some of which are significant. The discarded draft of the first page (I, 349-50) is entitled "Das Gesicht", that is, "The Vision", which was later changed to "Das Kloster oder der Vorhof"; for after a supernatural vision of Mathilde, Heinrich finds himself translated to a different kind of realm among people who can look back on earlier incarnations, who have died and yet seem to be alive in a new form of existence in a "forecourt" of heaven. "Das Lied der Toten" (I, 350-355) is all that now remains of the later development of this chapter.

There seems to be a case, therefore, for considering this chapter separately on its own terms, especially as it represents a significant departure from the mode of Part I as well as a development in literary method. These pages provide a model of Hardenberg's technique of fusing the plane of real events with the world of myth, which he saw quite simply as "freye poëtische Erfindung" (III, 668). In "Die Erwartung" the marvellous had still only been operative in the realm of dreams, or else in the Märchen told explicitly as a fantasy. There is, it is true, the Provençal chronicle in the hermit's cave where Heinrich recognizes his own portrait and sees future events, but this extraordinary circumstance is not developed or explained: the end of the chronicle is missing (I, 264-65). Hardenberg himself claimed a distinction of form when he was working on the second part of his novel: "Der zweite Teil wird schon in der Form weit poetischer als der erste," the reason for the change being that "die Poesie ist nun geboren," and there was to be "eine noch innigere Mischung" of the elements of novel and Märchen.[2]

In a review article of 1803, in which he outlines important recent developments in German literature, Friedrich Schlegel says that even as it stands *Heinrich von Ofterdingen* illustrates and proves his point that every novel should be constructed "nach Art eines Märchens," and that this, in fact, happens quite naturally in the case of a novel which is "wahre Mythologie":

> Glücklicherweise aber kommt mir ein Beispiel zu statten, welches jedem, der es studiren will, meine Behauptung deutlich machen und ihm den *Übergang vom Roman zur Mythologie* zeigen kann [my italics]. Es ist

der unvollendet gebliebene *Heinrich von Ofterdingen* von Novalis. Hätte er den Cyklus von Romanen, den er, um die Welt und das Leben aus den wichtigsten verschiedenen Standpunkten des menschlichen Geistes darzustellen, entworfen hatte, vollenden können, so würden wir daran ein Werk besitzen, welchem für die Bildung und Erregung der Phantasie kein anderes an Nützlichkeit gleich kommen dürfte, und welches uns den Reichthum der Alten an philosophischen Dialogen weniger beneiden lassen würde.[3]

What Schlegel meant by "Mythologie" in this context can best be understood from his "Rede über die Mythologie," the ideas of which were well known to Novalis as a part of the *Gespräch über die Poesie* published in the third volume of *Athenaeum* (1800):

> Und was ist jede schöne Mythologie anders als ein hieroglyphischer Ausdruck der umgebenden Natur in dieser Verklärung von Fantasie und Liebe... Denn Mythologie und Poesie, beide sind eins und unzertrennlich ... Denn das ist der Anfang aller Poesie, den Gang und die Gesetze der vernünftig denkenden Vernunft aufzuheben und uns wieder in die schöne Verwirrung der Fantasie... zu versetzen, für das ich kein schöneres Symbol bis jetzt kenne, als das bunte Gewimmel der alten Götter.[4]

As to the genre and medium of the novel itself, Schlegel saw what he called "das romantische Buch" primarily as the Socratic dialogue of the new age, incorporating "Lebensweisheit" as opposed to "Schulweisheit" *(Lyceum-Fragment*, 26). The new "mythology" in the novel was therefore to be characterized on the one hand by events seen in the transfiguring light of the imagination, the marvellous in nature, and on the other hand by philosophical insights conveyed largely in the form of conversation and dialogue.

Both these requirements are fulfilled in the opening chapter of *Heinrich von Ofterdingen,* Part II: the miraculous irrupts into the real world, the phenomena of nature and of the human mind are transfigured in the light of the imagination and at the same time subjected to philosophical inquiry in a more consistent way than was the case in Part I. The structural principle underlying the attempt to convey the mythological and also the philosophical dimension is that of the dialogue in two main and distinct forms. Among the last plans Hardenberg noted in the summer of 1800, "Allerhand poëtische Pläne," was the project for a novel in dialogue form recounting the events of a single day: "Begebenheiten Eines Tags. Ein dialogirter Roman" (III, 682). He had, it seems, given careful thought to the key position of dialogue within the narrative of fiction.

The chapter deals with the events of a late afternoon and evening at some time, perhaps a year or more, after the marriage of Heinrich and Mathilde and of her death. Heinrich had foreseen her death in a dream but we are told nothing about it in concrete terms: Hardenberg intended the transition from the first book to the second to be "dunkel — trüb — verworren . . . kein rechter historischer Übergang" (I, 341). Mathilde's death was to be nothing more than a function of its effect on Heinrich in his development as a poet. Within the strict economy of the fable, every single word was to be submitted to the test of relevance:

> In einem Roman... muß nur jedes Wort poëtisch seyn... Der Dichter hat blos mit *Begriffen zu* thun. Schilderungen etc. borgt er nur als BegriffsZeichen (III, 681 and 683).

Apart from the poem "Astralis", which is an introduction to the whole of the first section of Part II, the opening chapter consists basically of two dialogues of contrasting kinds, the first preceded by a vision of Mathilde which is granted to Heinrich, the second introduced by a brief description of the mountain home of his second interlocutor. The interchange which takes place between Heinrich and the supernatural at the beginning might also be seen as a kind of indirect dialogue in that Heinrich responds in the medium of a song to the voice he hears in the course of his vision. The first of the dialogues as such is a question and answer interchange between Heinrich and Cyane, the girl who appears after the vision, the second takes the form of a conversation between Heinrich and the scientist-doctor, Sylvester. This is largely philosophical. There is a minimum of background description and at no stage, although the sense of the landscape is vivid, is any natural setting an end in itself: it only serves to supplement the "Begriffe" to be conveyed within the dialogue and as a result of it. According to Hardenberg, "BegriffsZeichen" without immediate relevance to the basic concepts which are the stuff of poetry, are merely the equivalent of poetical music and painting:

> Es giebt poëtische Musik und Mahlerey - diese wird oft mit Poësie verwechselt, z.B. von Tiek, auch wohl von Göthe (III, 683).

The ideas conveyed in the dialogue between Heinrich and Cyane belong to the realm of myth, those of the second dialogue are part of the world of rational give-and-take in argument. Both are a form of creative interchange though each moves on a different level and both are intended, in Schlegel's terms, to form and stimulate the reader's imagination. A consideration of the substance and technique of the chapter as a whole, and of the way in which the dialogues operate, may help to cast some light on that transition from novel to myth which Schlegel saw in *Heinrich von Ofterdingen.*

Throughout the early part of the chapter, and until Heinrich is introduced to Sylvester, he appears as an anonymous pilgrim. "Das Ziel seiner Reise" is mentioned but we are only left to gather from subsequent events that he is, in fact, making a pilgrimage to seek healing at some mountain shrine. The pilgrim is a man without hope seeking to deaden thought by the exertion of his ascent into the mountains. Nature, and even his own thoughts, have ceased to speak to him in terms that he can understand he is numb with grief:

> Auf dem schmalen Fußsteige, der ins Gebürg hinauflief, ging ein Pilgrim in tiefen Gedanken. Mittag war vorbei. Ein starker Wind sauste durch die blaue Luft. Seine dumpfen, mannigfaltigen Stimmen verloren sich, wie sie kamen. War er vielleicht durch die Gegenden der Kindheit geflogen? Oder durch andre redende Länder? Es waren Stimmen, deren Echo nach im Innersten klang und dennoch schien sie der Pilgrim nicht zu kennen (I, 3l9-20).

These are the few terse sentences which have replaced a page of detailed circumstantial description, the "poëtische Mahlerey" of the earlier draft, "Das Gesicht" (I, 349-50), ultimately abandoned by the author in the interest of strict relevance. A comparison between the two versions shows just how much Hardenberg was still achieving technically during the last working months of his life and how great was his gain in poetic expertise and intensity. He had the heart to jettison an attractive, perhaps somewhat naive mountain décor, steep rocks in every direction, dark forests, alpine meadows with rare and highly coloured mountain flora, the sound of the bells of grazing cattle, rushing torrents echoing from out of the deep below, a few buzzards hovering over isolated firs, a strong wind soughing through the tree tops, a luminous sky with shifting sunlight. The indeterminate voices of the wind which, in the later version, resound in the pilgrim's heart, unfathomed as yet, are specified in greater detail in the original draft, "... so daß zuweilen die Endsilben und einzelne Worte einer menschlichen Sprache hervorzutönen schienen" (I, 350). The idea of an intelligible human language in nature, audible more especially to the poet, was important to Hardenberg, nor is it lost in the final version, but only hidden in a more subtle way as part of an interior monologue in question form. Was the wind trying to speak to him of the meaning of his childhood in the plains at the foot of the Wartburg - "War er vielleicht durch die Gegenden (variant: Ebenen) der Kindheit geflogen?" - or else of his journey towards the region of his greatest happiness - "andre redende Länder" ? The wind heralds the moment of creative change and of understanding the language of nature, a moment which cannot come until he has gained distance from the immediate past and turned to survey the new perspectives opened out by the ascent of his pilgrimage. Throughout the opening part of this chapter Heinrich is in the mythical landscape of Hardenberg's own *Hymnen an die Nacht* where this part of his life's journey is called "die Wallfahrt zum heiligen Grabe" and where the pilgrim carries the heavy cross of his grief, "drückend das Kreuz." The steep mountains he has to ascend are "Grenzgebürge der Welt," the highest point of endurance which, once reached and transcended, enables him to survey not only the old world of tragic events "wo das Licht in ewiger Unruh hauset", but also to catch a glimpse of the new land of longing to which his beloved has preceded him (I, 137). When Heinrich has reached this climax point of his pilgrimage the process of healing can begin. The pilgrim weeps, he finds himself again, "seinen Sinnen ward die Welt wieder gegenwärtig und alte Gedanken fingen tröstlich zu reden an."

Nature, too, now speaks to the pilgrim, as though in his own language but still mysteriously, in images. On the horizon beyond the towers of Augsburg the pilgrim sees the shining river: "Dort lag Augsburg mit seinen Türmen. Fern am Gesichtskreis blinkte der Spiegel des furchtbaren, geheimnisvollen Stroms." In their annotations the editors of the text point out that this is the river Lech[5], though they do not risk naming the wild mountain range supposedly so close to Augsburg. It is true that Hardenberg noted in the "Paralipomena", "Ein Dichter verliert seine Geliebte im Bade", even though this faintly comic jotting comes in the context of what seems to be a different story (I, 337). But even if he had intended a realistic bathing or boating accident of this kind in a geographically verifiable landscape, instead of an interior landscape of the mind, "eine innere Phantasie", as Heinrich himself calls this region (I, 279), the river of Heinrich's dream was also and primarily the stream of time rushing ever faster to carry away the frail bark, the exterior hull of Mathilde's earthly body, drawing it down into the whirlpool of illness and death: "Auf einmal zog es sie hinunter. Eine leise Luft strich über den Strom, der ebenso ruhig und glänzend floß, wie vorher" (I, 278). The stream of time is unruffled by Mathilde's death which is why it is "furchtbar, geheimnisvoll", but in its guise as death, as Acheron, it draws down the poet, too, below the surface of ordinary life to experience death by analogy in the unbearable pain of separation which transfers his own inner life to the realm of death: "'Wo ist der Strom?' rief er mit Tränen. - 'Siehst du nicht seine blauen Wellen über uns?' Er sah hinauf, und der blaue Strom floß leise über ihrem Haupte" (I, 278-9).[6] From his present vantage point in the mountains where the reality of his pilgrimage merges with the memory of his prophetic dream and the actual tragedy itself, Heinrich can look back from a distance in time and space at the mirroring surface of the stream which had, for a while, engulfed him too. As in the dream where, in the realm of death, "Blumen und Bäume redeten ihn an" and he felt at home, so too, forest and mountain now become meaningful again in the pilgrim's eyes, he understands their language as they speak to console him in terms which, at any rate as far as the reader is concerned, can do with some elucidation:

> Der ungeheure Wald bog sich mit tröstlichem Ernst zu dem Wanderer, das gezackte Gebürg ruhte so bedeutend über der Ebene und beide schienen zu sagen: "Eile nur, Strom, du entfliehst uns nicht - Ich will dir folgen mit geflügelten Schiffen. Ich will dich brechen und halten und dich verschlucken in meinen Schoß. Vertraue du uns, Pilgrim, es ist auch unser Feind, den wir selbst erzeugten — Laß ihn eilen mit seinem Raub, er entflieht uns nicht" (I, 320).

The river wears away stone and vegetation but it only exists as a river as long as the bedrock of its foundations and the forested banks on either side give it a tangible structure, geologically speaking. In this sense, though it is the "enemy" ("es ist auch unser Feind, den wir selbst erzeugten"), it can never escape from rock or forest for these are more enduring than the protean, evanescent element which makes up a stream of water as a recognizable entity ("Eile, nur Strom, du entfliehst uns nicht"). Forest and mountain then speak in turn as the more enduring phenomena of nature in which, by analogy, Heinrich is to put his trust, seeking comfort from them ("Vertraue du uns, Pilgrim"): the forest with its timbered sailing ships can master the stream and keep up with it, the rocks can break and arrest its course, even swallow it up and force it to disperse itself in underground channels. Forest and hills are therefore ultimately more powerful than the enemy river and will outlast it, that is to say, time, the river, cannot have final possession of its booty even in the realm of transience because the human soul outlasts time in the realm of eternity.

This is the way in which nature "speaks" to Heinrich when he learns to read its "Chiffrenschrift." This passage is an apt illustration of the technique of "Übergang zur Mythologie" with a background of geology. Even though the mood is entirely different, this concentrated, cryptic passage moves in a world of poetic personification linked with scientific truth which is kindred to the method of Goethe's "Mahometsgesang" where natural phenomena camouflage spiritual meaning in a seamless metaphor. Science entered quite naturally into the poetic creation of both Novalis and Goethe.

The pilgrim now finds that he can again speak to nature which has shown itself to him in its reassuring aspect. Thus the poet in *Die Lehrlinge zu Sais* had also discovered the reciprocity between man and nature involved in a mutual dialogue: "Wird nicht der Fels ein eigentümliches Du, eben wenn ich ihn anrede?" (I, 100) Heinrich turns aside from his direct ascent and thinking that he can see a human being, a monk, perhaps his own teacher from the Wartburg, kneeling at prayer under an oak tree, he walks up to the figure only to find that it is a rock whose shape had human semblance. He embraces it nevertheless as representing his friend, he speaks to this friend in the wilderness and pleads with the Blessed Virgin to intercede for him and give him some sign of comfort in his solitude. His prayer is heard, the sign is given in a song, a voice and a vision in the oak-tree, whereupon he himself sings a song of thanksgiving and dedication: he finds his own personal voice and vocation as a poet - "Die Poesie ist nun geboren."

How has Hardenberg succeeded in his first attempt to describe supernatural events in the context of ordinary life where earlier in the novel they occurred either in a dream or a Märchen? There are passages of great beauty in his account of the vision, but there is also a somewhat calculated simplicity which makes this part of the chapter less convincing than, for instance, the poet's vision by Sophie's grave in the third of the *Hymnen an die Nacht,* or the dream vision of Mathilde's death in the stream of time. As an overture to the vision, "klare Stimmchen ... wie aus tiefer, unterirdischer Ferne" are heard singing a short cradle song several times over. It describes the absorbed and reciprocal love of a mother and her child, the theme of the child being taken up again in a non-mythical context in Heinrich's dialogue with Sylvester. The idea of new life symbolized by childhood, is, in fact, the link between the two realms, and runs right through the whole chapter from Astralis's poem and the cradle song in the mythical world to the talk between Heinrich and Sylvester on the nature and the education of children. The two stanzas heard by

Heinrich are actually part of a Flemish Christmas carol,[7] so it seems that the reader's thoughts were meant to be directed, in the first place, to Mary and her divine child as representing the archetype of childhood in general. Though Heinrich afterwards identifies the voice that now speaks to him from out of the tree as that of Mathilde, it is clearly and at the same time the voice of Mary who has chosen to live there with her child as at a place of pilgrimage where people come to pray. She asks for a sturdy warm house to be built on this site, a church where prayer is to be valid and real. Her child has conquered and survived ("überwunden") death and this means that Heinrich need no longer grieve: "Härme dich nicht." Up to this point of the "vision" Heinrich has only heard a voice, but then along a beam of light that shines out through the tree he sees right into

> eine ferne, kleine, wundersame Herrlichkeit hinein, welche nicht zu beschreiben, noch kunstreich mit Farben nachzubilden möglich gewesen wäre.

The poet does, however, attempt to describe this little world of wonder, first of all the décor of the room which he sees and the kind of people in it:

> Es waren überaus feine Figuren und die innigste Lust und Freude, ja eine himmlische Glückseligkeit war überall darin zu schauen, sogar daß die leblosen Gefäße, das Säulwerk, die Teppiche, Zieraten, kurzum alles was zu sehen war nicht gemacht, sondern, wie ein vollsaftiges Kraut, aus eigner Lustbegierde also gewachsen und zusammengekommen zu sein schien (I, 321-22).

As in "Das Lied der Toten," also meant to form part of this chapter at a later stage, the realm of the dead is imagined as being furnished with concrete objects for everyday use:

> Lobt doch unsre stillen Feste
> Unsre Gärten, unsre Zimmer
> Das bequeme Hausgeräthe,
> Unser Hab' und Gut.
> Täglich kommen neue Gäste

Diese früh, die andern späte
Auf den weiten Heerden immer
Lodert frische Lebens Glut....
Tausend zierliche Gefässe
Einst bethaut mit tausend Thränen,
Goldne Ringe, Sporen, Schwerdter
Sind in unserm Schatz. (I, 351 and 353)

Hardenberg sees the realm of the dead as having exuberant vegetative and organic life and cohesion, "wie ein vollsaftiges Kraut;" death's fire of life continually renewed by new arrivals burns with ever increasing brightness. The inhabitants of this realm seem to be carrying on an intense though silent process of festive communication which, in the poem (verses 7, 8 and 4, 9) takes a physical, even sexual form, but in Heinrich's vision is just happily social:

> Es waren die schönsten menschlichen Gestalten, die dazwischen umhergingen und sich über die Maßen freundlich und holdselig gegeneinander erzeigten (I, 322).

Mathilde is standing right at the front of this stage-set gathering and shows by her smile and gestures - she places her hand on her heart - that she can see Heinrich even though she cannot, apparently, speak to him once she becomes visible: it was Mary, it seems, who had spoken from heaven itself as though with Mathilde's voice. Mathilde and the others whom Heinrich can now see are, in fact, still in the forecourts of heaven, one of the regions of the "Vorhof" of the chapter heading:

> Ganz vorn stand die Geliebte des Pilgers und hatt' es das Ansehn, als wolle sie mit ihm sprechen. Doch war nichts zu hören und betrachtete der Pilger nur mit tiefer Sehnsucht ihre anmutigen Züge und wie sie so freundlich und lächelnd ihm zuwinkte, und die Hand auf ihre linke Brust legte. Der Anblick war unendlich tröstend und erquickend und der Pilger lag noch lang in seliger Entzückung, als die Erscheinung wieder hinweggenommen war (I, 322).

What he sees restores Heinrich to something like his former self, though having both detachment and heightened awareness:

> ...und der Pilgrim sah sich wieder in einer vollen, bedeutsamen Welt. Stimme und Sprache waren wieder lebendig bei ihm geworden und es dünkte ihm nunmehr alles viel bekannter und weissagender, als ehemals, so daß ihm der Tod, wie eine höhere Offenbarung des Lebens, erschien, und er sein eignes, schnellvorübergehendes Dasein mit kindlicher, heitrer Rührung betrachtete (I, 322).

Because death has now been revealed to him as a form of heightened life, he sees its modes of existence in the earthly conditions familiar to him: people live in actual houses with useful goods and chattels, "das bequeme Hausgeräthe," all around them while earth presents itself to his eyes anew in those same terms: "die Erde lag vor ihm wie ein altes, liebes Wohnhaus, was er nach langer Entfernung verlassen wiederfände." In Hardenberg's romantic process of poetical "Potenzirung" and "logarythmisiren", what is remote and mysterious has been made familiar, the familiar signficant in a new way.[8] Now that the future and the past have merged for him in an entirely new kind of present, an eternal now which dictates a new sense of time, he is content to go on wandering through the gay, bright rooms of this house for a little while longer:

> Zukunft und Vergangenheit hatten sich in ihm berührt und einen innigen Verein geschlossen. Er stand weit außer der Gegenwart und die Welt ward ihm erst teuer, wie er sie verloren hatte, und sich nur als Fremdling in ihr fand, der ihre weiten, bunten Säle noch eine kurze Weile durchwandern sollte (I, 322).

In the fourth *Hymne* where Hardenberg describes the effects of his vision by Sophie's grave, he uses the metaphor of the world as a clock operated by the alternation of light and darkness:

> Gern will ich die fleißigen Hände rühren... unverdrossen verfolgen deines künstlichen Werks schönen Zusammenhang - gern betrachten deiner gewaltigen, leuchtenden Uhr sinnvollen Gang - ergründen der Kräfte Ebenmaß und die Regeln des Wunderspiels unzähliger Räume und ihrer

Zeiten (I, 137),

a vision which does not, as it were, leave the cosmic scale. It is perhaps worth while inquiring into the literary background which may be associated with the naive concreteness of the "Wohnhaus" metaphor and the precise detail of this miniature, brightly coloured next world seen by Heinrich along a beam of light. We are told by Karl von Hardenberg, Friedrich's brother, and this is also related by Tieck and Kreisamtmann Just in their memoirs of the poet, that he had always been an admiring reader of Johann Caspar Lavater whose writings, together with the Bible and Zinzendorf, were his staple reading in the last few months of his life.[9] No particular work is specifieed, though it is known that Hardenberg was also interested in the *Physiognomische Fragmente,* but judging from the context of Just's account that the poet derived great comfort from Lavater's writings in the time after the death of Sophie and Erasmus in 1797, the main work in question was probably *Aussichten in die Ewigkeit* which appeared in four volumes between 1768 and 1778. So great was the popular demand for Lavater's work that in I781 he published a shortened version of it, a single volume of some 300 pages.[10]

This treatise in the Pietist tradition but marked with Lavater's own brand of enthusiastic naiveté and persuasive power, was of a kind to appeal to Hardenberg and help him in a practical way to come to terms with the thought of his own death as it had helped him to bear the loss of Sophie and Erasmus earlier on. Even if one is fully aware of its purely speculative nature, the book has the fascination of a Baedeker read in advance of the journey, or even of a bold game of the imagination. The metaphysical playfulness which was an aspect of Pietism was evident in many parts of this book; it was therefore a work calculated to evoke Hardenberg's own "Spieltrieb," liable to come into operation even in the most solemn contexts. As the conclusion of the opening doctrinal chapters Lavater relates a friend's dream vision: his dead wife, not yet in heaven but "in den Vorhöfen der Ewigkeit," appears to him in a dream and tells her husband about the kind of life which departed souls lead in this place. All their powers of perception, cognition and moral insight are immensely heightened, they know what is happening to their loved ones on earth and can see them plainly but are unable to communicate with them except through their intuitions and through signs without the noise of words. Lavater's friend reports the message he received intuitively from his wife: "Sie wohne unter Millionen Seelen in Gegenden voll Heiterkeit, Stille und Betrachtung; aber im Himmel sey sie noch nicht; Gott habe noch nicht gerichtet. Lichtvolle Wolken verdecken noch zur Zeit ihren Augen diesen seligen Ort."[11]

The relevance of Lavater's ideas to Hardenberg's own thought patterns will be evident without pressing individual similarities, but Lavater's speculations on the eye with its heightened powers of vision in the "Vorhof " state of existence, are of particular interest. Heinrich sees his vision along a beam of light: "Da drang durch die Äste ein langer Strahl zu seinen Augen..." In his chapter concerning powers of sense perception in the forecourts of heaven, Lavater points out that even by means of unaided human vision the eye can take in at one and the same time a host of starworlds which are millions of miles apart; it is no great leap of the imagination, then, to envisage "Sehröhren" (organs of vision) which can enable yet further glimpses into and through these realms in outer space, "weil wirklich jetzt schon von diesen undenklich entfernten Körpern auf das Netz unsers irdischen sterblichen Auges Strahlen einfallen, und daselbst (nur nicht für uns) alle Punkte aller vorüberstehenden beleuchteten Körper mit einer Deutlichkeit zeichnen, wogegen die feinste Kopie eines Gemäldes eine Verunstaltung genannt werden kann."[12] The notion of the copy of a painting in connection with Heinrich's vision at the end-point of a ray of light is cognate to this "ferne, kleine, wundersame Herrlichkeit... welche nicht zu beschreiben, noch kunstreich mit Farben nachzubilden möglich gewesen wäre" (I, 321). By Mathilde's agency, Heinrich shares for the brief moment of his vision in the heightened powers of perception enjoyed in the "Vorhof" state of being. His vision represents a more specific, mythical "Steigerung" of that of the poet of the third *Hymne* who sees eternity mirrored in the eyes of his dead beloved: "Zur Staubwolke wurde der Hügel - durch die Wolke sah ich die verklärten Züge der Geliebten. In Ihren Augen ruhte die Ewigkeit" (I, 135).

In his healed state of mind following upon his vision, Heinrich is able to comply with the injunction he had been given earlier on: "Wenn du ein Lied zu meinen Ehren auf deiner Laute spielen wirst, so wird ein armes Mädchen herfürkommen...," and for the first time in this novel describing the making of a poet, Heinrich is seen in action in his destined role: "Der Pilger ergriff seine Laute und sang" (I, 323). In the song "Liebeszähren, Liebesflammen," the oak tree of Heinrich's vision where even the hard rock kneels in prayer, is now revealed as the Tree of Life, or the Cross, nurtured by Mary in her "garden enclosed" and made meaningful to the pilgrim by Mathilde's agency. Those who mourn will come as pilgrims to the Church founded in the high places where the Tree of Life has flourished and brought solace by a vision of eternity and light:

> Unvergeßlich sei die Stelle,
> Wo des Lichtes heilge Quelle
> Weggespült den Traum der Schmerzen. (I, 324)

In Heinrich's song of thanksgiving, Hardenberg has transposed into a concentrated lyrical statement the essential meaning of the vision told in prose. Heinrich has now taken up his role as a poet, he has been spiritually and emotionally prepared to penetrate further into the mythical realm, to enter into a fruitful dialogue with it at various levels.

When he has finished his song, Mary/Mathilde's prophecy comes true and Cyane, another incorporation of the blue flower of his dream, has materialized, standing by the rock and the tree, of which she is the visible messenger. Before she turns to Heinrich, she pays her tribute of worship at this emblematic altar of the tomb and the cross which is the place of her origin:

> [sie] trat unter den Baum, sah mit einem unaussprechlichen Lächeln hinauf und schüttete aus ihrer Schürze viele Rosen auf das Gras. Sie kniete still daneben, stand aber bald wieder auf und führte den Pilger fort (I, 325).

The conversation which now follows, a series of brief questions and answers, loses much of the unintelligibility generally ascribed to it if it is taken quite literally and in the mythical sense of Heinrich's vision and of his song:

> "Wer hat dir von mir gesagt," frug der Pilgrim. "Unsre Mutter." "Wer ist deine Mutter?" "Die Mutter Gottes."

So far, the mystery is an accepted one: at the foot of the cross God's mother became the mother of all mankind when Christ said "Woman, behold your son," and to the disciple, "Behold your mother." The next part of the dialogue, revealing the fact that Cyane has lived on earth before her present incarnation, enters the realm of paradox:

> "Seit wann bis du hier?" "Seitdem ich aus dem Grabe gekommen bin." "Warst du schon einmal gestorben?" "Wie könnt' ich denn leben?"

Death, it seems, is the indispensable condition of life; a genuine inquiry is "answered" by a rhetorical question, implying, and thus, in a way, bringing about the matter-of-course acceptance of a paradox which only makes sense in the domain of mystery. Hardenberg has here made use of what he considers one of the great prerogatives of the poet, "In Geheimniß Stand erheben," for, as he says, "Das *Unbekannte* ist der *Reitz* des Erkenntnisvermögens" (II, 590). In answer to Heinrich's question whether her life on this mountain is one of solitude, Cyane says "Ein alter Mann ist zu Hause, doch kenn ich noch viele, die gelebt haben." It seems that Heinrich, who has now been given the capacity to live in two realms of experience at the same time, and, as a poet, to mediate between them creatively, has entered the "zu Hause" of Cyane and Sylvester, the "Vorhof" inhabited by "the dead," that is, by those who have knowledge of a previous life, whether or not they are avatars in the true sense of the term. In becoming a poet, Heinrich has established a two-way traffic between the real world and the world of myth which he is now able to survey simultaneously from his "Grenzgebürge"; it is his task to transfer the infinite into the finite realm by means of language and the symbolical construction of the transcendental world here and now in the work of art.[13]

The intended ambiguity of Cyane's answer that she has come "aus dem Grabe" implies that she might be either a reincarnation in the world as we know it, or else in the "Vorhof" realm of the dead, or, as far as Heinrich is concerned, in both at the same time, as is his own case after the vision. His poet's mind has become its own place, a temenos, and for the time being a place shut off (this is the true meaning of "Kloster," the first part of Hardenberg's title). It is intended to be "höchst wunderbar, wie ein Eingang ins Paradies."[14] This country of the mind, "ein allegorisches Land" (I, 339), which Heinrich, and with him the reader of the novel, has now entered, cannot be understood in terms of logic, and this is what Hardenberg is trying to convey within the form of a dialogue which does not, and cannot make sense as one might expect in a novel. For the new kind of novel Hardenberg was trying to write was primarily "Realisirung einer Idee," and therefore "incommensurabel", also in some of its individual components:

> Der Roman, als solcher, enthält kein bestimmtes Resultat - er ist nicht Bild und Factum eines *Satzes*. Er ist anschauliche Ausführung - Realisirung einer Idee. Aber eine Idee läßt sich nicht, in einen Satz fassen. Eine Idee ist *eine unendliche Reihe von* Sätzen - eine *irrationale Größe* - *unsetzbar* (musik[alisch]) - incommensurabel (II, 570).

Cyane's answers to Heinrich's questions are designed to make him adapt himself consciously to the incommensurable sphere he has now entered. He learns that Cyane has been told about him by her former mother who is 'eigentlich dieselbe' as her real mother now, the mother of God, and who is also called Maria. Maria was the wife of the hermit count of Hohenzollern whom Heinrich had met on his journey:

> "Den kenn' ich auch." "Wohl mußt du ihn kennen, denn er ist auch dein Vater." "Ich habe ja meinen Vater in Eisenach?" "Du hast mehr Eltern." "Wo gehn wir denn hin?" "Immer nach Hause" (I, 325).

Cyane's brief, categorical answers are designed to create an atmosphere of unquestioning certainty. Her final reply is meant to confirm, on the "Vorhof" level, an insight Heinrich had already begun to apprehend right at the beginning of his journey towards his mother's home. At sunrise on the first day he turns to look at the homeland he has now left,

> Er sah sich an der Schwelle der Ferne, in die er oft vergebens von den nahen Bergen geschaut, und die er sich mit sonderbaren Farben ausgemalt hatte. Er war im Begriff, sich in ihre blaue Flut zu tauchen. Die Wunderblume stand vor ihm, und er sah nach Thüringen, welches er jetzt hinter sich ließ, mit der seltsamen Ahndung hinüber, als werde er nach langen Wanderungen von der Weltgegend her, nach welcher sie jetzt reisten, in sein Vaterland zurückkommen, und als reise er daher diesem eigentlich zu (I, 205, Part I ch. 2).

In Hardenberg's plans for the continuation of his novel, Heinrich does in fact ultimately return to the Wartburg, his home and origin, acting out the external, geographical mime of an inward mystical process, the final return from a journey which, from the moment of setting out, reveals itself as a way home.

There is, however, another level of meaning to be considered in connection with Cyane's answers. The idea of metempsychosis, or Hardenberg's version of it in a system of an infinite number of correspondences throughout time and space, is already present in "Die Erwartung". Not only does Heinrich recognize his portrait and scenes from his life in the hermit count's chronicle which comes from Jerusalem, but the Saracen captive, Zulima, discovers a resemblance between Heinrich and her poet brother who left Jerusalem to join a famous poet in Persia. But whereas these were merely pointers, there is now a real attempt to work out the implications of what Hardenberg in a note called "Verteilung Einer Individualität auf mehrere Personen" (I, 346). Metempsychosis as it is more commonly understood was a popular subject of speculation in the latter part of the eighteenth century, even, for instance, with Lessing, and the idea enjoyed a particular vogue in the Herder-Goethe circle at Weimar and Jena. Both Charlotte von Stein and Sophie von Kühn (who was known to members of this circle and visited by Goethe when she was ill in Jena) seem to have believed in it. Goethe and Hardenberg, without necessarily giving it formal credence, nevertheless toyed with the idea, looking on it as an emotionally satisfying symbol and a rewarding poetical ploy. It can serve to express the sense of a deep intuitive familiarity in a relationship which seems to defy any rational explanation except that of memories of a former existence. Goethe's "Ach, du warst in abgelebten Zeiten / Meine Schwester oder meine Frau,"[15] keeps to the plane of reasonable hypothesis, but in his Cyane-Heinrich dialogue, Hardenberg takes the idea much further into the realm of myth. Here everyone is related by specific and, as it may seem, mutually exclusive ties to everyone else, just as every road from anywhere to any other place is always, by definition, the way home. The doctrine of reincarnation which may seem questionable when held as a serious belief, has now been frankly mythologized by being translated into the terms of "Unendlichkeit" in the mode of Hardenberg's new experimental novel. This means that it is pointless to speculate about the logical content of this dialogue in an attempt to relate it to the approved doctrine of metempsychosis;[16] all one has to do is simply to allow the dialogue to create its effect of mystery, of ambiguity, of a statement valid only in the idiom of the new position now reached by Heinrich in the myth of his development as a poet - which is what the novel is about.

The verbal form of this dialogue resembles the cryptic interchanges of the Märchen in its folk form and also the surrealist question and answer interludes in, for instance, Goethe's "Märchen" or in Klingsohr's. In these cases the dialogue has the function of a successfully answered riddle which breaks down barriers for triumphant further action. In the first "Vorhof" dialogue, question and answer clear the way for Heinrich's further exploration of the new realm. The object is not to supply Heinrich, or indeed the reader, with information in the usual sense but to give him a new orientation by means of the creative disorientation which marks Schlegel's "Übergang vom Roman zur Mythologie". The effect is reinforced by the sense of solution unconsciously conveyed by an authoritative assertion, however paradoxical it may sound in its substance. Hardenberg makes much of what he calls "rhetorische Gewalt des *Behauptens,*" a literary device which helps the writer to carry conviction in the direction he intends.[17] Once this plane of creative disorientation has been reached and the new pattern established in the reader's mind, the novel can safely put the two-way traffic into operation and revert, as the author sees fit, to the kind of dialogue which does not look very different from that in Hemsterhuis's *Alexis,* or even Wieland's *Agathon,* a favourite novel of Hardenberg's in which the technique of philosophy by conversation is brought to a point of high perfection.[18]

The stage is now set for the first philosophical dialogue in the "Vorhof" mode, the talk between Heinrich and Sylvester. According to Lavater, the communication and interchange of ideas, "symphilosophieren", as Hardenberg and his friends called it, will be one of the main delights in heaven because everyone will be capable of giving artistic expression to an ever-renewed store of insights without any risk of boring his interlocutor. It is true that this "talk" will be silent: earthly language is necessarily successive in the realm of time whereas ideological interchange in the next world is immediate, "Gemälde und Sprache zugleich," "sichtbare Darstellung des Unsichtbaren, nichts als Offenbarung und Wahrheitssprache."[19] Sylvester and Heinrich were still dependent on words, but their talk was to convey a new and immediate intensity of insight, taking Heinrich a stage beyond his predominantly listening role in "Die Erwartung." Both the "Vorhof" types of dialogue had been foreshadowed in the first part of the novel, the Cyane-Heinrich pattern in the talk between Heinrich and Mathilde who, in their love, are already close to the transcendental realm where time has no power over them (I, 287-289), the Heinrich-Sylvester pattern in the talk about poetry with Klingsohr (I, 280ff). The new kind of "Gespräch" is a paradigm symbolizing the poet's own power to understand the world and reconstruct it by means of his art, and that is why the whole notion of dialogue is of such basic importance in the novel. At the point of Heinrich's arrival at Augsburg, it was said of him:

> Alles was er sah und hörte schien nur neue Riegel in ihm wegzuschieben, und neue Fenster in ihm zu öffnen. Er sah die Welt in ihren großen und abwechselnden Verhältnissen vor sich liegen. Noch war sie aber stumm, und *ihre Seele, das Gespräch,* [my italics] noch nicht erwacht (I, 268, Part I, ch. 6).

Klingsohr and Mathilde had then opened his lips and had unfolded into "unendliche Melodien" the chord of his response which had until then been unmodulated.

After his experience of grief and his vision Heinrich is fully prepared to take his share in bringing about the actual object of conversation between two people, that is, not just the imparting of information, and mutual expansion of knowledge but the creative modification of each separate point of view, a process leading to new discovery and changed attitudes for both speakers. Something new is to emerge "was beydes zugleich, und mehr, als Beydes einzeln ist," and this, as Hardenberg says in one of his *Dialogen,* is the definition of "ächte Mischung," as every true chemist knows, and it is also the aim and object of true dialogue.[20]

Hardenberg had, in fact, written formal dialogues as a literary exercise, never published in his life-time but intended for the *Athenäum* (II, 655 ff). They are totally different in kind from either of the dialogues in the second part of his novel. The *Dialogen* of 1799 are a sequence of complex fire-works of verbal brilliance, a word-play game in the ironical mode on literary and philosophical topics. There are moments of hymnic solemnity, as at the end of the fifth dialogue (II, 669), but this is exceptional. The sparring partners are "A" and "B." "A" is conservative and sceptical, he tends to get giddy on the rarified heights near the philosophical snow-line, "die ewige Schneelinie," favoured by "B", the rash and witty leader in the argument. These men are talking for the sake of talking and they do not visibly modify one another's opinions although this appears to be the aim of "B". In the second "Vorhof" dialogue, on the other hand, Heinrich speaking as a poet and Sylvester as a scientist, are each deeply aware of the other's approach and prepared to allow it entry into their own consciousness: "Mich hat die Beschäftigung mit der Natur dahin geführt," says Sylvester, "wohin Euch die Lust und Begeisterung der Sprache gebracht hat" (I, 334).

The conversation takes place in Sylvester's garden secluded among the ruins of an old castle. Here the two men sit and talk while Cyane prepares an evening meal. In an unforced sequence they cover a number of topics; the mention of Heinrich's father, also known to Sylvester long ago, of Heinrich's childhood and enlightened upbringing, leads the talkers on to a discussion of childhood in general and the significance of one's own native region and landscape. In the context of regional vegetation, flowers and plants are compared with children; Sylvester then considers the influence of clouds and weather conditions on all forms of organic and inorganic life. Extreme natural phenomena such as thunder and storms make man more deeply conscious of his own unique nature in its connection with nature in general. The concept of conscience, or consciousness, "Gewissen," is then analysed in its relationship to moral goodness, to ethics and finally to poetry, the basic function of which is to further virtue and goodness. This, the climax of the dialogue, opens out new perspectives for Heinrich's understanding of his role as a poet; as a final point of clarity reached by way of a careful progression of give-and-take in argument, Heinrich exclaims:

> Also ist der wahre Geist der Fabel eine freundliche Verkleidung des Geistes der Tugend, und der eigentliche Zweck der untergeordneten Dichtkunst, die Regsamkeit des höchsten, eigentümlichsten Daseins. Eine überraschende Selbstheit [identity] ist zwischen einem wahrhaften Liede und einer edeln Handlung (I, 332).

Throughout the talk the roles are clearly distinguished, Sylvester contributing in the main the natural philosophy, Heinrich translating this into his own poetical terms to the enrichment of their substance and to Sylvester's delight, while both at every stage interpret and expand the ideas put forward by the other. In part the talk takes the shape of question and answer in a straightforward interchange, and in any case, even when expanding a given point, each always talks *to* the other and not *at* or past him. They do not merely compete in juxtaposed philosophical disquisitions as do the voices in Hardenberg's *Die Lehrlinge zu Sais,* or go off tediously at a tangent, as in even the best of the eighteenth century philosophical dialogue novels. In "Die Erfüllung," the dialogue does at moments get fairly close to the "eternal snow-line," but, though complex, it always remains a living interchange between two people who go on developing their relationship while objectively furthering one another's reflections - the talk continues, therefore, to operate on an emotional as well as on an intellectual plane.

At the point which leads up to the climax-discussion about conscience, and where the argument begins to coalesce into something more concentrated as compared with the longer, smoother periods of the talk earlier on, Heinrich and Sylvester answer one another by putting further questions in the interests of a more incisive clarity; their speech units are brief, the rhythm creating an atmosphere of expectancy, even tension:

> "Macht mir doch die Natur des Gewissens begreiflich." [asks Heinrich]
> "Wenn ich das könnte, so wär ich Gott, denn indem man das Gewissen begreift, entsteht es. Könnt Ihr mir das Wesen der Dichtkunst [21] begreiflich machen ?"
> "Etwas Persönliches läßt sich nicht bestimmt abfragen."
> "Wie viel weniger also das Geheimnis der höchsten Unteilbarkeit. Läßt sich Musik dem Tauben erklären?". . .
> "Das Weltall zerfällt in unendliche, immer von größern Welten wieder befaßten Welten. Alle Sinne sind am Ende Ein Sinn. Ein Sinn führt wie Eine Welt allmählich zu allen Welten. Aber alles hat seine Zeit und seine Weise. Nur die Person des Weltalls vermag das Verhältnis unsrer Welt einzusehen . . ." (I, 330-31).

These terse sentences are "Stoßsätze", a word aptly coined by Hardenberg in another context.[22] Every part of this second dialogue, the philosophical content of which has recently been analysed in some detail[23] is an important distillation of romantic theory in various aspects and has also left its mark on poets and artists later on in the romantic movement and right on down the new century. Hardenberg's thoughts about children as prophets and as visible inhabitants of the Golden Age returned to earth moreover find close parallels in the thought of Blake, Coleridge and Wordsworth. The correlation of children with flowers which Hardenberg works out in striking and specific images was a revelation for Philipp Otto Runge, determining the whole course of his artistic development in his portraits as well as in the "Tageszeiten" sequence. Echoes of Sylvester's talk on clouds and weather conditions, as well as features of the method of both dialogues in expressing relationship, have reached as far as Stifter.[24]

The idea of conscience as it is here developed in a new and personal way, is linked with Hardenberg's own most consistently held theory of poetry as a force uniting this world with the transcendent realm, and as having the potential to change and even redeem the earth when the poet succeeds in transferring the infinite into the finite realm by means of language rightly structured. Some of what is here put forward provided the theoretical background of later romantic writing, in certain respects, for instance, for that of Arnim, of Brentano and more especially of Eichendorff's more simplified but basically identical view of the function of the poet and of poetry as he develops it in his lyrics, novels, and later on in his literary criticism.

The effectivness of this dialogue in determining personal artistic attitudes demonstrates the power of Hardenberg's theories in action, while within the novel itself, Heinrich's own continued poetical unfolding is shown as actually taking place in its successive stages. As in Part I of the novel, for instance in the evening walk to the hermit's cave, the outer world of nature was transformed into poetry, so in "Die Erfüllung" Heinrich himself actively shares in transforming philosophical and scientific ideas into poetry and artistic form: art is seen to change the world. In the final part of the talk Hardenberg again uses the term "Fabel" as synonymous with "Poesie" as a whole, as he did in the allegory of Klingsohr's Märchen. He prefers this term because, in the genre of the fable, the story and the moral, that is, the outward framework and the ethical idea to be conveyed, are still indissolubly one. In the cosmic metaphor of two heavenly constellations visibly united in a single revolution, Heinrich says: "Die Bibel und die Fabellehre sind Sternbilder Eines Umlaufs" (I, 333). Sylvester picks up this point so as to show, by his development of it later on, the actual thought process by means of which both of them have reached clarity, at any rate on this point and for the time being:

> Euch wird alles verständlich werden, und die Welt und ihre Geschichte verwandelt sich Euch in die Heilige Schrift, so wie Ihr an der Heiligen

> Schrift das große Beispiel habt, wie in einfachen Worten und Geschichten das Weltall offenbart werden kann; wenn auch nicht gerade zu, doch mittelbar durch Anregung und Erweckung höherer Sinne (I, 334).

In "Die Erwartung" the process by which poetry transforms the world was conveyed, in the main, by authorial comment, by nature description, by a poem or a conversation, all as reflected in the listening and learning mind of Heinrich, the developing poet; in "Die Erfüllung" a more complex stage of the process is conveyed by the movement and progress of thought within the dialogues themselves while commentary and description recede further into the background. They nevertheless have their more limited function. In "Das Kloster oder der Vorhof," the dominant metaphor for the birth of poetry in the bereaved Heinrich is that of new life flowering among ruins, an earthly vegetative variation of the cosmic image in Klingsohr's Märchen where Fabel's final constellation and emblem is that of the phoenix, new life being born out of the ashes of death. As an overture to Part II of the novel as a whole, Astralis, the star-child born to Heinrich and Mathilde, a mythical being corresponding to Fabel who herself is "mit Fleiß irrdisch" (III, 672 and I, 342), sings a song describing her conception, her birth and the role she is destined to play in the world:

> Es bricht die neue Welt herein
> Und verdunkelt den hellsten Sonnenschein,
> Man sieht nun aus bemoosten Trümmern
> Eine wunderseltsame Zukunft schimmern,
> Und was vordem alltäglich war,
> Scheint jetzo fremd und wunderbar. (I, 318)

It is typical of Hardenberg's novel-into-myth technique that the image in a poem or in a dialogue is forthwith carried over quite inconspicuously into an actual concrete situation within the narrative that follows. After the final answering words of the first dialogue, "Immer nach Hause," Cyane leads the way "home" to Sylvester's house, a place where new life flowers richly among the moss-grown ruins of the past:

> Sie waren jetzt auf einen geräumigen Platz im Holze gekommen, auf welchem einige verfallne Türme hinter tiefen Gräben standen. Junges Gebüsch schlang sich um die alten Mauern ... (I, 325).

In the same way as, in the mythical realm, Heinrich was able to look along the beam of light and see right into another world, so, with the poet's transforming eye, he can now see in these earthly ruins a terrestial vision of centuries of human history distilled into small shining minutes - the poet has transcended earthly time:

> Man sah in die Unermeßlichkeit der Zeiten, und erblickte die weitesten Geschichten in kleine glänzende Minuten zusammengezogen, wenn man die grauen Steine, die blitzähnlichen Risse, und die hohen, schaurigen Gestalten betrachtete (I, 325).

A further comparison then puts this metaphor into a cosmic relation, thus completing the first movement of Hardenberg's poetical technique of "Potenzirung" or "Romantisiren" of things first seen only in an earthly aspect:

> So zeigt uns der Himmel unendliche Räume in dunkles Blau gekleidet und wie milchfarbne Schimmer, so unschuldig, wie die Wangen eines Kindes, die fernsten Heere seiner schweren ungeheuren Welten (I, 325).

As this continuation shows, Hardenberg exploits the cosmic potentiality of his comparison only to bring it back to earth with his simile for the Milky Way, ". . . wie die Wangen eines Kindes," completing the sentence, however, by means of a rhythmically effective inversion so that the reader is left at the end with the idea of infinity. Hardenberg's way of using imagery in this double movement, his stylistic procedures here analysed, are fully representative of the "far more poetical form" of the continuation of the novel, as he himself saw it. The imagery itself might be called a kind of mythology in Hardenberg's own definition of the term, "Mythol[ogie] in meinem Sinn, als freye poëtische Erfindung, die die Wircklichkeit sehr mannichfach symbolisirt etc.," "die wirck[liche] Welt selbst wie ein Märchen angesehn."[25]

After this description of the ruins, Hardenberg continues the narrative in a matter-of-fact way, the change of rhythm in the prose marking the transition:

> Sie gingen durch ein altes Tor weg und der Pilger war nicht wenig erstaunt, als er sich nun von lauter seltsamen Gewächsen umringt und die Reize des anmutigsten Gartens unter diesen Trümmern versteckt sah. Ein kleines steinernes Häuschen von neuer Bauart mit großen hellen Fenstern lag dahinter. Dort stand ein alter Mann hinter den breitblättrigen Stauden und band die schwanken Zweige an Stäbchen (I, 325).

What makes up the special distinction of "Die Erfüllung" is not only the conjuring up of the mythical realm as the successful stylistic fusion of the two planes of "Wunderwelt" and "wirckliche Welt," already foreshadowed in "Die Erwartung." By the contrasting nature of his dialogues and their content, by the whole movement of his narrative proceeding on both levels at one and the same time, Hardenberg has stretched the capacity of the novel form in a new way, though whether he could ever have worked out a whole novel, or a number of further novels, on this original model, is another matter altogether. In what he did manage to complete, however, he has shown a possible way of making the transition from novel into myth in Schlegel's sense and of successfully mediating between two planes of experience. It is this process of mediation which makes the work of art creative in its effect on man's attitudes, the poet's essential task as Hardenberg described it in the *Lehrlinge zu Sais:*

> Die Außenwelt wird durchsichtig, und die Innenwelt mannigfaltig und bedeutungsvoll, und so befindet sich der Mensch in einem innig lebendigen Zustande zwischen zwei Welten in der vollkommensten Freiheit und dem freudigsten Machtgefühl (I,97).

---

[1] The MS of the draft, "Das Gesicht," is at the Freies Deutsches Hochstift, Frankfurt am Main, MS 9616. The MS of the opening chapter, with the exception of the poem "Astralis," formerly owned by Stefan Zweig and now

missing, is at the Nationale Forschungs- und Gedenkstätten, Weimar, H. 18 Folio SS, pp. 1-16. A part of the missing MS of the "Astralis" poem is reproduced facing p. 221. in vol. I of the original Kluckhohn-Samuel edition, *Novalis. Schriften, 4 vols,* (1929). - Except where otherwise stated, my quotations, indicated by volume and page number only, are taken from the new edition, *Novalis Schriften* edited by Paul Kluckhohn and Richard Samuel, 5 vols (1960ff.) Vol. I, *Das dichterische Werk* (I960); Vols II and III, *Das philosophische Werk* I und 2 (1965 and 1968). [Note that the pagination is unchanged for the main texts in the 1977 revised edition of Vol. I.]

2 Letters to F. Schlegel, 5 April and 18 June [1800], IV, 333 and 343 in the 1929 edition.

3 *Europa. Eine Zeitscbrift,* ed. by Friedrich Schlegel (Frankfurt 1803), vol. I, p. 56 (Reprint ed. by E .Behler, 1963).

4 Friedrich Schlegel, *Kritische Ausgabe seiner Werke* (1967), vol. II, ed. by Hans Eichner, p. 318, p, 313, p. 319. In his revision of the *Gespräch* for the 1825 edition of his works, Schlegel did not think his definitions of mythology sufficiently selfevident and he added a number of amplifications, of which the most helpful is that pointing to mythology as "... geltende symbolische Naturansicht, als Quelle der Fantasie, und lebendigen Bilder-Umkreis jeder Kunst und Darstellung" (p. 312, Note 10). There is also a longer explanation where Schlegel obviously had Novalis in mind (p. 320, Note 3).

5 "Man muß annehmen, daß darin Mathilde ertrunken ist, wie Heinrich in seinem Traum (oben S. 278, Z. 7ff) voraussah" (I, 611).

6 Helmut Schanze who compiled the computerized index of *Heinrich von Ofterdingen* has some interesting findings on the use of the notorious adjective "blue" in this novel: "Der Feststellung [Novalis's] *Alles blau in meinem Buche* widerspricht der nüchterne Befund im Index durchaus: Das Wort *blau* ist keineswegs so "häufig", wie man fürs erste annehmen könnte. Der Index führt insgesamt 21 Belege (von ungefähr 46,000 Wörtern) auf." With particular reference to the blue waves of the blue stream of Mathilde's death, the adjective is "einzig als Setzung in einem transzendenten poetischen Raum zu verstehen." The vivid colour adjectives in Klingsohr's

Märchen are similarly mythical and designed "einen autonomen poetischen Raum zu evozieren. Dies wieder ist einer der Gründe, welche die Faszination des 'romantischen Romans' ausmachen." "Zur Interpretation von Novalis' *Heinrich von Ofterdingen*. Theorie und Praxis eines vollständigen Wortindex", *Wirkendes Wort*, 20 (1970), 19-33, 24 and p. 26.

7 See Richard Samuel, *Die poetische Staats- und Geschichtsauffassung Friedrich von Hardenbergs* (1925), p. 227.

8 *Logologiscbe Fragmente*, II, no. 105, beginning "Die Welt muß romantisirt werden" (II, 545).

9 *IV*, 430 and 455 (1929 edition); see also Samuel, *Geschichtsauffassung*, *p*. 241.

10 *Aussichten in die Ewigkeit*, Gemeinnütziger Auszug aus dem größern Werke dieses Namens, Zürich, 1781. The edition I have used is a new unaltered one, Zürich 1841.

11 "Beilage aus der Handschrift eines Freundes von einem Traum," ed. of 1841, pp. 76-77. It is evident from Grimm's dictionary that the term "Vorhof" was current in 18th century Pietist usage and denoted a happy place as distinct from Catholic purgatory where waiting was more a matter of painful longing and purification. - The rest of Lavater's book is a detailed amplification of the kind of activities related in the initial vision out of which he creates a lively mythology of the transcendental. Some of the chapter-headings will give an idea of its nature and at the same time point to similarity with Heinrich's vision in his own "Der Vorhof": Chapter X, "Von den himmlischen Wohnungen," XII, "Von den himmlischen Körpern," XVII, "Von der Sprache im Himmel," XVIII, "Von den gesellschaftlichen Freuden des zukünftigen Lebens," XXI, "Beschäftigung der Seligen," XXV, "Über die Zeit": we shall be able to survey the events of aeons in a single glance "wie ein Gemälde," (p. 327).

12 *Aussichten in die Ewigkeit*, ch. XII, p. 154.

13 Cf. "Von der Bearbeitung der transscendentalen Poesie läßt sich eine Tropik erwarten - die die Gesetze der *symbolischen Construction* der transscendentalen Welt begreift" (II, 536).

[14] See the note in "Die Berliner Papiere," I, *"Ein Kloster,* höchst wunderbar, wie ein Eingang ins Paradies. Istes Kap[itel] ein Adagio" (I, 340).

[15] The poem beginning: "Warum gabst du uns die tiefen Blicke," addressed to Frau von Stein.

[16] Friedrich Hiebel, *Novalis,* 2nd revised ed. (1972), pp. 347f. On the subject as a whole in this connection, see Peter Kuepper, *Die Zeit als Erlebnis des Novalis* (1959), p. 79, note 28.

[17] "Es ist gewiß, daß eine Meynung sehr viel gewinnt, so bald ich weiß, daß irgend jemand davon *überzeugt* ist - *sie wahrhaft annimmt* freylich muß es auf eine Art seyn, deren Ursache nicht gleich in die Augen fällt... Rhetorische Gewalt des *Behauptens" (Das allgemeine Brouillon, No.* I 5 3, III, 269).

[18] For a useful recent discussion of the dialogue in the emergent novel of the eighteenth century, see Hans Gerhard Winter, "Probleme des Dialogs und des Dialogromans in der deutschen Literatur des 18. Jahrhunderts," *Wirkendes Wort,* 20 (1970), 33-51. See also *Der philosophische Dialog als literarisches Kunstwerk,* by R. Wildbolz, Sprache und Dichtung, 77 (1952).

[19] *Aussichten in die Ewigkeit, p.* 228 and p. 230.

[20] *Dialogen,* [3], II, 667.

[21] In his MS, Hardenberg originally wrote "Poesie" instead of the more complex "Wesen der Dichtkunst," and later on in the argument, he had first put "Moral" instead of "Tugendlehre" (Variants, I, 612). His aim, it seems, was to avoid the words more specifically loaded with set associations.

[22] The word occurs in the notes of 1797 on Hemsterhuis's philosophical dialogue, *Alexis:* "Nach ihm ist der Buchstabe nur eine *Hülfe* der philosophischen Mittheilung - deren eigentliches Wesen im *Nach*denken besteht. Der Redende leitet nur den Gang des Denkens im Hörenden - und dadurch wird es zum Nachdenken. *Er denkt* - und der *Andre denkt nach.* Die Worte sind ein unzuverlässiges Medium des Vordenkens. Die ächte Wahrheit

muß ihrer Natur nach, *wegweisend* seyn. Es kommt also nur darauf an jemand auf den rechten Weg zu bringen, oder besser, ihm eine bestimmte Richtung auf die Wahrheit zu geben ... Die Darst[ellung] der Philosophie besteht demnach aus lauter Themas, Anfangssätzen Unterscheidungssätzen - bestimmten *Stoß*sätzen - Sie ist nur für Thätige, für Wahrheitsliebende da - die *analytische* Ausführung des Themas ist nur für Träge oder *Ungeübte...*" (II, 373-74).

23 Charles M. Barrack, "Conscience in *Heinrich von Ofterdingen:* Novalis' Metaphysic of the Poet," *Germanic Review*, 46 (1971), 257-284. Barrack deliberately confines himself to a philosophical analysis of the dialogue and comes to the conclusion that for Heinrich, the poet, conscience appears in its true form as the ego's consciousness of itself, and that poetry itself can therefore be a manifestation of conscience. Although Barrack of set purpose does not enter into Hardenberg's philosophical position in its contemporary context, or into any formal aspect of style and language, I think that his careful analysis might have gained from a brief consideration of H. Wunderlich's important article on "Gewissen" in Grimm's *Wörterbuch*. From this it is clear that, linguistically, the transition from the more general meaning of "consciousness" or "knowledge of self" to a narrower ethical and religious notion corresponding to the Latin "conscientia," was a very gradual one and was by no means as settled by the end of the eighteenth century as it is now. This makes Hardenberg's identification of "Gewissen" with a poet's consciousness of himself as a poet, and therefore as poetry *tout court*, seem less arbitrary and also less original.

24 See Günther Weydt, "Ist *Der Nachsommer* ein geheimer *Ofterdingen*?" GRM, 39 (1958), 72-81, especially for Stifter's use of dialogue. Weydt's speculations, at least some of which are convincing, are developed more fully by Edmund Godde, *Stifter's 'Nachsommer' und der 'Heinrich von Ofterdingen'*. Untersuchungen zur Frage der dichtungsgeschichtlichen Heimat des *Nachsommers* (Diss. Bonn 1959).

25 III, 668, and III, 674 and I, 343, notes dating from the summer or autumn of 1800 when this chapter was being written.

Joseph Görres' Metaphorical Thinking

Görres is an acknowledged master of German prose style. What he says rather than how he says it, the astonishing variety of his literary, scientific, political and religious concerns, has however, and rightly, been the main focus of critical attention. But for Görres himself, the art of style and problems of communication always held considerable interest both in his thinking and in conversation, even when, and precisely because, he was so often forced to write at speed and under pressure. He broke new ground for journalism in that his own maintained a consistently high literary standard over a long period of years, more particularly in his "Rheinischer Merkur" (1814-1816) during the Napoleonic era. Taken as a whole, however, his writing is so disparate in scope and subject matter that anything like a comprehensive study of his style, essentially the key to any true understanding of this complex Romantic, would have to proceed along with a systematic analysis of a number of his most representative works as literary structures. Nothing of this kind has as yet been done. In a short inquiry it might be possible to make a beginning, to find a way in, by looking more closely at one dominant feature of Görres' style, style being seen as the formal aspect of the art of communication in language. Görres had a tendency to think and to express himself in metaphors. While this has always been recognized - indeed, it could hardly be missed - it has not been considered as part of his general and changing approach to language in his work as a whole. The purpose of this essay is to give some idea of the nature and development of this key feature of Görres' writing in his more formal literary work, his journalism being in rather a different case.

From the beginning of his career - he started university studies in medicine and science, and after a period of political activity, studied on his own, continuing to educate himself while teaching chemistry in Coblenz, science, philosophy and literature on an experimental basis in Heidelberg, and finally professing history in Munich - Görres always saw language in a primarily social context and as a two-way process: formed and structured by man, language is given an identity which then, in turn, proceeds to influence and to react upon personality, confirming, as it were, the Frenchman in his Frenchness, the German in his Germanic nature: "Sprache ist das große Band, das Individuen aneinander bindet; sie ist das nächste Erzeugniß des Spiels der innern physischgeistigen Organisation, also modifiziert in ihrer Konstitution nach den Modifikationen dieser Anlagen, und sie wirkt auch wieder rückwärts auf diese Anlage zurück." The context here is that of national identity and the Rhine as a natural frontier, but he goes on to make a general point about the relationship between verbalization and thinking: "Bestimmtheit, Schärfe und Nettheit im Ausdrucke der dem Geist vorschwebenden Ideen durch ein gelenkiges Organ, sind die unzertrennlichen Begleiterinnen einer lichten Vorstellungskraft, eines hellen unbefangenen Verstandes, der sich in seinen Konzeptionen spiegelt."[1]

Guido Görres claims for his father invariable clarity of exposition in his writings, this also being reflected in his handwriting, the prime gesture expressive of mental and emotional process. As an overall judgement, this perhaps rests on filial piety rather than on invariable objective fact; the most common and, it would seem, often justified criticism of Görres' literary work, as distinct from his journalistic writing, is its tendency to diffuseness and frequent obscurity. As to his handwriting, clarity is hardly its most marked feature, but rather, as with Novalis, the rhythmic vitality, the speed and vigour with which he flings his thoughts down on paper, the wide range of the extremes he reached in the upper and lower spheres into which this gestured reflection of his thinking and striving extends. There is, rather, a certain element of the personal hieroglyph about it, and this may also be said to characterize Görres' literary work as a whole. The hieroglyphic dimension is what Novalis found lacking in Lessing's prose: "Lessings Prosa fehlts oft an hieroglyphischen Zusatz", an accusation which could never be levelled at Görres, nor yet that, like Lessing, his vision was too acute so that he lost "das Gefühl des undeutlichen Ganzen, die magische Anschauung der Gegenstände zusammen in mannigfacher Erleuchtung und Verduncklung". [2] Görres' vision was always global in Novalis' sense, and while the resulting atmosphere of his writings is indeed often one of magical clairobscur, there is also some blurring of the edges where sharp outlines might have been demanded.

As an adjunct to Görres' global vision and an attempt to master it meaningfully, there was his strong, almost compulsive urge towards systematization; every topic, whatever its scope, had to be seen as fitting into a scheme from the start, as often as not whether the ways and means, and the organic development of gradually evolved proof and argument allowed of system or not. This tendency was strongly criticized by Tieck in his letter of 18 May, 1818, to Solger, when he writes about Görres' "Mißbrauch der Combinationsgabe". The most cogent example here is the systematized scheme introducing Görres' huge work on mysticism, worked out over eight years and some two thousand pages, but never reaching what he himself saw as the heart of the work, "einigende Mystik". Systematization is essential to clarity but when it arises from, or goes hand in hand with, a rather too markedly intuitive apprehension of phenomena, it can mask a certain lack of clear thinking.

It is here that metaphorical thinking and writing can prove helpful and also effective for communication, even though it has dangers of its own. In prose usage, especially, the metaphor implies a simpler thought process than a straight comparison: it can serve as a useful synthetic measure, a short cut for putting across an idea which has proved rather too complex for logical formulation. It is a rhetorical device, well known to preachers and politicians, which is more comprehensive and complex in its effect precisely because of that element which must necessarily remain unclear, even mysterious. A sustained analogy has this same effect of heightening emotional intensity, often at the cost of clarity; and while Novalis recommended analogy in the most positive terms as a magic wand, Schiller more cautiously saw it as a powerful but dangerous instrument for the analysis of events, and one which should be used only with the greatest circumspection.[3] Görres exploited both these poetical ploys to the full, and as he progressively mastered the art of metaphor and sustained metaphorical analogy, this reflected back on his own thinking in the sense of his dictum of language working "rückwärts auf diese Anlage zurück".

Görres had used features of imagery in his earliest writings, but where the comparisons were not stock ones, he tended to over-elaborate parallels in explicit detail, illustrating his stage by stage argument with pedantic thoroughness. In "Der allgemeine Frieden, ein Ideal" (1798; I, 1-78), a personal manifesto in which he prepared the ground for is final turning away from Jacobin sympathies as finalized in "Mein Glaubensbekenntnis" that same year, he gives a parallel between what he calls "polyarchische Demokratie", a form of liberal centralized government, and Linnaeus' sex classification of plants: "Ein merkwürdiges Analogon zu dieser Formenklassifikation liefert uns das linneische Sexualsystem", and so on (I, 23). The very rhythm is that of explanation in a class room. Algebraic equations, too, are used to elucidate social and political phenomena, and also for painlessly working out an "allgemeines Friedensschema", or what industrial relations groups now call a peace formula. In his "Resultate meiner Sendung nach Paris", produced in the face of disillusion with French power politics and the Terror, he began to write more mature prose and to use figures of speech which fit more easily and memorably into the flow of his exposition. He also shows himself aware of the possibly specious nature of oratorical imagery in political contexts:

> Da creirte man die Maxime: auch das Rad der Natur rollt hin und in seinen Speichen hängen Millionen zerißner Leichen [...] Tod also sey die Losung gegen innere, Tod gegen äußere Feinde! So ward der Terrorismus das Regulativ der Handlungsweise der Jakobiner. ("Resultate", 45)

But at the same time he thinks it quite in order to use similar rhetorical procedures to help his own people in their fight against pessimism and despair, a state of mind only fit for miserable creatures who sit cowering in their caves,

> wie ein Troglodyt in seinem Körper wohnt, und von der ganzen weiten Schöpfung nichts kennt, als seine Höhle, in der er die Stalaktiten und Tropfsteine für die Grundvesten der Welt hält [...] (76)

like men who are not forward-looking, open to the wider horizons of hope, and who understand

> daß alles, was geschieht, geschehen mußte; daß Sonnen erlöschen und Republiken dahinsterben nicht am Zufall, sondern nach den Gesetzen der ewigen ordnenden Natur. (76)

This is the first hint of the imagery of nature in its cosmic aspect which remained the staple background of all Görres' metaphorical thinking throughout the complex evolutions of his beliefs and up to his last published work within a few weeks of his death in 1848.

Of his fellow Germans he says: "Im Reich der Ideen schafft er sich seine Welt, dort labt er sich an den Bildern die er durch seine Sinne aus der äußern Sphäre in jene innere aufnimmt [...] Seine Kultur geht daher nach Innen weil er dort sich der meisten bildsamen Kräfte bewußt ist." (89) Detailed suggestions for setting up a "cisrhenanische Republik" then conclude the tract, creating a realm of fantasy as remote and unrealistic in its way as his school friend Brentano's "Ländchen Vadutz"; this new Rhineland project was the lost paradise of a young Republican's idealistic dreams. Görres detailed its constitution, laws and government with the same loving intensity with which Vadutz was described, complete with its "Wundergebirge der Geschichte, Fabel- und Märchenwelt", a never-never land of order and integrity. Görres' early political activity, as distinct from his mature intervention in Germany's affairs later on at the time of the Restoration, had a romantic private world aspect to it. As he relinquished direct political action at the end of the century, he allowed the image-making powers of an idealistic inner world which had hitherto found expression in the cut-and-thrust language of politics, to arise more freely and to spill over into his conscious thinking and writing. He was now ready for the impact which his reading of the Romantics made on him, Novalis, the Schlegels, and most of all, Schelling, whose work showed him that speculative and imaginative thinking could be effectively and convincingly combined, could serve, as in science, the field with which he was most familiar, as a valid basis for objective knowledge. He found here models of thinking and writing which profoundly confirmed him in his own basic cast of mind and thus were able to release a poetical vein in him. Not, of course, that he was a poet, or would ever have claimed such a status for himself. It is interesting, however, that it was precisely the same stage at which Wordsworth, similarly disillusioned by the Terror, found a new release of poetic power in the "Lyrical Ballads" (1798) and a return to the stability of true folk traditions.

Although a change in Görres' way of writing was already evident in the two collections of aphorisms of 1802 and 1803, the form itself being a departure from ideas presented as a sequently argued whole, the change did not become marked until the year following when he began to contribute literary essays to Christoph von Aretin's Munich periodical, "Aurora". It was in keeping with the new look that Görres chose to entitle these passing flashes of insight "Korruskationen", summer lightning, though this was neither the first nor the last time that he showed a taste for monolithic titles of symbolical import: "Rübezahl" (1798), "Athanasius" (1838). These essays were designed, in Aretin's words, to "shed light" on German literature; they included reflections on Lessing, Goethe, Schiller, Hölderlin, Jean Paul and Kleist, as well as comparative comments on all the main art forms as occasion offered. Görres was feeling his way towards new possibilities of expression. In the very first essay he sets up an analogy between modern literature and geological rock and fossil formations, speculating about the difficult task that future generations will have to assemble "die Gebeine unseres Mammuts" in order to make out what the original of this monster could possibly have looked like (I, 98). Continuing in this vein, he describes Jean Paul, "überhaupt ganz eigentlich der Repräsentant des Modernen", in terms of a lively landscape, and the comparison of French and German literature also proceeds on the basis of natural scenery contrasted. Then there is the revolution in politics, philosophy and poetry at the end of the century which suddenly disturbs the calm domestic bliss of "Poesie" in its house and garden redolent of bourgeois complacency: eccentric people come wandering into this tame and settled world, magicians speaking in riddles and murmuring strange spells:

Alte Marmorbilder stiegen von ihren Gestellen herunter, und wandelten nackt durch die Straßen; wunderliche Träume der Mitternacht, in denen Himmel und Erde ineinander laufen, von Äther, Dunst, Licht und Gold

> zusammengesetzt, liefen am hellen Tage herum; die Bäume fingen an zu sprechen, und die Kräuter und Blumen zu singen, jede auf ihre Weise, und der Winde Brausen artikulierte sich, und das Murmeln der Quellen [...] bisher ungesehene Vögel flogen aus dem Süden herauf, und brachten fremde, seltsame Gesangsweisen mit, und die Echos in den Bergen sprachen alle fremden Sprachen. (I, 115)

It is only a short step from Görres' criticism by metaphor and personification to Heine's techni-colour version of it, to his idea of Brentano's muse as the crazy Chinese princess, locked in her bell tower, who "laughs madly at us, filling our souls with gruesome delight and lewd terror".[4] Görres was a trend setter in this mode of criticism, not only for Heine, but for Gutzkow, who worked it to death, and for Eichendorff, who gave it his unmistakable aura of true poetry. Görres himself, however, has clearly been reading his Novalis, "Hyazinth und Rosenblüthchen" in particular, which is evident even in his new sentence rhythms, and in the fact that his style as a whole was beginning to assume a rather different aspect.

The great challenge to give an account to himself and to others of the stage he had reached in his thinking and in the new organization of his store of miscellaneous knowledge and experience, came when he announced his lectures at the university of Heidelberg for the academic year, 1806-1807. His first bout of university work lasted less than two years; by the autumn of 1808 he was back at his school in Coblenz. As a preliminary to his first year he published a fly sheet to announce the subject of his lectures, perhaps one of the most spectacular Romantic documents to have survived and not one of the best known: "Ankündigung Philosophischer und Physiologischer Vorlesungen im Winterhalbenjahre 1806-7. Von Professor Görres".[5] In view of his recent development, it comes as no surprise that Görres chose to compose it in the form of a single, long sustained and consciously mystifying analogy between the realm of the spirit and that of matter. This was his shop window and he does not intend to neglect the window dressing. He proposes to lecture on what might seem to be two disparate subjects. He therefore wants to show their "unity and homogeneity" and to demonstrate in the most intriguing way possible how closely interrelated these two fields in fact are, and necessarily must be: patterns of creative thought, shown in operation on matter as the world is gradually formed out of the dark formless void at the beginning, are mirrored in every manifestation of organic life, in the very substance of animal and human bodies with which physiology, the study of the form and function of all living things, is concerned. This creative spirit has left its mark on all matter and it is therefore pointless to try to understand one without the other. Görres' twin lecture courses, complementing one another, have as their object not only information to be purveyed; they are to be a means, rather, of eliciting personal, independent thinking in the minds of students, too often living "wie Automate im fremden Geiste"; the lectures are to instil enthusiasm and energy by establishing "kecke, kräftige, in sich gerundete Gebilde" in student minds. The choice of the collective plural, "Gebilde", rather than some more direct equivalent of "ideas", as one might have expected from an academic course, is interesting here, and characteristic for this new professor for whom thought tended to proceed most cogently, though not exclusively, of course, in interrelated clusters of images.[6]

Görres does not begin his announcement of some four octavo pages with any plain statement of intention but with a verbal mystification designed actually to set in motion the educative process he has in mind for his listeners. He is practising what Novalis, and any rhetorician, recognizes as the art of simple assertion: say firmly enough that a thing *is* so, and it actually *becomes* so. The first half of the announcement consists of two mammoth sentences, articulated only by commas and semi-colons, this last, if Adorno is to be believed, the now as good as obsolete form of punctuation which infallibly points to a sustained and therefore valid thinking process in the writer.[7] This first sentence describes the coming of light and life to the earth when it was void and without form, each successive stage of this advent being one of action, gradual at first, then increasingly swift and turbulent:

> [...] wie eine ferne Dämmerung um den Horizont des werdenden Universums spielt, und nun die Mitternacht vor dem neuen Licht ergraut, und die Finsternis sich in Schattenschemen bricht und wölkt, und der Elemente wunderbare seltsamgestaltige Welt sich in den dunklen Gewölben

> regt, und schlaftrunken, schwer und träg die Kräfte sich in der gebärenden Nacht zusammenfinden, und langsam, leise und schweigend in der Schöpfung geheimnisvollem Weben sich aneinanderfügen; wie dann die Scharen der Feuergeister sich stärker drängen, mächtiger die Glut durch die Schattengebirge blitzt, und hell die neue Zeit in den Feuerstreifen der ersten Aurore aufglüht, und kräftiger sich's im dunklen Reiche rührt und regt, bis der Lichtgeist selbst, über alles glorreich, herrlich über die Weltgebirge schreitet, und nun die Nacht erbleicht, und die Finsternis in die Tiefe des Stoffes sich eilig flüchtet; wie Erz und Stein im Morgenstrahl dann froh erklingen [...] (I, 138)

Each cosmic event comes to what is only an apparent end, the momentarily suspended process being indicated by a semi-colon followed by the comparative particle, "wie", which is also the opening and key word of the announcement as a whole: "Wie das All in seinem Wesen wurde, war und ist; [...]". The repetition of this punctuation manoeuvre for each successive process described in skilfully varied rhythmic patterns, creates growing tension and suspense until the mimed process is completed and the long withheld second term of the comparison is at last reached some fifty lines and a dozen semi-colons further on: "darüber und über noch ein mehreres giebt die *Philosophie* uns Zeugnis, die das Göttliche, das die *Religion* in seiner *Idealität* anschaut, in seiner *Realität* ergreift, und in diesem Eingreifen sich subjektiv als *Kunst,* objektiv als *Wissenschaft* darstellt" (I, 139).

Görres has now established a total synthesis, as he sees it, of all the abstracts he has here italicized: what he proposes to put across in his lectures is universalism. But in the meanwhile, one may well ask, what does "Philosophie" in a narrower sense mean in Görres' context? The answer is: "Unendlichkeit nach allen Richtungen, Progression nach allen Dimensionen des Realen ist das Wesen der Philosophie", which leads straight on to physiology. Görres sees physiology as the microcosm within the cosmos of "philosophy" which is most closely related to us as human beings, the immediate focus of all our reflexes as human organisms, teaching us how an inner, personal and individual life may be won from the immeasurable total of life as a whole:

> Das ist daher das Verhältnis der Philosophie und der Physiologie, Alleben

und Einzelnleben; Weltgeist und Menschengeist, Himmelsbahn und irdisch Pulsieren [...] Die Philosophie von ihrer natürlichen Seite genommen, will des Weltganzen innerste Verborgenheit aufdecken, wie das Geäder durch den großen Körper läuft, wie die Nerven sich durcheinanderschlingen, wieder voneinanderlassen, wie Faser mit Faser sich verwebt [...] Die Physiologie aber philosophisch genommen erkennt des Himmels Abglanz im Tropfen, der schwebend in der Erdenatmosphäre hängt, in der Tiefe der Leiblichkeit findet sie die Wunder der Ferne wieder, und des Firmamentes Widerschein, des Äthers Klarheit in der dunklen Nacht des Organischen [...] (I, 141)

Philosophy and physiology in partnership, help us, in Blake's terms, to "see the world in a grain of sand". It is clear that a mind having this kind of view of the correspondences between matter and spirit will be perfectly at home in the realm of "signatura" and will think metaphorically almost as a matter of course.

Eichendorff, one of the students who heard these lectures, took it quite for granted that a scientist should be "thinking in images", as he put it. And if one bears in mind Görres' own and the contemporary connotation of the term "philosophical", his project of lecturing on his two chosen topics as a single unity is not so surprising. Philosophy was not primarily "Weltanschauung"but "natural philosophy", that is, theoretical and applied science considered in its principles and theory. This use has survived in English, thus in the title of a leading scientific periodical, "The Philosophical Magazine", founded in 1798 to "diffuse Philosophical Knowledge among every Class of Society [. . .] and of every thing new or curious in the scientific World, both at Home and on the Continent", and still going strong.[8] The acta of the Royal Society are still called "Philosophical Transactions".

So one may say that the close proximity into which Görres puts his two subjects is objectively justified. His literary method, however, while it is significant for him as a writer, might be considered questionable: in a context where sober information was expected, there is mystery and metaphor. It is no longer common knowledge just how our academic forbears went about announcing their lecture courses - fly sheets are too ephemeral; but if the comparison is not lèse-majesté, there is always Schiller's inaugural of 1789 to remember, a brilliantly systematized and solemn statement of intent, working up to: "Und auf solche Art behandelt, meine Herren, wird Ihnen das Studium der Weltgeschichte eine ebenso anziehende als nützliche Beschäftigung gewähren. Licht wird sie in Ihrem Verstande und eine wohltätige Begeisterung in Ihrem Herzen entzünden".[9] Görres, the Romantic, was writing the kind of thing for which Novalis invented the term "lyrisches Philosophem" or "Minuspoesie"; and of the writer of lyrical prose, he says that if he is "ganz lebenstrunken, so werden es Dythiramben seyn, die man freylich als Dythiramben genießen und beurteilen muß".[10]

The "Ankündigung" can, in fact, best be understood as a kind of poetic mime in Romantic fashion. As far as Görres was concerned, the minds of his prospective student listeners were analogous to the void of primeval darkness without form upon the face of the deep, as in Genesis; creative light was now about to be shed on dark chaos by the agency of those "kecke, kräftige in sich gerundete Gebilde" which Görres hoped to fashion and call forth in unformed and uninformed minds. He had always been fascinated by the image of the formless void of primordial chaos and by the creative process which gradually, on the seven days of creation, transformed it into the structured order of a cosmos: "[...] erst wenn die Kräfte durch das Unendliche zum Ebenmaße gekommen sind", he says in the first of his "Korruskationen", "kann die wahre organische Schöpfung beginnen" (I, 98), and the opening section of "Religion in der Geschichte" which Görres contributed in his first Heidelberg year to Friedrich Creuzer's "Studien" (1807), is taken up with a protracted elaboration of the same topos. All the same, Görres was quite capable of seeing the Genesis situation in a rather less than solemn light. This is suggested by the satirical drawing done according to his design in the "Zeitung für Einsiedler" of 1808. Against a landscape background of Heidelberg, complete with castle, university buildings, hills and the river, an engaging monkey is shown conducting the opening bars of Haydn's oratorio, "The Creation", which, in the ten years since its first performance, had taken Europe, and Romantic Europe in particular, by storm.

It would perhaps be too daring to suggest that Görres wrote his "Ankündigung" with his tongue in his cheek, but as a Rhinelander, he could surely not have been devoid of humour: there is in fact much evidence to the contrary, especially in his letters. He must have been quite aware that the elaborate model he was here using as a means was oddly disproportionate to the simple end of, as it were, putting a notice in the local "University Reporter" (the name of the Cambridge variety of the genus). Nor can he have been under any illusion about the utter dreariness of the academic and intellectual situation in Heidelberg at that time, about all the philistine smugness and lack of imagination at which he and Brentano laughed so uproariously in their jointly devised "Entweder BOGS, der Uhrmacher", and that he himself managed to come to terms with in the splendid nonsense "Tollgewordener Epilog" to the "Schriftproben von Peter Hammer" (1808).[11] In his announcement, Görres was visibly enjoying himself, revelling in imaged complexity and fine writing, seeing to what lengths he could go, how far and how picturesquely he could relate his two fields of interest in a way that would attract notice, even scandalize, where necessary. He had the serious intention of instructing and educating, and the less solemn aim of shocking his potential hearers into receptiveness for something new and strange. "Ich muß gestehen, es ist mir ganz unbegreiflich, wie man Herrn Görres nach Erscheinung der beiliegenden Ankündigung den Hörsaal eröffnen konnte". This reaction by the editor of the periodical in which Görres' announcement was subsequently published, indicates that, as far as the local philistines were concerned, Görres had not failed to make his point.[12]

It is evident from Görres' writing during the Heidelberg years, especially from his work on German chap books and the critical essays, that his new way of thinking and writing had become a valid method for him of arriving at an objective vision of the world and of conveying his insight. It was not, however, primarily an attempt to make the abstract concrete, or vice versa, in Novalis' sense of "romantisiren" and the converse of "logarythmisiren";[13] his intention is to posit what he sees as a true correspondence and relationship, to enlighten the understanding of the reader, and with rhetorical intention, to affect his imagination, set it to work and stir his sensibility. In any case, his aim is not to etherealize a fact or a thought but to clarify it and thus to give it the accuracy of poetic truth. A process of this kind can be seen in action in the two dominant images he uses to characterize and give the feel of chap books. There is the language metaphor, by which they are "redende Stimmen der Vorzeit" the voice receding ever further and more mysteriously into the remote past, until one hears, as it were, only the language of the elements, "sinnvoll und bedeutend, aber nicht mit Menschenzungen, nicht mit artikulierten Tönen [. . .] dem innern Sinne ist ihr Verständnis nur gegeben" (I. 174f.). Then there is the vegetative image by which these books are as "Naturwerk, wie die Pflanze":

> Wie Halm an Halm auf dem Felde in die Höhe steigt, wie Gräser sich an Gräser drängen, wie unter der Erde Wurzel mit Wurzel sich verflicht, und die Natur einsilbig aber unermüdet immer dasselbe dort, aber immer ein anderes sagt, so tut auch der Geist in diesen Werken [. . .] das Volk lebt ein sprossend, träumend Pflanzenleben; sein Geist bildet selten und nur wenig, und kann nur in dem Strahlenkreise der höheren Weltkräfte sich sonnen, seine Blüte aber blüht alles unter die Erde in die Wurzel hinab, um dort wie die Kartoffel eßbare Knollen anzusetzen, die die Sonne nimmer sehen. Nicht ganz so unbegründet zeigt sich daher die Besorgnis, es sey da unten nichts zu suchen, als wertloses Geröllе, Kieselsteine, die die Ströme in den langen Zeitläuften rund und glatt gewälzt, schmutzige Scheidemünzen, die vielfältiges Betasten abgegriffen [...] (I, 147f.).

Provided one can come to terms with such Romantic notions of composite authorship, Görres' images - the voice speaking across the centuries, the hidden and crude life of the root system beneath the earth, the rounded, smooth stones, the worn coinage of small change- all these convey in concentrated, vivid fashion the general feel of these stories to which Görres was about to introduce the reader or his audience: his "Die Teutschen Volksbücher" was based on a lecture course. Görres was thereby himself helped to apprehend and organize what was to him new knowledge, purveyed mainly by Brentano and his library: Görres took the familiar course of lecturing and writing about a topic so as to find out something about it. As his literary horizon widened, his style gained in distinction and originality, which is clear from his essays in the “Heidelberger Jahrbücher”, particularly from his review of "Des Knaben Wunderhorn" where he tried to do for folk poetry something of the kind he had done for chap books, and from his analysis of what he saw as the "Hieroglyphik der Kunst" and "plastische Symbolik" of Runge's "Die Zeiten" (I, 203-222).

While this new-found and newly developed pattern of thinking remained with Görres to the end, it gradually became a less conspicuous and more truly integrated feature of his style, less of a mannerism than it at one stage threatened to become. His later religious writing (he remained aware of the distinction between "religion" and "theology," not trespassing into the latter) gave him plenty of scope for putting forward his theory on the subject of symbolism. There is, for instance, the chapter in the first volume of "Die Christliche Mystik" (1836) where he describes the "signatura" of the cross to be found "im Grundbau jeglicher Substanz", in the outstretched wings of a bird in flight, in the structure of trees, plants and leaves (II, 494ff.); and in "Die Wallfahrt nach Trier" (1845) his discussion and defence of the astonishing concourse of pilgrims to venerate the relic of Christ's "Tunica", the seamless robe, leads him to examine the whole topic of symbolism and the way it has been integrated into the liturgy and worship of the Church.

But while religious symbolism was a main preoccupation of his later years, there was one field of comparison which remained a constant with him and on which he drew readily all through his life - that of astronomy: "Der Himmelsbau" was the title of one of his philosophical lectures in 1807, and his unfinished essay, written a few weeks before he died, has a star title. The firmament and its pattern of immutability within a fixed and ever recurring cycle of regular change was the archetype of stability, that is, before Einstein. At the conclusion of his "Kritik der Praktischen Vernunft" (1788), Kant had posited his great parallel between the starry sky and the moral law innate in man: "Zwei Dinge erfüllen das Gemüt mit immer neuer und zunehmender Bewunderung und Ehrfurcht, je öfter und anhaltender sich das Nachdenken damit beschäftigt: der bestirnte Himmel über mir und das moralische Gesetz in mir". In the detailed analogy which follows - it is never a metaphor - Kant seeks to invest the moral law with the certainty and the stability inherent in the laws that govern the movement of the stars. In the same way, Görres' aim was to lend to the second term of his analogies and metaphors in this field, in whatever sphere it happened to be - literary, political, mystical -, an atmosphere of scientific truth, an aura of transcendence, as "an der großen Sternenuhr" (I, 177). Like Kant, he involved the laws of cosmology as an aid to constructive thinking and action, but also with a rhetorical intent of persuasion. At the beginning of "Der Allgemeine Frieden" (1797), he sees himself as a "Kosmopolitiker", in analogy to the "Kosmologe" he is about to analyse, he says, and to explain political "constellations" and laws, starting out from an original state of chaos, always significant for him, and then enabling himself and others, as he hopes, to see events in the two realms - the firmament and the political world - as "völlig analog in einer Art von chymischen Wechselwirkung" (I, 10). Twenty-five years later, he begins his account of European history, "Europa und die Revolution" (1821), with an introduction entitled "Orientierung". Taking your bearings by fixed stars, by the movement of winds, clouds and tides, "in Zeiten, wo die sittliche Welt in allen ihren Tiefen bewegt erscheint und die Gesellschaft in großen Wellen schlägt und brandet", was hardly a dead metaphor in Görres' time. He pursues the image with skill and tact throughout the simple systematic time-sequence of the inquiry as a whole - "Vergangenheit", "Gegenwart", "Zukunft", - and keeps the idea of a ship guided by the stars ever in the background.

In his introduction to Melchior von Diepenbrocks's translations from the Dominican mystic, Heinrich Suso, (1829), he sees mystical experience as a firmament only very partially explored from our earthly observatories: "Unvollendet sind die angelegten Sternkarten geblieben, die uns heimisch machen sollten in jenem Geisterhimmel", while at the same time, the natural sciences are making startling advances and uniting to solve the physical, geological and cosmological mysteries of the universe. It was Görres' aim, though not his fully accomplished achievement, to charter this mystical firmament and to work out fully the star maps he found so incomplete compared with the scientific blue-prints of his time.

Finally, as though to complete a circle, Görres began his last work, "Die Aspekten an der Zeitenwende - zum neuen Jahre 1848", with a reprint of an essay written for the "Rheinischer Merkur" almost a whole generation, as he says, previously: "Der Sternenhimmel in der Neujahrsnacht von 1815-1816". He was here enlisting the aid of a familiar model, that of the traditional almanach, popular to this day, with its use of weatherlore and astrological data for more or less crude prognosis of the year to come. Görres' prognosis, however, was not to be by means of astrology itself but only by the symbolical import of the figures and signs man has from time immemorial projected into the night sky. Beginning with a lyrical evocation of darkness and light over the earth, he goes on to read the permanent significance of the familiar night constellations "in diesem großen apokalyptischen Panorama", Orion, Libra, Taurus, Scorpion, Lion and so on, "stehende Typen alter großer Geschichtsformen", which can predict the future only in so far as they represent basic human impulses - justice, industry, aggression, tyranny - in action and interaction in the affairs of men. Long years have passed since the Napoleonic era when his first essay was written,

> [...] aber der Sternenhimmel hat nicht gealtert in dieser Zeit [...] das ganze Werk wird von der Strenge des Gesetzes umfaßt; der Finger Gottes hat den Dekalog dieses Gesetzes mit Lichtzügen in dem Äther vorgeschrieben, und die Erdkräfte, seine Werkzeuge, die elektrischen Feuersmächte, Windeswehen und Wasserströmung, und die Verwandtschaften in der Tiefe haben ihn in den Steintafeln der Erde nachgeschrieben. (II, 724f.)

This is the setting in which he begins his - unfinished - analysis of what the year 1848 might hold for the world he knows.

The thought of life as a storm-tossed sea with stars in heaven to guide the wanderer's ship, remained with Görres to the very last, it seems. A day or two before he died on 29 January of that same year, he laughingly refused the offer of a little skull-cap to keep his head warm: "Willst du mir wohl deine Ulysseskappe aufsetzen!" he said to his son-in-law. "Soll ich noch einmal das Steuerruder auf die Schulter nehmen, noch einmal die Weltfahrt? Das wäre eine stürmische Fahrt! Nein, dazu ist es zu spät. "

---

[1] Resultate meiner Sendung nach Paris im Brumaire des achten Jahres. Koblenz im Floreat J. VIII (i.e. May 1800). 82f. As the critical edition of Görres' works Gesammelte Schriften, ed. W. Schellberg and others, Cologne 1926 onwards, has not been available to me, I have based my work, wherever possible, on Wolfgang Frühwald's admirable recent selection, Joseph Görres, *Ausgewählte Werke in zwei Bänden.* Freiburg/Basle/Vienna 1978. References

by volume and page in the present essay are to this selection which has presented complete texts as far as possible, carefully introduced and annotated. For texts not in this selection, I have used Lord Acton's original editions now in the Cambridge University Library. For a number of personal details I have used his copy of Johann Josef von Görres, *Ein Denkmal aus seinen Schriften auferbaut*, ed. by J. A. Moriz Brühl, Aachen, 1854, especially the introduction by various authors.

2 Novalis, *Schriften*. Ed. by Paul Kluckhohn and Richard Samuel. Continued by Hans-Joachim Mähl and Richard Samuel. New edition, 6 vols., Stuttgart 1960 onwards. II. 537.

3 *Die Christenheit oder Europa*. Novalis III. 518; *Was heißt und zu welchem Ende studiert man Universalgeschichte?* Schiller, *Werke*. Ed. by Ludwig Bellermann. 14 vols. Leipzig n.d. VIII. 26.

4 *Die Romantische Schule*. Heinrich Heine. *Sämmtliche Werke*. Ed. by Ernst Elster. 5 vols. Leipzig n.d. V. 308.

5 The original fly sheets cannot now be traced. The text, (I, 138-142) is based on the reprint in: *Heidelberg und seine Umgebung im Sommer 1807 in Briefen von R. Reinbeck*. Tübingen 1808, 203-212. The copy in the British Library is from Ludwig Tieck's Library.

6 Oskar F. Walzel's "Görres' Stil und seine Ideenwelt", in *Euphorion*, 10, 1903, 792-809, is still the most useful inquiry into Görres' use of various figures of speech in his early Heidelberg writings but does not include the "Ankündigung". The most perceptive recent comments on Görres' style are those by W. Frühwald, *Die Sprache*, (Anhang, II. 921-930).

7 Th. W. Adorno, *Noten zur Literatur I*. "Satzzeichen". Frankfurt am Main 1958, 168f.

8 I am indebted to Professor Sir Nevill Mott, a former editor of the periodical, for helpful comments on this point and for lending me his copy of the original first volume of the *Philosophical Magazine* for 1798.

9 Schiller, VIII. 28.

10 Novalis, II. 462.

11 Cf. the essay by the present writer, " 'Ein literarisches Mondkalb': Joseph Görres' 'Tollgewordener Epilogus' to his 'Schriftproben von Peter

Hammer' ". In: *German Life and Letters*, XXXIV, 1 (1980), Special Number for Leonard Forster, 108-16.

[12] Quoted by W. Frühwald from Reinbeck's work, Note 5 above (II. 801).

[13] Novalis, II. 545.

Carus' »Neun Briefe über Landschaftsmalerei« (1831)

*Werk und Form in romantischer Perspektive**

Carl Gustav Carus (1789-1869) teilt das Schicksal vielseitig begabter Spätromantiker, die oft gerade durch ihr künstlerisch orientiertes Universalstreben als Romantiker gelten, und eben deshalb auch nur selten in der Fülle ihrer Gesamtleistung erfaßt und gewürdigt werden. Auch hier kommt nur *ein* Werk von Carus zur Sprache; es ist dies aber ein repräsentatives Werk und bedeutet in Carus' Gesamtentwicklung so etwas wie das Integrationssymbol eines Vielseitigen, der sich nicht nur als Naturwissenschaftler, praktischer Mediziner, Psychologe und Lehrer auszeichnete, sondern auch als Landschaftsmaler, Schriftsteller und Kunstkritiker der Malerei, der Dichtung und der Musik. Geschildert werden soll, wie Carus, in Kunstsachen und in der Literatur der Jünger Goethes, dabei aber auch der wahlverwandte Freund Caspar David Friedrichs und Ludwig Tiecks in Dresden, sich mit dem für ihn so tief bedeutsamen Verhältnis zwischen Natur und Landschaftsmalerei auseinandersetzte. Dazu gehört auch Einsicht in die Persönlichkeit, welche diese ganz originelle Kunstkritik bedingte und gestaltete.

Was ist für Carus, im Zusammenhang dieses Werks, Natur, was ist Landschaft, was ein Kunstwerk? Carus hatte eine gewisse Abneigung gegen das Wort »Landschaft«; er fand es prosaisch, ja »handwerksmäßig«, eher also anklingend an Landschaft als wirtschaftliches Gelände, als sozial zusammengehörendes Ganzes, einfach als Landstrich, was es ja auch, laut Grimm, bedeuten konnte und kann. Carus drängt also vom Anfang an auf den von ihm geprägten Terminus »Erdleben«, d. h. Landschaft dynamisch und von innen, von der Natur selbst aus gesehen und nicht vorerst vom Standpunkt des menschlichen Auges als Szenerie. Natur deutet zu allererst auf Leben, auf ein an sich Lebendiges; das Wort hängt ja mit dem Lateinischen »nascor« (natum) zusammen, also mit Geburt, mit Geborenwerden,

Lebendigwerden und am Leben sein. Für Carus war die Natur ein Lebewesen mit einer wahren Physiognomik, der Erdoberfläche; Natur ist »lebendige Offenbarung fortwirkender göttlichen Ideen, so daß Erde und Wasser nichts anderes ist in unserem Planeten, als Fleisch und Knochen und Blut unseres eigenen Körpers ... Leben ist stetiges Einleiben des Urbildes in das Werdende, der Idee in die Natur«[1].

Was ist nun für Carus ein wahres Kunstwerk? Wir müssen, wie er meint, das gemalte Bild als kleinen Kosmos sehen können, als eine in sich geschlossene Welt im Kleinen, Schöpfung einer uns verwandten, von uns zu umfassenden geistigen Kraft, also der Schöpfungskraft des Künstlers; er muß die überzeugende Fähigkeit haben, im Kunstwerk ein neues, organisch zusammenhängendes Ganzes zu gestalten und daher zu erschaffen. Und was ist nun insbesondere ein Landshaftsbild, oder, wie er es nennen will, ein Erdlebenbild? Erst im dritten Brief seines Werkes kommt er behutsam an eine Definition heran: Es ist »Darstellung einer gewissen Stimmung des Gemütslebens (Sinn) durch die Nachbildung einer entsprechenden Stimmung des Naturlebens (Wahrheit)«[2].

Landschaft, so könnte man ganz allgemein sagen, ist ein Stück Natur in malerischer Sicht. Landschaft entsteht erst, indem der Betrachter die Natur als Ausschnitt sieht, als »zusammenhängenden Landstrich«, um mit Grimm zu sprechen, »mit Rücksicht auf den Eindruck einer solchen Gegend auf das Auge«. Während Sinn für Natur so alt ist, wie die Menscheit selbst, so ist die künstlerische Darstellung von »Landschaft« etwas viel Späteres. Sie bedeutet an sich schon Trennung von jenem ursprünglichen, einheitlichen Fühlen der Allnatur, eine bewußte Auswahl, die der Künstler vornimmt, um Natur zur Landschaft zu gestalten, sie im kleinen Kosmos seines Bildes neu zu erschaffen, so daß — und nun zurück zu Carus — der Betrachter »hineingezogen wird in den heiligen Kreis des geheimnisvollen Naturlebens« und der Geist sich erweitert (III, 46)[3].

Das also sind die Grundbegriffe, Natur, Landschaft und schöpferisches Bild, Themen, die Carus dann allmählich in ihren ästhetischen, künstlerischen und geschichtlichen Verzweigungen ausbaut. Wollte man etwa rein den Sachgehalt der Landschaftsbriefe wiedergeben, so entstünde ein unzutreffender

Eindruck des Werks in seiner ganzen Wesensart. Es soll der Wahrheitsgehalt, das Künstlerische erfaßt werden, und um mit Goethe zu sprechen, das »Wie«, nicht nur das »Was«, beides hier eng ineinander verschlungen. Wie bei manchen romantischen Kunstwerken dieser Art, die auch Kunstkritik sein wollen, ähnlich wie z.B.Wackenroders sonst so verschiedene *Herzensergießungen*, handelt es sich hier eher um Kleists »allmähliche Verfertigung der Gedanken«, wenn nicht beim Reden, so doch im inneren Gespräch. Es ist ein schriftlicher Gedankenaustausch und Dialog des Briefstellers der Landschaftsbriefe, Albertus genannt, mit dem fiktiven Briefempfänger, Ernst, der aber seinerseits nicht in Briefen, sondern nur in der inneren Auseinandersetzung von Carus mit sich selbst zur Sprache kommt. Es sind dies die beiden Namen von Carus' ältestem, schon als Kind verstorbenen Sohn: »Ihm wollte ich in den Namen dieser stillen Betrachtung noch eine Art Totenfeier, aber ganz insgeheim . .. halten«, heißt es in einem Brief an einen vertrauten Freund[4]. Das ruhige, jahrelange Gespräch (die Landschaftsbriefe reichen von 1815 bis 1831) mit dem alter ego, dem nur in der Phantasie als erwachsener Sohn lebenden Gesprächspartner, schafft allmählich Klarheit für Carus über Wesen und Funktion seiner Kunst. »Alle Forschung« meinte er später einmal, »ist ein Zutagefördern eines Verborgenen aber schon in uns Vorhandenen, ein Bewußtwerden des vorher Unbewußten«; und der Eingangsatz seiner gleichzeitigen Dresdener Vorlesungen über die Psyche lautet: »Der Schlüssel zur Erkenntnis vom Wesen des bewußten Seelenlebens liegt in der Region des Unbewußtseins«; dies klingt heute selbstverständlich, damals aber war die genaue Formulierung einer solchen Einsicht neu und auch »romantisch«[5].

Literarisch läßt sich die Briefform unsystematisch gestalten: es gibt hier nicht nur eigentliche Briefe, sondern auch gesonderte Aufsätze, genannt »Beilagen«, z. B. »Andeutungen zu einer Physiognomik der Gebirge«, »Von Darstellung der Idee der Schönheit in landschaftlicher Natur«, »Vom Aufbruch des Elbeises bei Dresden, 1821«; dann auch »Fragmente eines malerischen Tagebuchs«, also genaue Farben- und Stimmungsnotizen Carus' für später auszuführende Bilder. In großen Tagebüchern legte er sich von Jugend an über alles in seinem Leben und Denken ausführliche Rechenschaft ab und las es dann wieder in gemessenen Abständen, ein Verfahren, das an den sanftmütigen Obristen in Stifters *Letzter Mappe* erinnert; der Obrist hatte das, ähnlich wie Carus, als unfehlbares Bildungsmittel, als fruchtbare Selbstanalyse entdeckt.

Es handelt sich also hier um keine regelrechte Abhandlung, sondern um ein literarisches Potpourri, »ein Kunstgebild der echten Art«, romantisch in dem Sinne, daß sich, wie im Fall der stimmungstragenden Einzelmenschen in den Bildern Friedrichs und auch Carus', eine Ichfigur, sozusagen ein einsamer Wanderer im Raum der Kunstästhetik, Künstler und Kritiker zugleich, auf ganz persönliche Weise in den Vordergrund rückt, um sich allmählich in das gesamte Phänomen der Landschaftskunst hineinzudenken, in ihr Wesen und Ziel, ihre mannigfaltige Behandlungsweise in der Vergangenheit und die Möglichkeiten einer neuartigen Entwicklung in der Zukunft. In solchen Stichworten faßt Carus im letzten der Briefe annähernd—denn er denkt hier immer nur annähernd und kreisend, nicht geradeaus systematisch—den ungefähren Inhalt seines Werks zusammen. »Eins ist jedoch übrig«, meint er dann noch, ». . . der lebendige Mittelpunkt . . . das Leben des Künstlers selbst, sein Verhältnis zur Welt, zum Menschen« (IX, 169). Womit Wackenroders Klosterbruder anfängt und was er dann durchgehend aus der Chronik Vasaris und aus der eigenen Erfahrung ausführt, das kommt bei Carus, wie es scheint, erst zum Schluß. Liegt aber das Subjektive in den Landschaftsbriefen weniger offensichtlich an der Oberfläche, so geht es doch auch hier um das persönliche Problem, ja um die Problematik des romantischen Menschen und Künstlers selbst: Wie kann Carus seine Naturmalerei in seine übrige Tätigkeit »einverleiben«, seine Naturansichten in seiner Kunst »darleiben«—es sind dies Lieblingsworte des Naturwissenschaftlers, der immer biozentrisch, vom körperlichen Leben aus, dachte, nicht an erster Stelle logozentrisch. Sein persönliches Anliegen weitet er zur allgemeinen Fragestellung aus: Wie läßt sich meine Passion, die Landschaftsmalerei, mit meinen beruflichen Pflichten und Forschungen, die mich genau so leidenschaftlich interessieren wie die Kunst, vereinbaren und integrieren? Läßt sich hier eine sachliche, nicht nur eine rein persönliche Verbindung zwischen Kunst und Wissenschaft aufstellen? Zwischen Naturstudium, wie es z. B. Novalis in den

Lehrlingen zu Sais schildert, und der Kunst, der künstlerischen Gestaltung der gewonnenen Einsichten in die Natur, ins Naturleben?

Wie es Novalis darum zu tun war, die Poesie mit Geschichte, Philosophie und seinem naturwissenschaftlichen Beruf als Minenassessor zu vereinbaren, und Eichendorff, auf weniger philosophischer Ebene, mit dem Bürobetrieb des Staatsdienstes, in dem er eben ausharren mußte, so stand auch Carus zwischen der ärztlichen Praxis und Lehrtätigkeit und seiner Malkunst. Wackenroders Joseph Berglinger und Eichendorffs Otto gingen an ihrer Kunst zugrunde; Eichendorff schuf sich den Taugenichts, Carus dagegen schrieb die Landschaftsbriefe, seine Tagebücher und große Bände poetisierender Naturwissenschaft, sich auf diese Weise eine persönliche Reife erringend, die es ihm ermöglichte, in den Frühmorgen- und Mußestunden ruhig an seinen Bildern und Kohlezeichnungen bis ans Ende eines langen, überaus reichen Berufslebens weiter zu arbeiten.

»Es trat in diesen Briefen«, wie Carus später in seinen *Lebenserinnerungen* bemerkte, »eine eigenthümliche Vermählung von Wissenschaft und Kunst hervor... wo sich mir Natureindrücke zu poetisch-bildlichen Darstellungen allmählich metamorphosierten«.[6] Er empfindet die unkünstlerische Formulierung von Gedanken über Kunst als inneren Widerspruch, ringt also um das genaue Wort, die stets angemessene Form für seine Gedanken, »so daß sie in der Seele des Lesers gleichsam neu und vollständig aufgebaut werden«.[7] Der Gesamtaufbau des Werks ist eindrucksvoll in der neuartigen künstlerischen Struktur, als »abgerundeter Kreis«, wie Carus selbst seinen Briefzyklus nennt. Wesen und Ziel der Kunst überhaupt und dann der Landschaftskunst insbesondere werden in den ersten drei Briefen besprochen, die verschiedenen Behandlungsweisen und die geschichtliche Entwicklung dieser Kunstform folgt in den Briefen IV und V. So weit kam das 1815 begonnene Werk, bis Carus 1822 die Gebirgswelt der Schweiz kennenlernte, während er schon in der Zwischenzeit auf Caspar David Friedrichs Anregung an die Ostsee und nach Rügen gefahren war. Das waren also die ersten großen Land- schaftserlebnisse außerhalb der engeren sächsischen Heimat — er stammte aus Leipzig, lebte dann ständig in Dresden. Jahrelang blieb sodann die Arbeit an den Briefen liegen; Carus konnte sich die Möglichkeit einer künftigen Entwicklung der Gattung nach dem von den Holländern, und ganz besonders von Claude Lorrain erreichten Höhepunkt, nicht vorstellen. Die Dresdener Galerie besaß, und besitzt noch heute, zwei herrliche Claude-Lorrain-Bilder, *Flucht nach Aegypten* (1647) und *Acis und Galatea* (1657), die Carus heiß liebte und später auch kommentierend beschrieben hat[8].

Im Vortrag wurden keine Bilder gezeigt, und das mag befremden. In ihrer Zeit sollten Carus' Landschaftsbriefe für seinen Leserkreis vorerst als geistiges Anschauungsmaterial dienen, als Lesewerk und Anleitung zum Nachdenken über Natur und Kunst. Das traf auch ganz den Erwartungshorizont des damaligen Lesers, der höchstwahrscheinlich nur wenige der von Carus erwähnten Landschaftsbilder kannte, und dann vielleicht eher in der Form eines Sepiadrucks oder Kupferstichs, also ohne Farbe. Ein solcher Leser bekam also wenig Vergleichsmaterial zu sehen, wie das jetzt durch gute Farbreproduktionen und Dias als selbstverständlich und auch notwendig angesehen wird. Carus aber,— denn für ihn und seine Zeitgenossen war Gemäldebeschreibung, ob in Prosa oder im Gedicht, eine allgemein akzeptierte, literarische Gattung,— mußte sich auf Wirkung und Überzeugungskraft des Wortes, der Sprache, verlassen, also auf Beeinflussung des inneren Auges seines Lesers; damit kommt seinem literarisch-strukturellen Verfahren auch größere Wichtigkeit zu. Heute ist man mit Museen in aller Welt so verwöhnt, daß es Mühe kostet, aber eine die es lohnt, sich in die viel weniger museale Lage des damaligen Kunstliebhabers zu versetzen, auch wenn er das Glück hatte, in Dresden zu wohnen, in München, Paris oder Wien. Ohne Bildvorweis also lenkt sich die kritische Aufmerksamkeit nicht nur auf Idee und Argument, sondern auch auf Struktur und Darlegungsweise. Carus hat hier in seiner charakteristisch formulierten Vereinigung von Natur- und Kunstwissenschaft, ähnlich wie auch Goethe, durch dieses Verfahren bahnbrechend gewirkt und Neues geleistet.

Zurück zu dem von Claude Lorrain erreichten Höhepunkt und zu Carus' Frage: Was nun und wie weiter in der Entwicklung der Landschaftsmalerei? Den Standpunkt der rein symbolischen Stimmungslandschaft, wie bei dem Freunde Friedrich und im eigenen Frühwerk, hatte Carus überwunden; er empfand das nun, auch für die Kunst im allgemeinen, als ausgearbeitete Manier, dem ein neuer Ansatz, eine frische, innerlich noch nicht ganz geklärte Anschauungsweise, folgen sollte und mußte. Die Briefe stockten, bis Carus durch die Lektüre von Goethes Wolkengedichten, *Howards Ehrengedächtnis,* in der Zeitschrift *Naturwissenschaft überhaupt* (1820—1822), vom Kunstwerk als Stimmung zum Kunstwerk als informierter Gestalt den neuen Weg fand. Durch Goethes dichterische Vermählung von genauer metereologischer Wissenschaft und Poesie—der englische Quäker Luke Howard hatte als erster die Wolkengestalten klassifiziert und ihnen die Namen »Cumulus«, »Cirrus«, »Stratus« usw. gegeben—gingen Carus plötzlich die Augen darüber auf, wie sich die eigene naturwissenschaftliche Kenntnis mit künstlerischer Landschaftsgestaltung vereinigen ließe und auf welche Weise ihm und seiner Kunst da Neuland eröffnet werden könnte. Diese Entdeckung stellt er als spannendes psychologisches Erlebnis in den Briefen VI und VII dar. Schließlich kommt er in den beiden letzten Briefen, VIII und IX, auf den Künstler als Menschen zu sprechen und auf das eigene erneute Verständnis der gesamten Landschaftskunst, die er nun in »Erdlebenkunst« umgetauft hat und deren neuer Name schon an sich Manifest und auch Programm ist. Es wird nun Einiges näher ausgeführt.

Carus' indirekte, kreisende Denkweise ist schon erwähnt worden. Er war sich ihrer vollkommen bewußt und in einer Art von Entschuldigung, die zugleich captatio benevolentiae ist, gesteht Albertus dem Freund, daß in den einzelnen Briefen »Ordnung und genügendes Umfassen vergebens zu suchen seien«, womit Carus auch recht hat. Aber es fällt ihm nicht ein, mit der Kunstkritik der Akademien und ihrem ästhetischen »Wort- und Schellengeklapper in Büchern und vom Katheder aus« zu wetteifern (I, 22). Er will vor allem selbst suchen und entdecken, nicht dozieren; auch will er Freude machen an der Kunst und selbst froh weiter malen und schriftstellern. Weit wichtiger als systematische, progressive Feststellung ist ihm dichterische und besonders auch aphoristische Formulierung seiner Einfälle und Eindrücke. Und das große darzulegende Thema jedes einzelnen Briefes ist im Grunde genommen die Natur selbst in ihrer Beziehung zum schauenden Menschen, zum Künstler.

Als Stimmungsleitmotiv und auch als Strukturprinzip für den gesamten Briefzyklus setzt Carus daher den Kreislauf der wechselnden Jahreszeiten, um auf diese Weise den Leser unauffällig in das organische und zeitliche Naturgeschehen miteinzubeziehen. In der Winterszeit, im Frühling, Sommer und Herbst, wird dann in den einzelnen Briefen die künstlerische Widerspiegelung der Natur im kleinen Kosmos des schöpferischen Kunstwerks besprochen. Damit greift Carus auf den in der Dichtung, Musik und Kunst beliebten Jahreszeiten-Topos des achtzehnten Jahrhunderts und der Romantik—James Thomson, Haydn, Friedrich —zurück. Die ersten beiden Briefe schreibt Albertus im Winter und gibt für den Innen- und Außenraum Einstimmungen: »Der Schnee rieselt naßkalt am Fenster nieder, tiefe Stille umgibt mich ... die in den langen trüben Abenden des Vorwinters zeitig angezündete Lampe verbreitet anmutiges Dämmerlicht um mich her . . .« (I, 17). Später wird der Morgenspaziergang an strahlenden Wintertagen, der Elbe entlang, beschrieben, »das zierliche Spielen des Lichts zwischen blauem Himmel und schneebedeckter Erde ... mit mannigfaltigen, schön gebrochenen Farben, welche hier dem geübten Auge sichtbar werden . . . dort blitzt ein helles Schneelicht auf einer Felsenkante, noch mehr hervorgehoben von dem bräunlichen, mit allerhand Moos und Flechten sparsam gezierten Gestein . . .« (II, 27 f.). Froh vertieft sich Carus in jedem Brief in »das ruhig kreisende Naturleben«.

Im Zusammenhang mit dem Begriff und dem neuen Terminus »Erdleben«, gibt Carus einige Erklärungen. Während sich Tierwelt und Pflanzenreich ohne weiteres als »Leben« ins menschliche Bewußtsein einordnen lassen, ist das für die geognostischen Grundformen der Natur, also für Erdboden, Steine, Felsen und Gebirge, als schon Vorhandenes und nicht ersichtlich Werdendes, weniger selbstverständlich. Diese Grundformen »sind ein Leben von solcher Unermeßlichkeit für unsere Kleinheit, daß Menschen es kaum als Leben erkennen oder gelten lassen wollen« (II, 34). Der Wissende, der Naturforscher aber erkennt und fühlt, daß von allen Naturbereichen lebendige Wirkung ausgeht, doch ist es ein anders geartetes Leben: »Durch das Wechseln der Tages- und Jahreszeiten, den Wolkenzug und alle Farbenpracht des Himmels, das Ebben und Fluten des

Meeres, das langsame aber unaufhaltsam fortschreitende Verwandeln der Erdoberfläche, das Verwittern nackter Felsgipfel, deren Körner, alsbald herabgeschwemmt, allmählich fruchtbares Land erzeugen, das Entstehen der Quellen, nach den Richtungen der Gebirgszüge sich zu Bächen und endlich zu Strömen zusammenfindend, alles folgt stillen und ewigen Gesetzen . . . wir fühlen uns in ein stilles, in sich gekehrtes, gleichförmiges, gesetzmäßiges Leben mit einbezogen ... in den ungeheueren Kreis von Naturereignissen. Tritt denn hin auf den Gipfel des Gebirges, schau hin über die langen Hügelreihen, betrachte das Fortziehen der Ströme und alle Herrlichkeit, welche Deinem Blicke sich auftut ...«. Dies sind ganz allgemeine Naturbegriffe, Worte, wie auch Eichendorff sie liebt, Bilder nach Friedrich und Carus im Riesengebirge: ». . . es ist eine stille Andacht in Dir, Du selbst verlierst Dich im unbegrenzten Raume . . . Dein Ich verschwindet, Du bist nichts, Gott ist alles« (II, 35 ff.). Das also ist für Carus Beschaffenheit und Wirkung des »Erdlebens« und somit sollte es auch für den wirklich schöpferischen Künstler weit mehr als nur Landschaft im üblichen Sinn bedeuten.

Über die Wirkung des Erdlebens im Bereich des Vegetativen und besonders der Pflanzen spricht Carus auch als Heilwirkender und Psychologe. Was geht vor im menschlichen Gemüt bei der Betrachtung des kleinen Kosmos im Erdlebenbild? Mit dem Samenkorn, der Blume, dem jahrhundertelangen Wachstum der Bäume, gehen wir beruhigt und unbewußt ein in den Kreislauf der Natur. Vor einem Claude Lorrain z. B. atmen wir unwillkürlich tief ein, wir leben neu auf in dieser heiteren südlichen Luft, im sonnendurchtränkten, doch mildem Licht und im Schatten der hohen Baumkronen. Nicht nur beruhigend aber wirkt das abgebildete Pflanzenreich, es kann auch betäuben, ja tödlich kann die Blüte sein und eine völlige Auflösung, den Tod, herbeiführen: die Höhle des Traumgottes ist »mit unendlichen Kräutern und Mohnen« ausgekleidet, es ist dies die Nachtseite des Erdlebens. Philipp Otto Runge wird in diesem Zusammenhang nicht erwähnt, auch weiß man von Carus selbst nicht, ob er die großen Blätter der »Zeiten«, etwa durch Tieck oder durch Goethe, in dessen Besitz sie waren, kannte, doch ist dies anzunehmen. Vor allem klingt hier am Ende des zweiten Briefes Joseph Görres' Nachdichtung der »Zeiten« in seinem Aufsatz von 1808 über die

Plate 5 A self-portrait by the author, completed in 1822.

vier Blätter Runges nach. Carus aber warnt hier vor dem Sog ins Unbewußte, vor der Todessehnsucht, die auch ihm in seinen jungen Jahren nicht fremd war. Und neu ist, daß in der Kunstkritik die körperlich-sinnliche Wirkung des malerisch dargestellten Erd- und Naturlebens auf diese Weise analysiert und betont wurde. Bewußte Erkenntnis der physischen sowie auch der geistigen Einflüsse der im Bild erscheinenden Naturformen kann, wie er meint, manchen Aufschluß geben, und uns »das recht eigentlich Klar- und Anschaulichwerden unseres Standpunktes in dieser Welt . . . gewähren« (III, 41).

Carus' eigener Standpunkt war stets sozial und auf das Wohlergehen seiner Mitmenschen hin orientiert, denn schon durch seinen Beruf gehörte er ganz der Gesellschaft an. Auch die Natur als künstlerisches Objekt im Landschaftsbild verstand er als Lebensgemeinschaft mit Mensch und Tier: »Der Jäger, im Morgennebel über Felsen klimmend, wird den Sinn der Landschaft klarer andeuten; eine einsame, in Betrachtung der stillen Gegend verlorene Gestalt wird den Beschauer des Bildes anregen, sich an dessen Stelle zu denken; der Pilger wird die Idee der Ferne, ja das Nichtzuermessende der Erdfläche uns zurückrufen; immer aber wird die Landschaft das belebte Geschöpf bestimmen, es wird aus ihr selbst notwendig hervorgehen und zu ihr gehören müssen, solange die Landschaft Landschaft bleiben will und soll« (III, 60 f.). Der Mensch in der Natur soll also der Natur angehören, ihr verwandt sein, sich aber nicht von ihr überwältigen lassen.

Nachdem Carus in den Briefen IV und V die geschichtliche Entwicklung und den nun erreichten, scheinbar nicht zu übertreffenden Höhepunkt der Landschaftsmalerei beschrieben hatte, wollte er, als verantwortungsvoller Mediziner, seiner Untersuchung und der Diagnose auch noch eine Verordnung folgen lassen: ein Heilsplan soll entworfen werden, um die Landschaftskunst vor der Schablone, den »Kursivlettern« der geistlosen Manier, ja vor der »Landschaftskarikatur«, wie er das nannte, zu retten. Hervorragende symbolische Landschaften wie die Friedrichs, der zwar nie genannt wird, haben ihre eigene künstlerische Berechtigung; aber es gibt da, wie in Carus' eigenem Fall in früheren Tagen, so viel bloß »sentimentale« Landschaftskunst, wo kein Weg weiterführt. In diesem

Zusammenhang führt Carus ein Beispiel aus Tiecks *Franz Sternbald* an und beschreibt das Bild des Klausners, der einsam im Wald seiner gefühlsüberladenen, religiösen Kunst lebt: im engen Tal wandelt ein Pilger zur Höhe, wo im Mondenlicht das Kreuz einer Kirche schimmert (vgl. 99 f.). Von Carus selbst gibt es ähnliche symbolische Bilder, ganz zu schweigen vom Tetschener Altar und dem Kreuz an der Ostsee, doch jetzt versteht Carus die Kunst, wo »die Natur als Symbol, als Hieroglyphe nur geachtet wird«, anders; eine christlich-sittliche Idee im Bilde reicht nicht hin, meint er, denn wir müßten uns auch, ob Christ oder Nicht-Christ, »ganz abgesehen von jener Idee, an der treu ausgesprochenen Szene *dieses* Naturlebens erfreuen können«, sonst gibt es keinen »wahren Übergang zur Anschauung«, und die Idee bleibt »eine bloße Lattenbrücke«, die, künstlerisch gesprochen, zusammenbricht, wenn wir sie beschreiten wollen (vgl. V, 101).

Den wahren Übergang zu Neuem in seiner Kunst, die fest gezimmerte Brücke also, fand Carus, wie schon angedeutet, in Goethes dichterischer Verklärung und Formulierung eines wissenschaftlichen Phänomens, der Wolkenklassifikation Luke Howards; auch für Goethe war das eine überaus freudige Entdeckung, die ihn künstlerisch anregte, wie schon von jeher die Wolkengestaltung überhaupt[9]. Ohne Himmel und Wolken gibt es kaum Landschaftskunst. Das Verlockende an den Wolken, und ganz besonders für Carus in diesem Übergangsstadium seiner persönlichen und künstlerischen Entwicklung, ist wohl das Gesetzmäßige im Vergänglichen und nur scheinbar Grenzenlosen: Durch die anschauliche Gestaltung der Wolken scheint das Gestaltenlose, das Unendliche des Himmels, auf einmal mehr faßbar. Goethe hat Carus den Weg gewiesen zu einer »auf höhere Erkenntniß gegründeten Kunstschönheit«, wo sich ein Erdlebenphänomen, die Wolkengestaltung, »in höherer geistiger Wiedergeburt« als Kunst verklärt (VI, 121 ff.). Kunst dieser Art, so heißt es bei Carus, ist orphisch, ist mystisch, denn die Natur, »die am lichten Tag Geheimnisvolle«, ist dem Künstler nun als exakte Erkenntnis aufgegangen, er ist eingeweiht und integriert in ihr wissenschaftliches Geheimnis. Des Künstlers nun sehendes Auge erfaßt »ein geheimes Verhältnis unter diesen stillen Geschöpfen« der Natur, er wird sich der Verschiedenheit der

Substanzen in den Naturdingen deutlich bewußt und lernt das wirkliche Verhältnis zwischen Form und Substanz in der Natur erkennen. Im gemalten Bild und dessen Wirkung als Kunst kommt sein neu integriertes Wissen dann zum Ausdruck.

Es muß betont werden, daß Carus nur die Wolkengedichte Goethes in dieser naturwissenschaftlichen Art kannte, nicht aber z. B. *Im ernsten Beinhaus* (aus dem Jahre 1826, aber erst nach 1832 erschienen), wo die Form dem Adepten—auch Carus gebraucht öfters dieses Wort aus der Alchemie—Orakelsprüche spendet, da sich ihm die gottgedachte Spur in der Form offenbart; oder die Dornburger Lyrik (1828), wo sich im September-Gedicht: »Früh, wenn Tal, Gebirg und Garten / Nebelschleiern sich enthüllen ...«, die drei Grundfarben (blau, gelb, rot) in der lyrischen Evokation des Sonnenaufgangs darstellen und einverleiben. Das also wäre die orphische, naturwissenschaftlich informierte Dichtkunst; wie aber sollte sich das ins Malerische umsetzen, wie sollte die von Carus erträumte Erdlebenbildkunst aussehen und wie der neue Künstler? Natürlich hat dieser vor allem ernstliches Naturstudium zu betreiben, genau wie der Figuren- und Historienmaler zu allererst und ganz selbstverständlich Anatomie studieren muß. »Ist nun aber die Seele durchdrungen von dem inneren Sinn dieser verschiedenen Formen, ist ihr die Ahnung von dem geheimen göttlichen Leben der Natur hell aufgegangen, und hat die Hand die feste Darstellungsgabe sowie auch das Auge den reinen scharfen Blick sich ausgebildet, ist endlich die Seele des Künstlers rein und durch und durch ein geheiligtes, freudiges Gefäß, den Lichtstrahl von oben aufzunehmen, dann werden Bilder vom Erdleben einer neueren höheren Art, welche den Beschauer selbst zu höherer Naturbetrachtung heraufheben, und welche mystisch, orphisch in diesem Sinne zu nennen sind, entstehen müssen, und die Erdlebenbildkunst wird ihren Gipfel erreicht haben« (VIII, 166). Diese Koda, den Abschluß des vorletzten Briefes, könnte man wohl berechtigterweise ein neuartiges, romantisches Kunstbekenntnis nennen.

Überlegt man nun, ob und wie dieses prophetische Desideratum sich etwa in der Landschaftsmalerei erfüllen könnte, so wäre es vielleicht angebracht, hier an einen der größten englischen Landschaftskünstler zu erinnern, der 1836 an der

Londoner Royal Institution Vorlesungen über Landschaftskunst hielt und dabei als seinen Leit- und Grundsatz Folgendes niederlegte: »Die Malerei ist eine Wissenschaft (a science) und als Untersuchung der Naturgesetze sollte sie auch betrieben werden (should be pursued as an inquiry into the laws of nature). Warum, also, sollte man die Landschaftsmalerei nicht geradezu als einen Zweig der Naturwissenschaften ansehen (as a branch of natural philosophy), wo Bilder nur die Experimente sind (of which pictures are but the experiments)?«[10] Diese Grundsätze stammen von John Constable (1776—1837), der eingehend Geologie, Pflanzen- und Witterungskunde studierte, und besonders die Wolkenformen nach Luke Howard und Thomas Forster mit wissenschaftlicher Einsicht erfaßte und in seinen Bildern dargestellt hat. Als eine ähnliche Grenzfigur wie Carus selbst, zwischen dem achtzehnten Jahrhundert, der Romantik und dem angehenden Realismus, war Constable in seinen Landschaftsbildern auch bewußter Exponent der romantischen Ideen von Wordsworth und Coleridge in den *Lyrical Ballads* (1798). Der mit Andacht und wissenschaftlichem Verständnis erschaute Himmel mit seinen Wolken war für Constable der Grundton der Natur, ihre maßgebende Skala und auch der Hauptgefühlsträger, »the sky is the key-note, the standard of scale, the chief organ of sentiment«. Im Bilde »Hampstead Heath«, werden in der Gestaltung des Himmels und des Geländes, wo bei einem Teich Instandsetzungsarbeit vor sich geht, Constable's naturwissenschaftliche Kenntnisse und Ansichten überzeugend zum Ausdruck gebracht. Ein Besuch in der Constable Gallery des Victoria und Albert-Museums in London, wo die schönsten seiner Bilder in wunderbarer Beleuchtung ausgestellt sind, könnte gut als Bestätigung von Carus' Ausführungen in den Landschaftsbriefen gelten. Durch diese Lektüre lernt man Constables Bilder und ihr eingreifend neues Verständnis von Himmel, Meer, Land und Baum besser zu verstehen und wirklich neu zu erfahren. Hier ist Naturwissenschaft durch Kunst weit über allen Realismus hinaus verklärt, und eben das wollte Carus ja darlegen und auch für sich selbst und für die Kunst im allgemeinen erreichen.

Daß Carus diesen englischen Zeitgenossen und seine wissenschaftlich orientierte Landschaftskunst, wie es scheint, nicht kannte—Constable stellte nur in London und in Paris aus —

tut nichts zur Sache, denn es sollte ja nur angedeutet werden, daß sich Constables große Erdlebenbildkunst in eben dieser Übergangsepoche mit Carus' neuem Postulat für diese Kunstform deckte. In seiner schönen kunsthistorischen und komparatistischen Studie, *Wolkenbilder und Wolkengedichte der Romantik* (1960), hat der damals in London lebende Kurt Badt das überzeugend erörtert und illustriert. Für Carus selbst bedeutet dieses Postulat die einzige Entwicklungsmöglichkeit für die Landschaftskunst im allgemeinen und auch für die eigene Malerei. Vergleicht man z. B. seine frühen symbolischen Bilder, die er selbst »mehr Hieroglyphe als Naturbild« nennt, mit seinen späteren Wolkenstudien, mit seiner überaus genauen, wunderschönen Zeichnung der Stalaktitengrotte auf der schottischen Insel Staffa, oder mit seinen Bildern der Felsgestaltung dort am zerklüfteten Meeresstrand, mit den Kohlen- und Bleistiftzeichnungen von Stonehenge, des geheimnisvollen Druidenkreises in der Salisbury Plain (Carus machte 1844 eine Englandreise als Leibarzt des Königs Friedrich August von Sachsen und kam übrigens auch nach Cambridge), so sieht man in diesen Zeichnungen vergleichsweise einen eindrucksvollen Beweis und Niederschlag der in den Landschaftsbriefen neu gewonnenen Einsichten[11].

Zurück nun zur künstlerischen Entwicklung Carus' und zum persönlichen Hintergrund der Gestaltung seines Werks, dessen Struktur und Tragweite nun beschrieben worden sind. Von 1816 an stellte Carus jährlich auf der Dresdener Akademie und dann auch auf Goethes Einladung in Weimar Landschaftsbilder aus. Gleichzeitig fertigte er für seine medizinischen Textbücher über Zootomie, Gynäkologie und vergleichende Anatomie hervorragend schöne Zeichnungen auf Kupfer an[12]. Er war gelernter Künstler und weit mehr als nur ein Sonntagsmaler. Von seiner Schülerzeit am Leipziger Thomasgymnasium an hatte er sich zielbewußt im Zeichnen und Malen ausgebildet, so daß oft, wie es in einem frühen Tagebuch heißt, sein »ganzes Wesen gewaltsam in diesen Zirkel hineinstrebte, das prosaische Leben zurückstoßend«, was zu depressiven Stimmungen führte. Aber die Malerei selbst brachte da, wie er erklärt, unerwartet Rettung: ». . . ein Kunstwerk vermag gleichsam als Ausdruck und Gleichniß des gesamten Seelenlebens dem Geist ... einen Spiegel vorzuhalten. Wie oft ist es mir daher gelungen, das innerste

Geheimnis der Seele von schwerer Trübung zu reinigen, indem ich dunkle Nebelbilder, in Schnee versunkene Kirchhöfe und Aehnliches in bildlichen Compositionen entwarf«, die dann »Erleichterung, ja Befreiung zu schaffen pflegten« (LE. I, 128). Er malte sich gesund.

Bezeichnend aber für die Richtung seiner später in den Landschaftsbriefen ausgeführten Ansichten ist, daß er nicht nur Stimmungshieroglyphen malte, sondern vom Anfang an auch Wissenschaftliches, z. B. ein farbig illustriertes Inventar von allen aufzufindenden Schwämmen und Pilzen in der Leipziger Umgebung. Die beiden Richtungen, Wissenschaft und Kunst, liefen in seiner persönlichen Entwicklung parallel und unvereint nebeneinander her, bis er sie durch die Ausarbeitung der Landschaftsbriefe selbst und durch das Modell der Wolkengedichte Goethes schöpferisch integrieren konnte. Von Jugend an malte und zeichnete er im Freien und bekam dadurch exakte Kenntnis und dabei auch inniges Verständnis der Natur. Als sich im Sommer und Herbst des Jahres 1813 die entscheidende Schlacht bei Leipzig vorbereitete, war Carus schon als junger Wundarzt in einem französischen Lazarett tätig und erzählt, wie er sich vor den schauderhaften Eindrücken —die er übrigens glänzend beschreibt—ins benachbarte Rosenthal flüchtete, um sich zeichnend und malend in dieser Waldeinsamkeit geistig wieder herzustellen, um »ein ewig gesetzmäßig Fortschreitendes« als »Gegengewicht in der Seele zu gewinnen ... gegen den unruhigen Wogenschlag des Menschenlebens . . . Da lag der große Eichenwald in seiner tiefen Ruhe, das Leben der Vögel drang durch die Zweige, die Wiesen wallten in dem vollen Wuchse ihrer Pflanzen, die Wolken zogen so ruhig ihren Weg . . . und so hatte man das Gefühl, die Erde lebt ihr stilles unbewußtes Leben nach ewigen Gesetzen von Tag zu Tag dahin, und alles, was wir Übermütigen als Weltbegebenheiten preisen, es drängt sich auf so schmalen Landstraßen und in verhältnismäßig so kleinen Ortschaften zusammen . . .« (LE, I, 125).

Wer mit Eichendorff vertraut ist, braucht kaum den vergleichenden Hinweis: »Beschauen Sie recht den Wunderbau der hundertjährigen Stämme da unten«, sagt Friedrich zur verzweifelten Romana, »die alten Felsenriesen und den ewigen Himmel darüber . . . wie da die Elemente, sonst wechselseitig vernichtende Feinde ... Freundschaft schließen und in weiser Ordnung und Frömmigkeit die Welt tragen und erhalten . . . weit erhaben über den kleinen Menschen in seinem Hochmute« (*Ahnung und Gegenwart.* III, 19). Was Eichendorff im Gedicht, im gleichzeitigen Roman (1815) aussprach, das brachte Carus damals in Bildern wie seiner Rosenthaler *Frühlingslandschaft* (1814) auf die Leinwand; Eichendorff dichtete sich den Kriegs- und Berufsgram von der Seele, und Carus betrieb dafür Maltherapie.

Bei dem jungen Mediziner und Künstler kam auch noch ein oft verzweifeltes Suchen nach religiöser Gewißheit dazu, das durch die einerseits wissenschaftliche und andererseits künstlerische Vertiefung in die Landschaft, in die Natur, durch den Versuch im ewig Wechselnden ein Bleibendes zu erkennen, auf die Spitze getrieben wurde. »Wer hat dich, du schöner Wald, / Aufgebaut so hoch da droben?«—das war für Carus keine rhetorische, also schon beantwortete Frage, wie für Eichendorff, keine Gelegenheit zu einer leicht hingeworfenen Ironie, wie bei Robert Musil; da lautet Ulrichs exakte Antwort im Gespräch mit der gefühlvollen Diotima: »Die Niederösterreichische Bodenbank ... und den Meister, den Sie loben wollen, ist ein bei ihr angestellter Forstmeister. Die Natur ist hier ein planmäßiges Produkt der Forstindustrie« (*Der Mann ohne Eigenschaften.* Zweiter Teil, 67). Für Carus aber war das eine existentielle Frage auf Leben und Tod, die er schließlich dann durch einen behutsamen Entheismus, oder durch den Begriff der »Gottinnigkeit«, wie er es nannte, lösen konnte. Sein starkes Gottesbewußtsein galt einem überpersönlichen, überkonfessionellen Schöpfergott, der durch seine Schaffenskraft die Natur belebt und erhält. Der Künstler aber ist, auf seine menschliche Weise, ebenfalls ein Schöpfer. Deshalb, und eben auch durch sein intensives, ja leidenschaftliches Studium der Gott-Natur—und das waren weder für Goethe, noch für Carus, zwei gesonderte Begriffe, sondern nur ein einziger—war sein Gottesverständnis für Carus' dichterische Schilderung der Erdlebenbildkunst so überaus wichtig. Die ganze Erde war für ihn wirklich ein Lebewesen, das aus Gott, in ihm und durch ihn lebte und bestand, und durch den Künstler schöpferisch auf die Menschen wirkte; als Mittler bewahrte er stets die Beziehung zum

Menschen, zum Realen, und zu fest war Carus im Organischen beheimatet, um sich je im Transzendentalen zu verlieren.

»Wie tief und gründlich Sie das organische Gebild erfassen«, in den »so wohl gedachten als schön geschriebenen Briefen, wie scharf und genau Sie es charakteristisch darstellen . . .«, schrieb Goethe an Carus nach der Lektüre der ersten paar Briefe im Manuskript (April, 1822) in einem Brief, den Carus dann 1831 seinem Werk voranstellen durfte, (S. 11—13). Auch sein eigenes Vorwort weist darauf hin, daß es ihm nicht nur um die Kunst selbst zu tun ist, sondern vielmehr exemplarisch um das eigene, sich stets verwandelnde Verhältnis zum Künstlerischen überhaupt. Im ersten Satz schon heißt es: »Wer gewohnt ist mit Aufmerksamkeiten den verschiedenen Entwicklungszuständen seines eigenen Innern zu folgen, wird bald eingestehen müssen, daß die Bilder dieser einzelnen Zustände sich untereinander wenig gleichen . . . nur einem tieferblickenden Auge wird bemerklich, daß immer noch aus demselben Ich die verschiedenen äußeren Formen hervortreten, so wie etwa eine und dieselbe Wurzel zu verschiedenen Zeiten verschiedengeformte Blätter hervortreibt« (S. 7 f.). Carus ließ die Landschaftsbriefe ganz allmählich als organischen Bestandteil des eigenen Wesens in seinem Gemüt heranwachsen; und schon mit dem Titel des Werks fängt das Organische, die verhüllte Naturverwandtschaft, an. Warum ausgerechnet n e u n Briefe, neun Haupteinheiten, denn es gab da außerdem noch manche Exkurse und Beilagen? Und dann explicite im Untertitel: »Geschrieben in den Jahren 1815 bis 1824«, also neun Jahre, obgleich das Buch dann erst 1831 erschien? Nur schwer konnte Carus sich zur Trennung von seinem Werk, zu dessen eigentlichem Geburtstag in der Öffentlichkeit entschließen. In seinen Lebenserinnerungen steht, daß er sich dann am Ende mit Johann Heinrich Mercks Zuruf an den jungen Goethe in ähnlichen Publikationsschwierigkeiten Mut machte: »Frisch auf die Zäune!« rief Merck, »so trocknen die Windeln!« (LE, I, 320). Diese ganzen Jahre lang arbeitete Carus tagein tagaus als Vorstand der Geburtshilfeanstalt Dresdens, ja er wohnte auch sozusagen vor Ort in einer Dienstwohnung mit der eigenen, kinderreichen Familie, und 1820 erschien die erste Auflage seines bahnbrechenden Lehrbuchs der Gynäkologie. Dabei hatte er, wie so mancher Romantiker und—laut Oskar

Seidlin, auch Thomas Mann—Sinn für versteckte Zahlensymbolik und einen ausgesprochenen Spieltrieb.[13] Die Triadik, die Dreimal-Drei-Zahl, die es ihm besonders angetan hatte, spielte schon in seinem zweiten Landschaftsbrief eine wichtige Rolle, die Dreiteiligkeit also der menschlichen Psyche—Gefühl, Erkenntnis, Wille—die drei Grundfarben, drei Grundtöne, drei Naturreiche, usw.[14] In seinem nächsten Buch, der natur- wissenschaftlichen Fortsetzung der Landschaftsbriefe, hat Carus es dann, dem Gegenstand der Forschung entsprechend, mit einer weiteren Zahlenmystik, der Quaternität, zu tun. Die Vier-mal-Vier-Zahl hängt zusammen mit den vier chemischen Bestandteilen der Erde selbst, Sauer-, Wasser-, Kohlen- und Stickstoff, mit den zwölf Monaten der jährlichen Bahn der Erde um die Sonne, also mit dem Planetarischen und Tellurischen des Erdlebens; daher lautet der Titel dieses neuen Buches *Zwölf Briefe über das Erdleben* (1841)[15].

Ausführungen über kryptologische Titel dieser Art, die Carus selbst natürlich als Rätsel belassen hat, scheinen vielleicht etwas weit entfernt von romantischer Kunstästhetik, aber als Spiegel der naturwissenschaftlich biozentrischen Einstellung des Autors mögen sie doch auch zum richtigen Verständnis dieses ganz originellen kunstkritischen Werks der Spätromantik beitragen. Daß Carus sich von solchen Späßen in gesetzteren Jahren etwas erholt hatte, zeigt sich schon an der zweiten Ausgabe des Werks von 1835, wo der Titel nun einfach und auch genauer *Briefe über die Landschaftsmalerei* lautet und die Neunzahl sowie die dreimal drei Jahre im Untertitel stillschweigend verschwinden.

Im *Buch der Freunde* bei Hugo von Hofmannsthal heißt es einmal: ». . . den Leser mitzuerschaffen ist der verhüllte aber größere Teil der schriftstellerischen Leistung.« Durch die Briefstruktur und die Möglichkeit eines immer wieder neuaufgenommenen Dialogs zwischen Albertus und Ernst, auch bei dem ansprechenden und ganz unprätentiösen Ton, ist es Carus tatsächlich gelungen, seinen Leser in Hofmannsthals Sinn mitzuerschaffen, ihn auf seinen Standpunkt umzustimmen. Carus' »Vermählung von Wissenschaft und Kunst« ist »ein schöpferischkünstlerisches Verfahren«, das, wie er später selbst zugibt, ihm nicht auf jeder Seite gelingt. Doch lassen sich die Landschaftsbriefe im Vergleich mit anderer romantischer

Kunstkritik immerhin auch sehen, denn die neuartige Auffassung von Kritik als Kunstwerk, als Dichtung, und überhaupt die künstlerische Formulierung des rein Wissenschaftlichen, ist ja in der Romantik beheimatet. In ähnlichem Sinne, und dabei auch mehr oder weniger als persönliches Bekenntnis, schreibt Friedrich Schlegel sein *Gespräch über die Poesie,* sein Bruder ein Gespräch über Gemälde, schreiben Tieck und Arnim über Minnelieder oder Volkslieder, Joseph Görres seine Phantasien über Runges »Zeiten« oder über die teutschen Volksbücher, Eichendorff dann, viel später, die Geschichte der deutschen Literatur. Carus bewegte sich, von Goethe ausgehend, zwischen der Romantik und dem naturwissenschaftlichlen Realismus des neunzehnten Jahrhunderts und ist sich dessen auch bewußt. In einer geognostischen Metapher aus dem Inneren des Erdlebens beschreibt und begrenzt Carus in seinen *Lebenserinnerungen* die eigene romantische Einstellung im Vergleich mit der des Freundes Ludwig Tieck: »War doch die romantische Poesie, die in ihm einen ihrer leuchtenden Brennpunkte fand, auch mir tief ins Herz gewachsen, es glühte ihre Empfindung und Richtung bei tausendfältigen Gelegenheiten und in vielen Bildern und Gedanken gleich feurigen Erzadern in meinem Innern, ja es war in mir, wie in Tieck, doch auch wieder dieser Glutstrom durch Felslager des Wissenschaftlichen überdeckt und gemildert« (LE, I, 211).

* Der am 15. Juli 1982 in Würzburg auf dem Internationalen Eichendorff-Kongreß gehaltene Vortrag blieb im allgemeinen unverändert. Die Anmerkungen wurden hinzugefügt.

1 Carl Gustav Carus: *Zwölf Briefe über das Erdleben.* Stuttgart 1841. S. 31 u. 18.

2 Carl Gustav Carus: *Neun Briefe über Landschaftsmalerei. Geschrieben in den Jahren 1815 bis 1824. Zuvor ein Brief von Goethe als Einleitung.* Leipzig 1831. Hg. und mit einem Nachwort begleitet von Kurt Gerstenberg. Dresden o. Jg. (1927). Neuauflage 1955. Brief III, S. 49. In der Folge zitiert mit Brief- und Seitenzahl, hier also: III, 49.

Verläßlicher, auch für die Ausgabe von 1831, ist der Faksimiledruck der zweiten Ausgabe (1835) mit einem vorzüglichen Nachwort und Bibliographie: *Briefe über Landschaftsmalerei. Zuvor ein Brief von Goethe als Einleitung.* Faksimiledruck nach der 2. vermehrten Ausgabe von 1835, mit einem Nachwort hg. von Dorothea Kuhn. = Deutsche Neudrucke. Reihe Goethezeit. Hg. von Arthur Henkel. Heidelberg 1972. Diese Ausgabe, mit Angaben über die Unterschiede der beiden Ausgaben von Carus, mit dem originalen Druckbild (vgl. z. B. Carus' häufige Anwendung des Sperrdrucks für Emphase; vgl. auch die von Gerstenberg ausgelassenen Seiten aus C. G. Nees von Esenbecks *System der Pilze und Schwämme,* die Carus im Brief VII als Beispiel für die Möglichkeit dichterischer Prosa über Naturwissenschaftliches bringt) ist der Edition Gerstenbergs vorzuziehen.

3 Allgemein zum Begriff »Landschaft« vgl. den noch immer grundlegenden Aufsatz von Georg Simmel: *Philosophie der Landschaft.* In: *Güldenkammer. Norddeutsche Monatshefte* 3, 1912. S. 635—645. Insbesondere für die Romantik: Helmut Rehder: *Die Philosophie der unendlichen Landschaft.* DVjs. Buchreihe 19. Halle 1932. Für die Entwicklung des Begriffs in der Kunst überhaupt: Kenneth Clark: *Landsdape into Art.* London 1949 (und weitere Auflagen), ferner die einschlägigen Einträge in: *The Oxford Companion to Art.* Hg. von Harold Osborne. Oxford 1970. Carus selbst beruft sich selten auf andere Autoritäten außer Goethe; es ist aber aus hier nicht zu belegenden Gründen anzunehmen, daß ihm u. a. die folgenden kunstkritischen Werke bekannt waren und ihn auch beeinflußt haben: Johann Heinrich Merck: *Über die Landschaftsmalerei* (1777) Ndr. Göttingen 1965: *J. H. Merck's ausgewählte Schriften zur Schönen Literatur und Kunst. Ein Denkmal.* Hg. von Dr. Adolf Stahr. Oldenburg 1840. S. 189 ff.— Karl Ludwig Fernow: *Über die Landschaftsmalerei* (1803). In: *Römische Studien.* Bd. II. Zürich 1806. S. 11—130.—F.W.J. Schelling: *Das Verhältnis der bildenden Künste zur Natur.* Rede gehalten in München an der Akademie der Wissenschaften am 12. X. 1807. In *Philosophische Schriften.* Erster Band. Landshut 1809.

4 Aus einem unveröffentlichten Brief vom 26. 2.1831 an den Freund Regis, zitiert bei Marianne Prause: *Carl Gustav Carus. Leben und Werk.* Berlin 1968. S. 46. M. Prause gibt einen illustrierten Katalog des gesamten künstlerischen Werkes von Carus; besonders erhellend ist die Nebeneinanderstellung einiger seiner Werke mit jenen von Friedrich. In den Anmerkungen, besonders zum Katalog, wird ein reiches Quellenmaterial verwertet. Außer bei D. Kuhn, M.

Prause und in der Dissertation Berna Kirchners: *Carl Gustav Carus. Seine »poetische«. Wissenschaft und seine Kunsttheorie, sein Verhältnis zu Goethe und seine Bedeutung für die Literaturwissenschaft.* Bonn 1962, sowie als Teil eines kurzgefaßten, aber aufschlußreichen Portraits von Carus bei Roger Cardinal: *German Romantics in Context.* Studia Vista. London 1975. S. 125—133, sind die Landschaftsbriefe, besonders auch in ihrem literarischen Aspekt und in der Struktur, wenig zur Sprache gekommen.

5 Carl Gustav Carus: *Mnemosyne. Blätter aus Gedenk- und Tagebüchern.* Pforzheim 1848. S. 25, und *Vorlesungen über die Psyche,* gehalten im Winter 1829/30 zu Dresden. Leipzig 1831; unter dem späteren Titel: *Psyche. Zur Entwicklungsgeschichte der Seele.* Leipzig 1846—als Kröner Tb. hg. von Rudolf Marx. Leipzig o. J.

6 Carl Gustav Carus: *Lebenserinnerungen und Denkwürdigkeiten.* Leipzig 1865—66. 4 Bde. Band I, S. 181 u. 158, im folgenden zitiert als »LE« mit Band- und Seitenzahl, hier also: LE, I, 181 u. I, 158.

7 Unveröffentlichter Brief an Regis vom 19. XI. 1820, zitiert bei M. Prause (vgl. Anm. 4) S. 45.

8 Carl Gustav Carus: *Betrachtungen und Gedanken vor auserwählten Bildern der Dresdner Galerie.* Dresden 1867. Auch A.W.Schlegel hat diese beiden Claude Lorrain-Bilder beschrieben und besprochen, in: *Die Gemälde. Gespräch,* Athenaeum II. Berlin 1799.

9 Vgl. z. B. Albrecht Schöne: *Über Goethes Wolkenlehre.* In: *Der Berliner Germanistentag 1968. Vorträge und Berichte.* Hg. von K. H. Borck und R. Henns. Heidelberg 1970. S. 24—41.— Auch Werner Keller: *»Die antwortenden Genrebilder«. Eine Studie zu Goethes Wolkengedichten.* In: JbFDH 1968. S. 191—236.

10 Charles Robert Leslie: *Memoirs of the Life of John Constable Composed Chiefly of his Letters.* London 1843. Hg. von Jonathan Mayne. Oxford 1951 und 1980, Kap. XVIII: Notes of Six Lectures on Landscape painting, delivered by Constable at Hampstead and at the Royal Institution. S. 289—331, besonders S. 323. Vgl. auch die Bemerkungen von George Turnbull in einem kunstkritischen Werk des frühen 18. Jahrhunderts, das Constable gut kannte: »Landscapes are Samples or Experiments in Natural Philosophy ... they serve

to fix before our eyes beautiful Effects of Nature's Laws, till we have fully admired them, and accurately considered the Laws from which such visible Beauties and Harmonies result.« In: George Turnbull: *A Treatise on Ancient Painting*. London 1740. S. 146.

11 Vgl. M. Prause, Anmerkung 234, S. 70, über Stonehenge, und Katalog Nr. 66 bis 71: »Bilder aus England und Schottland: Weymouth, Bodmin, Staffa, Warwick Castle«. Vgl. auch Carl Gustav Carus: *England und Schottland im Jahre 1844*. Berlin 1845 und dessen englische Übersetzung von S. Davison: *The King of Saxony's Journey Through England and Scotland in the Year 1844*. London 1846. Man vergleiche z.B. die Bilder aus England mit den vier frühen symbolischen Bildern, die Carus 1815 in Dresden und später in Weimar ausstellte: *»Weide im Herbstnebel«, »Friedhof mit Kind«, »Eingang zu Dantes Hölle«, »Waldeinsamkeit«*. In diesem letzten Bilde »... ist ein Waldstrom, welcher zwischen felsigen Ufern unter großen und überschattenden Eichen und Rotbuchen sich durchdrängt, auf einer lichten Graspartie zwischen Eichenbäumen sind ein paar Rehe gelagert, und über dem Strom schweben vor dunklem Waldgrün ferner Bäume einige Möwen« (Carus' eigene Beschreibung, zitiert bei M. Prause, S. 167).

12 Eine Bibliographie der Werke von und über Carus sowie ein ausgezeichneter Überblick seines beruflichen und künstlerischen Werdegangs (mit Tafeln) bei Heinz-Egon Kleine-Natrop: *Carl Gustav Carus. Ausgewählte Aspekte seines Lebens hundert Jahre nach seinem Tod*. In: *Nova Acta Leopoldina* 1970 (N. F. 36, Nr. 198). S. 199—247.

13 Siehe Oskar Seidlins schönen Aufsatz: *Das hohe Spiel der Zahlen: Die Peeperkorn-Episode in Thomas Manns »Zauberberg«*. In: *Klassische und Moderne Klassiker*. Göttingen 1972. S. 103—126.

14 Vgl. Joseph Needham und Lu Gwei-Djen: *Science and Civilization in China*. Cambridge 1982. Bd. V,5. S. 173—177, wo das chinesische Prinzip, »kung-fu«, im Zusammenhang mit der romantischen Naturphilosophie erklärt wird und überzeugend auf eine direkte Beeinflussung Goethes, Okens, Carus' usw. durch chinesische Ideen hingewiesen wird. Ich bin Joseph Needham (von Gonville and Caius College) dankbar für seine freundliche Enträtselung von Carus' »dreigeteilten innern Organisation, welche Physiologen im Menschen finden« (Brief III, 25); Carus nimmt einfach an, daß sein gebildeter Leser genau wissen wird, um was es sich handelt. Needham bespricht hier auch

anders konstituierte Dreiteiligkeitssysteme in der Geschichte der Naturwissenschaft und eröffnet dem naturwissenschaftlichen Laien damit ein weites und faszinierendes Feld.

15 Typisch für Carus ist es, daß er in solchen Spielen seine Naturwissenschaft und das Künstlerische als Einheit sieht; seine Landschaftsbriefe sind also dem Sinn und Zweck nach ein Integrationssymbol. — Für die naturphilosophische Zahlenmystik und weitere Spekulationen dieser Art, siehe an verschiedenen Stellen in *Romantische Naturphilosophie*. Ausgewählt von Christoph Bernoulli und Hans Kern. Jena 1926, besonders auch die Ausführungen über die embryonische und die plazentarische Periodeneinheit, S. 227 ff. Vgl. auch die relevanten Hinweise bei K. E. Rotschuh: *Naturphilosophische Konzepte der Medizin aus der Zeit der deutschen Romantik.* In: *Romantik in Deutschland.* Ein interdisziplinäres Symposion. Hrsg. von Richard Brinkmann, Sonderband der DVjs., Stuttgart. S. 243-266.

Ludwig Tieck and Dante

Ludwig Tieck as critic, scholar and translator is so closely associated with German medieval poetry, with Shakespeare and the Elizabethan stage, with Cervantes and the Spanish mystery drama, that linking his name with Dante and the Commedia may come as something of a surprise. Tieck was certainly less familiar with Dante's work than he was with these other areas of world literature, nor does its impact on his mind compare in importance with that made by Shakespeare and Cervantes, the other two persons of the Romantic Trinity; nevertheless, it is possible to discern in Tieck's long poetical career a clear and developing line of interest in the Divine Comedy which has never been considered as a whole or in sequent detail. While showing Tieck, the romantic poet and critic, in a new context, this relationship in its various aspects is also a new chapter in German romantic awareness of Dante.

Tieck's name is, in fact, rarely mentioned at all in connection with Dante, or else his knowledge of the Commedia is unfavourably compared with the greater Dante expertise of his friends in the group of Romantics converging on Jena as the eighteenth century, and all it stood for, merged into a new era.[1] Yet Tieck was the only actual poet among them to be drawn to Dante; the others were either critics like the Schlegel brothers, who also wrote verse, or else philosophers like Schelling and Fichte, joined later on by Solger and Hegel. All of these had a new critical understanding of Dante's work, virtually rediscovering it at a time when there were no adequate translations, and attempting to fill the gap by rendering isolated passages of the Commedia. But Tieck, in his double capacity as poet and critic, was later on in the 1830s, associated with another man's life commitment to Dante, that of Prince John of Saxony, "Philalethes", the translator and commentator of the whole Commedia. As a witness to Tieck's involvement both as poet and scholar in the "Academia Dantesca", assembled by the Prince in Dresden to discuss in draft his translation of the Purgatorio, the

Purgatorio, the stage he had reached by about 1834, there are Tieck's notes on cantos VI to XXXIII, preserved in Philalethes' Dante-Apparat in Dresden and now published for the first time as a whole. A critical examination of these notes, prefaced by a closer look at Tieck's early, more poetical, "Romantic" assimilation of Dante before his later textual involvement, should result in a more complete and therefore a juster view of Tieck's awareness of Dante than has hitherto been possible.

Furthermore, the fact that Tieck, "Altmeister" of Romanticism, was so helpfully associated in consultation with Philalethes, should confirm this translator's work as in some important ways a Romantic undertaking, later but essentially cognate with the other great pioneering translations which were the result of new critical attitudes and horizons. While Italian critics have tended to see Philalethes as part of the "riscoperta romantica" of Dante, this has not been stressed in the same way outside Italy. It is, in fact, Tieck who represents the living link with Romantic discovery in this respect, as he, in his own person, at a later stage continued to be what he had always been, the classic case of the Romantic. His attitude to Dante is therefore of particular interest in the context of the Prince's translation and of his discussion circle where Tieck not only contributed his poetically informed views on individual renderings but also had the important role of reading aloud the proposed translation, and, where this was indicated, the Italian original. Reading as Tieck read - his one-man readings of plays, poetry and prose were famous throughout Europe is not possible without true insight into the text: "Der Dichter tat mehr als Vorlesen . . . Indem er las, schaffte er dichterisch von neuem".[2]

This leads to a first basic and concrete point, too simple, apparently, to have merited the attention it deserves: Tieck knew and spoke Italian well. He did not have a mere reading knowledge of it as was the case with his friends at Jena; he knew what Italian actually sounded like, surely essential for understandig Dante as a poet and as a master of rhythm, rhyme and the musical flow of verse, all the aural qualities of poetry to which Tieck himself was particularly alive and sensitive. Not only had Tieck spent a year in Italy, (1805-06), but he was widely read in Italian literature and history, being immersed at the actual time of the Purgatorio translation in the Italian chronicles he was reading for his novel,

Vittoria Accorombona (1840). Linguistic gifts were all a part of his great histrionic ability; he was also sufficiently aware of the whole nature of language, and of the way a poet uses his instrument, to realize that a foreign tongue actually has to be learnt, known and used if a poet's whole intention is to be critically appraised and understood.[3]

Another relevant fact rarely remembered is that Tieck started out as a student of theology, even though a reluctant one. He soon gave up actual courses in favour of literature and classics, but it is evident throughout his long and changing poetical career that a foundation of theological knowledge and even interest remained, that a cast of mind had been conferred which made him particularly receptive to the age of faith to which Dante belonged, and to medieval civilization, unimaginable without theological structures. Tieck had a strong sense of the numinous and of what he called "Mystik", seeing this as essential to any insight into the philosophy of religion. At a time of retrospect in Dresden which coincided with his own renewed study of Dante, he explains that although unlike many of his friends, he had not taken to philosophy as a discipline but nevertheless saw it as akin to mystical theology; of this, he said, he had more immediate knowledge as he considered it to be closely related to poetry, or "Poesie".[4] For Tieck, "Mystik", cognate as it is for him both to philosophy and to poetry, may be said to represent the wide background-spectrum of spirituality against which Dante, the poet, set his Commedia, the work to which Solger, the philosopher and Dante lover with whom Tieck exchanged views on such matters, in fact applied the summary description, "diese hohe Mystik".[5] It was through his friendship with Solger that Tieck, in middle life, returned to Dante in a new and more informed way, simply because he became more aware of what philosophy might have to offer to the poet. However, in spite of this more conscious thinking which resulted from his contact with Solger, Tieck found that he could not finally come to terms with Dante as a whole and give him whole-hearted love, as Solger did, or Philalethes or Carl Gustav Carus, his friend in the Dresden Dante circle. But he was, at least, deeply aware of the problem: it was, in the end, only Dante the poet, and the Commedia as a supreme poetic symbol that stirred his admiration and always kept his allegiance.

At an earlier stage of his career, the Commedia was for Tieck an intuitively grasped general concept rather than a firm possession of the mind. As such he saw it, as he also saw the far better known world of Shakespeare's plays, as a realm of the imagination to be entered and used at will in his own poetical creations and as a part of them. Dante and other Italian poets figure in his satirical play, *Zerbino, oder die Reise nach dem guten Geschmack (1799),* where Dante's obscurity and, generally speaking, his "Schnurrpfeiffereien" are the target of the Philistine's cheap wit, of a man who prides himself on not even having read the Commedia: " hat so eine Comödie, gleichsam ein Gedicht über die Hölle geschrieben . . ." "Hölle und Paradies! Und alles so umständlich, wie ich mir habe sagen lassen". This is the bird's eye view of Dante according to the enlightened non-reader of his work at the end of the century.[6]

The really significant analogy for Dante's work in Tieck's earlier writing lay in the realm of pictorial art, the main subject of revelation in the essays and the novel planned with Wackenroder.[7] Franz Sternbald, Dürer's disciple, is discussing allegory with the Italian poet, Florestan, and arguing that its use is also justifiable within the artist's domain: ". . . hier kann der Maler gleichsam über die Grenzen seiner Kunst hinausschreiten, und mit dem Dichter wetteifern". Indeed, the artist even has the advantage over the poet because he can visibly associate what in real life is successive and disparate: life and death, youth and age, the various seasons, men of all centuries. The artist can structure a totality which the eye can take in as a great whole happening simultaneously, "wie man auch nichts aus seiner Verkettung reißen darf". Florestan agrees with this argument, and as an example of allegory in painting, he describes Orcagna's "Triumph of Death" in the Campo Santo at Pisa, with its synchronicity of spring, love, dance and pleasure on the one hand, and with winter, death and decay on the other. The whole picture is dominated by the contemplative hermit on his bare rock as a counterpart to the grotesque figure of death pointing his scythe at open graves and rotting corpses. "Dieser Künstler", Florestan adds, "hat den Dante mit besonderer Vorliebe studiert, und in seiner Kunst auch etwas Ähnliches dichten wollen". The only poet known to Tieck who has managed to structure in a single work of art this universal totality, the synchronicity of life and death, of this world and its poetically imagined sequel in the next, is Dante. The Commedia is here seen as cognate and correlative to a work of art in a different medium where the artist, a "poet" in his way, has taken over the role of the allegorical poet.[8]

In the *Phantasien über die Kunst für Freunde der Kunst,* (1799), published the year after *Franz Sternbalds Wanderungen,* Tieck again sees Dante within the context of a work of art, this time comparing the structure and the effect of the Commedia with that made by Michelangelo's "Last Judgement" in the Sistine Chapel in Rome. After first linking the two names in a general way, and before describing the painting itself, he begins his essays with an impressionistic characterization of Dante's metre, the terza rima; this serves as a preparation, putting the reader into a receptive frame of mind for Michelangelo's "poem". Tieck now points to the aural impression of Dante's poetry, that sense of continuity, of process and of gradual but inevitable development conveyed by the interwoven rhyme and the steadily continuous movement of Dante's chosen rhythm, the terza rima. This then becomes an analogue to the Christian drama of the redemption revealed in the successive interrelated scenes of the painting: the Divine Comedy as a whole becomes a metaphor for Michelangelo's vision of the Last Judgement, each work of art in its different medium illuminating the other in a poetical association:

> Tritt mit dem heiligen Schauer in die Sestina hinein, und die erhabenen prophetischen Terzinen werden dich anreden, dein Geist wird himmelwärts fortgeführt, kein Stillestand, keine Nebensache, kein Ruhepunkt, auf dem das Auge haften könnte. Die ganze Welt, Vergangenheit und Zukunft sind hier in eine übermenschlich kühne Dichtung zusammengedrängt.

Michelangelo portrays the progressively revealed, interrelated totality of past, present and future in God's plan for humanity which Dante also portrays, each artist, the one in word and rhythm, the other in form and colour, functioning as the herald and prophet of Catholic Christianity:

> Dante singt in prophetischen, wunderbar verschlungenen Terzinen seine Dichtung, nirgend ein Stillestand, nirgend wo die Pracht der gewaltigen Verse aufhörte, immer tiefer wirst du in die geheimnisreiche Allegorie hineingeführt, hier findest du keine Nebensachen, keinen Ruheplatz, auf dem der Dichter stille steht, alle Kräfte spannen sich zum großen magischen Eindruck, aller Reiz ist vernachlässigt, die Erhabenheit nimmt dich in Empfang, die Wunder des Christentums, die mystischen Geheimnisse verschlingen sich in ihren unbegreiflichen Zirkeln und nehmen dich mit sich fort. Eben solche Beschaffenheit hat es mit dem Gedicht des Buonarotti . . . nirgend liegt so der tiefe allegorische Sinn verborgen . . . sein Gemälde ist der Schluß aller Dichtung, aller religiösen Bilder, das Ende der Zeiten.[9]

It may not be immediately obvious that this kind of rhapsody is, in fact "criticism"; Romantic criticism by metaphor is, however, a distinct and influential literary form in its own right, which, if not actually pioneered by Tieck and Wackenroder - Herder had something similar though less sustained - was effectively popularized by them, taken over by Görres and Eichendorff in their critical writing and worked up to a kind of caricature of itself in Heine's witty and lurid personifications in his account of German Romanticism.[10] This form of criticism served the purpose of giving the reader a brief, intuitive and memorable view and impression of a work of art, a poet, an artist as yet unknown to him. It enriched his imaginative experience of art which was the whole purpose of Romantic criticism, used in this particular case for both Dante and Michelangelo.

A rather different kind of Dante reminiscence, but still an aural one, comes in two of Tieck's contrasting experiments in the use of the terza rima, one in his most Romantic play, *Leben und Tod der heiligen Genoveva. Ein Trauerspiel, (1799),* and the other in the poem, "Die neue Zeit" (1800), Tieck's welcome to the new century in his *Poetisches Journal* of that date. Like A.W. Schlegel, according to whom, however, as distinct from himself, Tieck was not only a versifier but "ein dichtender Dichter", Tieck was highly skilled in the use of Spanish and Italian verse forms and rhythms, adapted to German. In his essay of 1803 introducing his translation of German medieval love lyrics, he not only shows profound insight into medieval civilization and poetical writing as a whole at a time when, culturally speaking, Europe was still more or less one, but he also reveals precise knowledge of metre, of rhyme and of the historical development of rhythmic forms in Europe. He is aware, at a time when this critical awareness was new, of the close relationship between Provençal and Italian poetry, so relevant to Dante. In connection with Dante and the terza rima, he stresses the lack of any true progeny, either in Italy or elsewhere in Romance literature: ". . . jener steht mit seinem wunderbaren episch-mystischen Streben allein".[11] At two important moments of his *Genoveva* Tieck uses the terzina and thereby enhances the literary effect he intended, that is, the creation of an atmosphere suggestive of Dante's world, of the transcendent and of prophecy.

At the end of the battle on French soil against the invading Saracens, the Major-Domo of the Frankish armies also has to fight against his own merely personal ambitions for kingship and worldly grandeur. He wins this battle too, and is then supported and confirmed in his right moral attitude by the visit of an Unknown Messenger, "Ein Unbekannter", whose identity remains a mystery. This man speaks in prophetic terza rimas, foretelling the kingship of the Major-Domo's son and the glorious empire of his grandson, Charlemagne. The Unknown has seen this splendid future in the stars:

> Was in den Himmelskreisen sich bewegt,
> Das muß auch bildlich auf der Erde walten,
> Das wird auch in des Menschen Brust erregt.
>
> Natur kann nichts in engen Gränzen halten,
> Ein Blitz der aufwärts aus dem Centrum dringet,
> Er spiegelt sich in jeglichen Gestalten,
>
> Und sich Gestirn und Mensch und Erde schwinget
> Gleichmäßig fort und eins des andern Spiegel,
> Der Ton durch alle Creaturen dringet.[12]

Now the name of Tieck's Carolingian Major-Domo of the Dark Ages is Karl Martell, Charles the Hammer, (688-741); no Dante reader could come upon this name without a thought of the moving encounter between Dante and his royal friend, Carlo Martello, in Paradiso, cantos VIII and IX, this namesake of a remote ancestor centuries ago. Just as Carlo Martello is the link between the young Dante in Florence, and Dante, the pilgrim poet in Paradise, so too, the Unknown, speaking in a prophecy, is Karl Martell's link with the realm beyond the stars in a cosmic dimension.

This effective Dante evocation is followed by another similar one to heighten the atmosphere at the end of the tragedy. The speaker, "Ein Pilgrim", is in fact the ghost of Otho, killed in Karl Martell's great victory earlier in the play and now returning to earth to comfort and reassure his own close friend, Genoveva's remorse-stricken widower, Siegfried. The situation is the more poignant in that the Pilgrim is also the father of Golo, the villain responsible for the tragedy of Genoveva's unjust banishment. It is a Commedia situation, the dead and the living engaged in a constructive dialogue: the link of new understanding is gradually formed between the two friends who speak in alternating terzinas, the verse groups increasing in length as understanding grows in the sorrowing Siegfried. The movement of the terzinas with their interlocking rhymes points to a progressive sense of solution as Siegfried is gradually restored to hope and to faith in God's forgiveness.[13] As in *Franz Sternbald* and in the *Phantasien,* but even more directly, Tieck has again used a Dante evocation to reinforce his own literary intention.

Genoveva was written at speed in the autumn and winter of 1799 when Tieck was living, for a time, with A.W. Schlegel and Caroline in Jena. The Italian language and Italian poets were being studied in common as part of the shared reading sessions which were the order of the day; the Commedia was thus again in Tieck's mind, stimulating him to another use of the terza rima, this time in the light-hearted and satirical vein. "Die neue Zeit" (1800), a poem of fifty-two terzinas and a final quatrain, heralds the rush of spring and beauty to a grey world as the old century of the Enlightenment, with hard and reluctant birthpangs, brings forth the new Romantic era and the infant century. In the first half of the poem, the aged mother herself laments in giving birth, then the poet speaks in his own person with a rousing call to new poetic action. The effect aimed at in this miniature allegory in terza rimas is to convey the inevitable movement of old times changing into new, a mime of the close but grotesquely incongruous relationship between old and new, mother and child, false idols of poetry on the way out and true gods appearing.[14]

On their own terms, then, Tieck's poetical Dante analogues could take their place next to the more orthodox critical comments on Dante by both the Schlegels, Schelling's analysis of the Commedia as a total philosophical structure or Hegel's brisk exposition of it in a single page of his *Aesthetik*.[15] Tieck's method was just another way of evoking a creative response to a great work of art. The whole phenomenon of the Nazarene brotherhood of painters in Rome, quite apart from the fact that it included much actual Dante illustration, is proof enough of the effectiveness of this form of artistic criticsm.

Prompted by the same generalized and intuitive view of the Commedia, Tieck also tried to clarify, by a comparison, the nebulous Romantic project of a grand composite epic on nature which had been the subject of discussion between him and Novalis: a new scientific and philosophical discovery was to be integrated with a poetical account of the developement of man and his future evolution in an entirely new artistic synthesis. The only possible, if remote model for this for ever unrealized Romantic project of "transzendentale Poesie" was, in Tieck's view, and also in Friedrich Schlegel's, to be found in Dante's epic: "Dantes prophetisches Gedicht ist das einzige System der transzendentalen Poesie, immer noch das höchste seiner Art" (Athenaeum Fragment, 247). The realm and landscape of eternity in Dante's theological, Christian perspective was now to find a parallel in the Romantic panorama of myth and Märchen, the background against which the real world of history, science and philosophy was to be explored by a wandering pilgrim-poet who was also a scientist and a philosopher. As one of the possible literary projects which the Italian poet, Florestan, describes to Franz Sternbald, he tells him about a "Geisterspiel" where human beings are to be largely replaced by the various forces of nature: "Kennst du Dante's großes Gedicht? Auf eine ähnliche, ganz allegorische Weise ließe sich vielleicht eine Offenbarung über die Natur schreiben, voller Begeisterung und mit prophetischem Geist durchdrungen" (Part

II, Book 1). The fact that all this is vague and unspecific does not invalidate it as a seriously held Romantic idea: on the contrary. And it is significant, perhaps ironical in true Romantic fashion, that the Commedia with its taut architectural structure and logically rounded development was selected as the one potential model for this most amorphous, if imaginatively appealing Romantic project. Tieck's suggestion, unspecific as it was in detail, is moreover the only remotely practical one ever made about how this figment of the Romantic imagination might ever be worked out in poetical practice.

At a later stage, and less nebulously, Tieck came to believe that Novalis, had he lived, might have been capable of writing a Romantic equivalent of the Commedia, an epic narrative transposed from its Italian background of Christian eschatology to one which, though also medieval and Christian, was in the same way to transcend time and space, putting its main emphasis on natural science and philosophy, on history recreated and prophetically experienced in advance as a great poetical present, as "geistige Gegenwart".[16] Tieck's important essay introducing his new edition of Friedrich von Hardenberg's works in 1815, was written when he was in contact with Solger and again thinking about Dante in the context of "poetische Mystik". In the light of these insights, Tieck now reconsiders the nature of what had actually been written of *Heinrich von Ofterdingen* before the author died, and he enters into the extraordinary plans for its completion. He believed that even in the unfinished novel Novalis had already begun to create a new linguistic medium, an original form, style and method resulting from his attitude to real life, namely that it was already and in itself a revelation of what was, as it seemed, inconceivable and beyond nature. This attitude of what he called "romantisiren" had helped Novalis to discover and perfect "einen neuen Weg der Darstellung", a style which, in its translucent clarity and simplicity, expressed and described what was above nature as something quite ordinary and everyday.

This analysis of a "new style" is, perhaps the most significant point about Tieck's Dante comparison in this essay. He thought that, like the author of the Commedia, Novalis had succeeded in formulating things unheard of before and that therefore, in describing the new poetical realm, he was actually in the process of creating it. This realm was the meeting place of reality and the transcendent, the Romantic poet's proper domain. Both the project and its literary method were so new that the only possible analogy for the completed *Heinrich von Ofterdingen* that Tieck could point to was the Commedia, the work whose intrinsic nature, style and structure Tieck had so well grasped on an intuitive level. Novalis himself, however, hardly knew Dante, and was not working on any model:

> So erfand er, von Beispielen unbestochen, einen neuen Weg der Darstellung, und in der Vielseitigkeit der Beziehungen, in der Ansicht der Liebe und dem Glauben an sie, die ihm zugleich Lehrerinn, Weisheit und Religion ist, darin, daß ein einziger großer Lebens-Moment und Ein tiefer Schmerz und Verlust das Wesen seiner Poesie und Anschauung wurde, gleicht er unter den Neueren allein dem erhabenen Dante, und singt uns wie dieser einen unergründlichen mystischen Gesang, sehr verschieden von jenem mancher Nachahmer, welche die Mystik wie ein Ornament glauben an und ablegen zu können.[17]

A central point in Tieck's comparison was that he saw the function of Novalis' Sophie, "zugleich Lehrerinn, Weisheit und Religion", as a parallel to the role of Dante's Beatrice, a focus of many meanings for the poet who was working out his earthly and heavenly destiny. Literally, she was the beloved who had died young, symbolically, she was both the revealer and the agent of mystical union with the transcendent and the divine: "in ihren Augen ruhte die Ewigkeit".[18] Manifold relationships, "Vielseitigkeit der Beziehungen", had been established between this world and the mythological dimension beyond it; by the new style and the whole movement of the narrative proceeding simultaneously on both levels, Novalis had already stretched the capacity of the novel form in a new way: Tieck's Commedia analogy is perhaps less far fetched than it may at first seem.

At a later stage, too, when Tieck had long been established in Dresden and was already a member of the Dante circle, he is again led to associate Novalis and Dante in his thinking; this time it is in the context of their relationship to their epoch. In his novella, *Die Sommerreise,* published in 1834, but reflecting, in a fictional correspondence, events of 1803, that is, the Romantic era, Tieck expresses views of Dante which show a closer relationship of study or at any rate something that went beyond the metaphors of earlier times. According to the letter writer in the novella, artists like Runge and C.D. Friedrich, whose symbolic art needs interpreting if it is to be fully understood, nevertheless remain one in heart and mind with their contemporaries at an epoch like the Romantic one, where imagination and reason are in close alliance; they are accepted even if not fully understood. Was this also the case, asks the letter writer, overtly identified with Tieck himself, when art and poetry were much more exclusively the product of reason, of "Verständigkeit", which meant that the poet was writing for a much more select readership, for an elite, on whom greater intellectual demands could be, and were in fact, made?

> . . . man sieht . . . wie Ein Geist immerdar sich im Zeitalter in Gegenden und Gemüthern meldet. Die Novalis auch nicht kennen oder verstehn, sind doch mit ihm verwandt. War es denn auch so zur Zeit des Dante?

That is, could Dante ever have been readable in a popular way? And did people in general have a sense of kinship with him, relate to him as the Romantic writer liked to see himself relating to the great beating heart of the people? The writer of the letter doubts this:

> So weit ich jene Jahre kenne, entdecke ich dort diese Verwandtschaft nicht. Dieser große Prophet hat in seinem Geheimnis dieses Streben, Sache und Deutung, Wirklichkeit und Allegorie immerdar in Eins zu wandeln, auf das mächtigste aufgefaßt.

In Dante, matter and meaning, historical reality and allegory, are a close-knit unity which the reader is left to unravel as best he can. And because, as Tieck sees it, the essential poetry of Dante cannot be segregated from the interpretation it needs, reading him necessarily becomes a most demanding but creative effort, calling for something far more than merely grasping what is being said:

> Ihn verstehn und fühlen setzt voraus und fordert eine große

> poetische Schöpfungskraft; mit dem gewöhnlichen Auffassen ist hier nichts gewonnen.

At this point the writer — and it is clear in this novella-à-clef that here Tieck is speaking in his own person — demurs a little in a spirit of mock modesty:

> Soll man sich aber selbst so loben? Im Briefe vielleicht. Und doch gemahnt es mich, als sei dies kein Lob. Nur Geweihte sollen Dante's Gedicht lesen. Es ist ja keine Bürger- und Menschenpflicht.[19]

Overwhelmed, perhaps, by the demands — theological, philosophical and historical — that his Purgatorio reading made on him, and makes on any committed reader centuries later, Tieck has not altogether appreciated to what extent the allegorical method was generally understood all over Europe, and has therefore not conceded that the Commedia could, and still can be read by people of varying degrees of culture and at various levels: "genuine poetry'" according to T.S. Eliot "can communicate before it is understood . . . it is better to be spurred to acquire scholarship because you enjoy the poetry, than to suppose that you enjoy the poetry because you have acquired the scholarship".[20]

By the time Tieck wrote *Die Sommerreise,* reading and studying Dante had become for him, if not "Bürgerpflicht", then at least "Hofpflicht", as Prince Johann's reader and one of his most valued advisers. Yet there is no evidence in the years that followed, that Tieck ever completely overcame the basic doubt and hesitation about Dante that he expressed so graciously in his novella and with perhaps that characteristic little touch of irony about his own attitude, his own failure. He joined the ranks of "consecrated" readers while this was expected of him, he worked willingly and well, at certain points even with enthusiasm, contributing much of interest in matters poetical and linguistic. But after this period of concentrated textual study, there is no evidence that he had formed the habit of returning to Dante for his own personal pleasure or edification, as he did so constantly to his other preferred poets. One must accept as final this remark of his old age to Rudolf Köpke, his Eckermann:

„. . . mich stört sein theologisches und philosophisches System, so tiefsinnig es auch sein mag, im Gedichte. Es stieß mich ab wenn mich anderes ergriff. Ich kann sagen, Dante ist mir stets nah und fern zugleich gewesen.[21]

* * *

From about 1828 to 1840 Tieck was a member of the Dante circle convened by Philalethes, Prince John of Saxony, to discuss the Purgatorio instalment of his translation of the complete Commedia, published in 1834,1840 and 1848. For Tieck, these years were marked by a concentrated and systematic study of Dante's text, the evidence for which lies in the written comments he made on Johann's draft translation of the Purgatorio, cantos VI to XXXIII. These comments, together with the notes of some of the other members of the Academia Dantesca, as the group was called in Dresden, are preserved in Philalethes' Dante Apparat which is still, in part, at the Sächsische Landesbibliothek in Dresden.

The story of the Academia and its members, among whom were some of Tieck's personal friends — Rumohr, his companion in Italy in 1805-06, and one of the fictional characters in *Eine Sommerreise,* Baudissin, his assistant, together with Dorothea Tieck, in the Schlegel-Tieck Shakespeare translation, Carus, the Romantic scientist, court physician and painter, Karl Förster, a teacher and himself a Petrarch and Dante translator, sometimes Raumer, the medieval historian, and often Frederick Augustus, John's elder brother who succeeded to the throne in 1836 — this story has been attractively told, for the most part in this periodical, by John's grandson, Duke John George of Saxony. The Academy is also mentioned in the contemporary memoirs of Carus, Förster and Baudissin, and finally in the more recently published memoirs of Philalethes himself.[22] Perhaps the most objective account in letters and memoirs comes from George Ticknor, an American Romance scholar from Harvard who visited Dresden in 1835-36, was invited to several of the Dante meetings and subsequently corresponded with John, whose English was excellent, for many years. This correspondence was also edited by the Prince's grandson.[23] The American found Tieck "more genial and agreeable" than some of the other members and it was the excellence of his reading that impressed him most of all. There can be no doubt that the way Tieck read contributed much, as time went on, to the quality of Johann's translation, that it helped him to gain distance from his work and see it in a truer poetical perspective. Tieck's reading was consciously simple — "einfach" is the word he himself uses to describe it — not fine declamation but, rather, understatement, no dramatic intrusion on the poet's word:

> Der Ton des Vorlesers darf nie die Grenzen dessen überschreiten, was ich immer den edlern Konversationston genannt habe. Auch im Tragischen darf das nicht geschehen, sonst wird es falsches Pathos und Manier, einzelnes wird herausgerissen und der Eindruck des Ganzen geht verloren.[24]

Tieck has here defined himself as what might be considered an ideal Dante reader: medieval poetry, as Tieck so well knew, was primarily intended for the living voice of an informed and sensitive but selfless reader who understood the text in all its nuances. And the Purgatorio is perhaps the most difficult part of Dante's poetic pilgrimage, purgation being rather less exciting and also more subtle than either damnation or bliss.

During the earlier stages of his work, Philalethes used himself to read his draft aloud at the meetings; his first invitation to Tieck was one for him to read aloud the whole of his "letzte Correctur" of the completed Inferno translation. John finished this on Easter Saturday, 1830, the date which he assumed to be the 530th anniversary of Dante's own emergence from hell. The practice of sending the draft round for criticism does not seem to have begun, it would seem, until he reached canto VI, the first canto on which any notes, apart from a brief comment or two by Baudissin, have been preserved in the Dresden holdings of the Dante Apparat. From this canto onwards there is a complete set of notes from Tieck which are, on the whole, the most detailed as they were also intended for the viva voce discussion after Tieck's reading. John marked his manuscript draft with neat capital letters in the margin, T, F, C, B, where there were comments by Tieck, Förster, Carus and Baudissin. The notes from Förster, "an excellent Italian scholar", according to Ticknor, and from Baudissin, are nearly all brief, straightforward suggestions for linguistic improvements. Both men write concisely, as a rule suggesting complete alternative lines or phrases for any which they criticize. While John rarely adopted a whole line of this sort, he was almost invariably open to Tieck's more discreet and tentatively put "thinking aloud" approach, as also to his suggestions about individual words and their right positioning according to Dante's poetic intention. Carus did not send in full and regular comments at all, just dashing off a few cogent, mostly technical pieces of information, scientific, medical and also astronomical details, much out of the way knowledge which enriched the Prince's commentary in an original way. Tieck's notes are by far the most interesting from the literary and critical point of view, though often discursive, containing flashes of inspired Dante commentary or brilliant excursions very slightly off the point. Where the others tended to look on their work as a practical task of correction, Tieck engaged in an imaginative, literary dialogue. His verbal contributions at the meetings seem to have been much the same. Förster says of him:

> Tieck hingegen schweift ab, er ist ein trefflicher Dichter aber ungenügender Dichtererklärer, er hält sich selten an die Worte und den eigentlichen Sinn, [a criticism disproved by many of Tieck's written comments] die reiche Phantasie dichtet gerne anmutig Manches hinzu, der Flug geht weiter und kehrt wohl endlich ab. Oft schon habe ich den Faden wieder an den gewaltigen Webstuhl geknüpft.[25]

Tieck's brilliance as a literary adviser and commentator lies precisely in the excursions which Förster, an affable pedagogue, deprecates. It was impossible for Tieck just to fault-find and correct. He did not want to risk "die Gefahr, etwas in den Ton eines Pedanten zu fallen. Doch hoffe ich bin ich nie in den (eine Gefahr die nahe liegt) ganz nichtsnutzigen eines mäkelnden Rezensenten gerathen", he writes at the end of his comments on canto XII, then following this up, with true pedagogic skill, by generous praise:

> Je mehr man diese Arbeit studiert, die von Liebe und Enthusiasmus unternommen wurde, die keine Mühe und Anstrengung scheut, je mehr überzeugt man sich, daß noch keine Uebersetzung der Bestimmtheit, Schärfe und dem Tiefsinn des großen Originales so nahe gekommen ist. Tieck.

It is worth while remembering the human situation at the back of all this work: the Prince was in his early thirties, a literary amateur, Tieck in his sixties and a writer of European fame. About his whole person there was an atmosphere of poetry, "das Poetische", and this is what Johann, who, from an early age felt that his own mind had what he calls "eine poetische Richtung", so greatly valued in Tieck, and needed for the tremendous poetical task he had set himself. With engaging modesty, he realized clearly that he himself was not a poet even though he wrote much verse: ". . . ich brachte es eigentlich nie weiter, als zu einem erträgichen Gelegenheitsgedicht . . . Es gab aber dieses Treiben meinem ganzen Wesen eine poetische Richtung".[26] But his Dante translation, to which he could never devote more than the spare time of a busy government official, was a life commitment of an extraordinary kind which drew him on irresistibly. By his choice of words in the successive prefaces to his translations, he reveals this powerful attraction: - "ein unbeschreiblicher Drang", "unbewußt", "unwiderstehlich", - as he tries to explain what it was that made him embark on the translation:

> Das charakteristische Gepräge eines höchst eigenthümlichen, bedeutenden Mannes in einer höchst eigenthümlichen Zeit, . . . eine Sprache, die um so mehr den Geist des Dichters wiedergiebt, als er sie selbst erst schaffen mußte, die hohe moralische Würde und der unendliche Fleiß der Ausführung zogen mich unwiderstehlich an.[27]

The view now taken for granted, that Dante's language was a new and personal creation in its time and, in fact, the essential condition of his new poetry, was a fresh insight in German Dante studies; it was firmly established in Tieck's mind, however, who had used it in trying to explain Novalis' achievement, and also continually recurs to the originality of Dante's language and usage in his notes on Johann's translation.

Tieck's notes take various forms but the general pattern is that of a specific linguistic query to begin with, either followed by a suggestion, usually framed as a question or put in the subjunctive tense with tentative phrases like "wohl nicht?", "vielleicht . . . ", "könnte es . . .?", "mir scheint . . .", "ich möchte doch zweifeln ob . . .", or often by a reflection of a more general kind on the point at issue (as for instance at canto xviii, 61). But Tieck does not only question; he praises good renderings, for all this is part of the dialogue, and he likes to share his delight in some specially attractive Dantean passage. This may then turn into a brief essay about Dante as a poet and the poetry of his time (canto xxiv 55 and 62), or into exclamations of praise: "Niemals kann man den Geist des großen Dichters genug bewundern", he says about canto xxv and Dante's dogma-into-poetry account of the creation of man: "Wie klar und tief ist dieser wunderbare Gegenstand hier abgehandelt, wie in den wenigen Versen erhöht, und wie präcis jeder Ausdruck, wie scharf gestempelt jedes Wort in seiner philosophischen Bestimmtheit — und doch wie spielend gleichsam, wie harmonisch und graziös in dem Geflecht der wohlklingenden Reime". Basically, it is still Dante the craftsman and the poet whom Tieck finds most attractive, as in the days of Franz Sternbald, the *Phantasien* and of *Genoveva;* but more detailed concentration on the text has shown him that Dante's greatness as a poet consists precisely in this apparently effortless fusion of poetry and conceptual exposition. All is not solemn hard work, however; there are entertaining excursions into out of the way fields of knowledge, culled from rare books in his library. There is information, for instance, on tunny fishing nets in Spain (canto xxxii 6) and there is expert wine-lore, pointing to more than merely scholarly expertise in the subject (canto xxiv 24). In this connection, "e purga per digiuno/ l'anguille di Bolsena e la vernaccia", Tieck quotes Holinshed's chronicles, the *Journey to Spain* by G. Baretti, Francesco Redi's *Bacco in Toscana,* and finally his own wine-tasting experience in the Rhineland to prove that "Firnewein", the rendering then adopted by Philalethes, would be the right word for "vernaccia". By such excursions, and by the charm of their presentation, Tieck has turned a potentially dull list of suggestions into a lively and personal communication.

When Tieck decides to venture on a point of interpretation, as for instance, for "das . . . von Dante beliebte Wort *nodo*" (canto xxiv 55), which he sees as a pun, he gives an ingenious, if somewhat Shakespearean explanation: Bonaguinta and his friends "tied themselves up in knots", just as the "concetti" tie up words in precious knots. Dante himself here provides literary history, explaining the evolution of the "dolce stil nuovo" out of the artificial "concetti" evolved in contrast to the coarseness of the popular prose style. But this is where Tieck understands and clearly defines Dante's mediating role as a poet:

> Nun scheint mir, daß Dante derjenige war, der den derben Prosaismus, die Ausdrücke des gemeinen Lebens, alles was dort barbarisch klang, in Bedeutsamkeit, Tiefsinn und Adel verwandelte. Jene concetti aber verwarf er ganz, nahm den großen, naiven Ausdruck wahrer Empfindung, und ächter Tiefsinn, mystische Vieldeutigkeit vertrat bei ihm die Stelle jener poetischen Witzeleien.

Tieck prefaces this cogent characterization of Dante's style by stressing how hard it is to sort out the rapid changes of poetic style and language in Italy, an "unermeßliches Feld für den Sprachforscher". Dante is unique in that he unites these two great strands of poetical tradition in such masterly fashion, using "das Große wie das Kleine auf wahrhaft göttliche Weise zu seinem Zwecke". Philalethes, often using Tieck's formulations, incorporated the main points of these in two important notes (cantos xxiv 55 and 62).

Thus Tieck's critical understanding of literary phenomena and of the organic development of poetry as a craft, was of the greatest value to Philalethes, primarily a historian, a man of a philosophical and ethical cast of mind whose interest was in the conceptual content of the Commedia rather that in its poetical form and literary method. Tieck's continual, vivid awareness of Dante, the poet, was perhaps his most important contribution to this translation. This is confirmed by Philalethes' almost invariable adoption of the more poetically acceptable and valid renderings so tactfully put forward, or merely indicated as possible. Tieck drew the translator's attention to words and phrases poorly rendered, unsuitable or not sufficiently close to the Italian or to Dante's order and intention, and then he left Philalethes to find his own way. To have done otherwise would, as Tieck, the poet and translator realized, have risked robbing the translation of its organic unity and given it a patchwork look. Tieck was an experienced literary midwife, and his Socratic role in conversation is also well attested; the written notes were, of course, merely a preparation for the live discussion which followed the "lettura".

Tieck's more specifically linguistic comments all bear witness to his understanding, not only of the whole complex process of translation, but of the special difficulties facing a German in translating from a Romance language. Here he spoke from experience: "Unsere Sprache ist oft noch ganz unerträglich philosophisch", he writes of a difficulty that has come up in canto xiii 14, and in comparing ponderous German alternatives to Dante's translucent clarity. Even his remarks on seemingly trivial points of language, on minor figures of speech, for instance on dead metaphors (IX, 33, XII, 79), all emanate from a well-versed translator aware of the need for constant vigilance and faithfulness in every detail. This is especially clear when Tieck insists that Philalethes should, wherever possible, avoid altering the exact positioning and sequence of Dante's words and phrases, (thus canto xv 142, "Die Umkehrung im Deutschen schwächt das Bild und den Eindruck"). In such cases Tieck tried to make the Prince feel the importance of accurate placing by giving him, not his own different translation, but a paraphrase of the passage as a whole. In this way he reconstructed the process of thought in Dante's mind as he conceived a particular image, and then explained the effect which each successive part of the image was meant to have on the reader: Tieck's note on canto xi 91 ff is an excellent example of this procedure. In such contexts, Tieck also at times makes strikingly accurate observations about the priority of sense impressions in the reader and the need, therefore, to respect Dante's whole intention in his word-order and his choice of words in translation: thus in the note on canto xiii 34, where Tieck prefers the exclamation "Siehe!" rather than Philalethes' suggested "Horch!" for Dante's "Oh!" —, "Oh!", diss'io, "padre, che voci son queste?", - ". . . Weil das Auge, schneller und geistiger als das Ohr, sich auch nach jedem Geräusch umwendet. — Gewiß eine große Kleinigkeit, um es so zu bemerken". However, the translator finally decided on the bleak but accurate, "O, sagt' ich, Vater, was für Stimmen sind das?". Most often, however, such subtle Tieckian reflections or paraphrases helped Philalethes to come up with a good rendering of his own, in harmony with his personal approach but guided by a poet's insight.

Some of the linguistic notes could hardly have been of direct use to the translator but were all part of Tieck's way of creating the right atmosphere; they stemmed from his own satisfaction in thinking about the use of words. Again and again, for instance, he comes back to the extraordinarily concentrated value of Dante's expressions, his "mystische Vieldeutigkeit", seeing this poetical ambiguity and richness in Malaspina's image of an opinion being "nailed into one's head",

> che cotesta cortese oppinione
> ti fia chiavata in mezzo de la testa
> con maggior chiovi che d'altrui sermone, (viii 136-138)

which Philalethes renders:

> Eh' diese Meinung, die du freundlich äußerst,
> Dir mitten in das Haupt wird eingeschlagen
> Mit stärkern Nägeln noch als And'rer Rede,

and on which Tieck comments:

> Vortrefflich, daß die Uebersetzung genau den Text und die etwas harte Metapher am Schluß wieder gegeben hat: die Nägel, das Einschlagen hier sollen allegorisch an Vieles erinnern; auch, daß Wohlthaten Schmertz neben der Dankbarkeit erregen: was der landflüchtige Dante empfindlich erlebt hat. Überhaupt ist in diesem Gesang, vorzüglich in der lezten Hälfte, der männlich starke Ton vortrefflich gefunden und gehalten.

Tieck even apologizes for stressing this favourite point of his so often: "Verzeihung, wenn ich immer wieder die mystische Worterklärung vielleicht zu hoch anschlage" (after canto xi 33), but he rightly felt that this was precisely the most valuable kind of help he, as a fellow poet, could give: an intimate understanding of Dante's superb craftmanship.

In order to give the greatest possible help to the translator, Tieck loyally tried to come to terms with Dante's theological and philosophical speculations, and to a limited extent, as the notes show, he succeeded; but they suggest even more conclusively that his heart was not in these things. His notes were primarily intended to stimulate an artistically fruitful and creative reaction in the Prince so as to improve his translation; in this he certainly achieved his object. However, the greatest value of the notes, apart from the immediate occasion they were meant to serve, lies in their ease and charm, in their flashes of poetical insight into Dante's writing and in their incidental and instructive entertainment value. They also point to the development of Tieck's understanding of Dante now that he was having to relate closely to the text rather than seeing the Commedia in the more numinous metaphorical generalities of earlier days. And finally, his notes show quite conclusively that Tieck was fully aware of the essential and indivisible unity of thought and poetry in the Commedia and that he made a distinction between the truth of this fact and his own personal feelings about it. The final paradox of "Dante ist mir stets nah und fern zugleich gewesen", reflects the character of his mind which could not, and in fact did not want to coordinate aesthetic enjoyment with speculative thought.

Note: Tieck's notes on *Purgatorio* vi - xxiii, edited, and provided with a commentary by E.C.S., appear in *Deutsches Dante Jahrbuch*, 60 (1985), 7-72.

[1] W. P. Friederich, *Dante's Fame Abroad*, Rome 1950, quotes Th. von Bernhardi's erroneous piece of gossip, that Tieck never read Dante and considered the Comedy as a glorification of the Catholic church, p. 461, C.Ch. Fuchs, "Dante in der deutschen Romantik", DDJ 1933, vol. 15, pp.61-131, makes only a brief passing mention of Tieck but is most useful about the understanding of Dante in the Jena Romantic circle to which Tieck belonged. As a proof, however, of how much remains to be discovered about Dante reception at this time, particularly in a political context, see Marcella

Roddewig, "Dante in der Dichtung des Freundeskreises von Hölderlin: Sinclair, Stäudlin, Reinhard, Boehlendorff", DDJ 1973, vol. 48, p. 79-106. - There is no entry for Tieck in the Enciclopedia Dantesca.

2 Rudolf Köpke, *Ludwig Tieck. Erinnerungen aus dem Leben des Dichters.* 2 Teile, Leipzig 1855, II, p. 178.

3 Tieck learnt Italian as a schoolboy in Berlin from a close Italian friend, and then systematically studied both Spanish and Italian at Göttingen in connection with his art studies under Fiorillo, Köpke I, 59 ff. From his "Reisegedichte eines Kranken", written during the full year he spent in Italy, 1805-06, it is evident that he knew Italian well enough to talk himself out of, and into, predicaments both amusing and awkward.

4 "Viele beginnen mit der Philosophie, und manchem, der nur in den Formeln stehen bleibt, verschließt sich durch sein Forschen der Sinn für die Mystik auf immer, zuweilen auch der für Poesie. Und doch wird nur der Philosoph gründlich und befriedigend lehren können, der die Mystik kennt und liebt, wie nur ein ächter Mystiker genannt werden kann, der auch in der Vernunft und ihrem Vermögen die göttliche Kraft erkennt und verehrt". *Ludwig Tieck's Schriften*, Berlin 1828-54 (1829), Vorbericht, p. lxxiv, an autobiographical summary of his poetical development.

5 K.W.F. Solger, *Nachgelassene Schriften und Briefwechsel*, hrgb. von Ludwig Tieck und Friedrich von Raumer, Leipzig 1826, 2 vols., I, pp. 122 and 124. Cf. also II, p. 212.

6 *Schriften*, X, pp. 271 f.

7 It is in the domain of art that Dante was, in fact, more intimately known and loved in the Romantic era than in the literature of the time. One has only to read, for instance, Ludwig Richter's *Lebenserinnerungen eines deutschen Malers*, Leipzig 1885, to realize what an important part Dante played in the imagination of this younger contemporary of Tieck's in Dresden, stimulated by the work of Nazarene artists in Rome

8 *Franz Sternbald*, II. Theil, 1. Buch, 6. Kapitel.

9 Wilhelm Heinrich Wackenroder, *Werke und Briefe*, Heidelberg 1967,

Phantasien über die Kunst für Freunde der Kunst, hrsgb. von Ludwig Tieck, Hamburg 1799, pp. 165 f.

[10] Cf. by the present writer, "Joseph Görres' Metaphorical Thinking", in *Literaturwissenschaft und Geistesgeschichte*, Festschrift für Richard Brinkmann, Tübingen 1981, pp. 376 f.; also included in the present volume.

[11] *Minnelieder aus dem Schwäbischen Zeitalter*, neu bearbeitet und herausgegeben von Ludwig Tieck, Berlin 1803, p. xxi, (Neudruck, Hildesheim 1966).

[12] *Leben und Tod der heiligen Genoveva. Ein Trauerspiel.* Jena 1800. Schriften, II, p. 67. The Unknown's speech consists of thirty terzinas, a short canto, one might say, with feminine rhymes predominating over the masculine, more difficult to achieve in a Germanic language.

[13] *Schriften* II, p. 267-269.

[14] *Gedichte von Ludwig Tieck*, Neue Ausgabe, Berlin 1841, p. 551-557. "Die neue Zeit" reads like a half comic counterpart of Novalis' "Astralis", the poem introducing Part II of "Heinrich von Ofterdingen" where the reign of poetry is to be established on earth. It was written at the height of the friendship between Novalis and Tieck and of the Jena Romantic encounters.

[15] Cf. Note 1, the article by C.Ch. Fuchs, p. 61 f., 76 f., 89 f., 101 f.

[16] *Novalis Schriften*, hgb. von Paul Kluckhohn und Richard Samuel, Zweiter Band — *Das philosophische Werk I*, Stuttgart 1965, "Vermischte Bemerkungen", 123, p. 468; cf. too Nicholas Saul, "Novalis's 'geistige Gegenwart' and his essay 'Die Christenheit oder Europa'", MLR 77 (1982), 361-377.

[17] *Novalis Schriften*, Vierter Band, *Lebensdokumente*, "Ludwig Tiecks Vorrede zur dritten Auflage von Novalis Schriften", Stuttgart 1975, pp. 559 f.

[18] *Novalis Schriften*, Erster Band, *Das Dichterische Werk*, "Hymnen an die Nacht, 3", Stuttgart 1977, p. 125.

[19] *Ludwig Tieck's gesammelte Novellen*, Berlin 1853, vol. VII, p. 19.

[20] *T.S. Eliot*, Selected Essays, London 1949, p. 238 and 237.

[21] Rudolf Köpke, *op. cit.*, II, p. 213.

[22] Johann Georg Herzog zu Sachsen, "König Johann von Sachsen und die Dante Forschung seit 100 Jahren", DDJ 1921, vol. 6, pp. 62-74; "König Johann von Sachsen als Dante Forscher", *Neues Archiv für Sächsische Geschichte*, vol. 43, Dresden 1922, pp. 201-220; "König Johann von Sachsen, Philalethes", DDJ 1934, vol. 16, pp. 113-129. *Johann von Sachsen*: *Lebenserinnerungen des Königs Johann von Sachsen. Eigene Aufzeichnungen des Königs über die Jahre 1801 bis 1854*. Hgb. von Hellmut Kretzschmar, Göttingen, 1958. See also the well documented essay by Roger Paulin, "'Höfisches Biedermeier'. Ludwig Tieck und der Dresdner Hof", in *Literatur in der sozialen Bewegung, Aufsätze und Forschungsberichte zum 19. Jahrhundert*, hgb. von Alberto Martino et al., Tübingen 1977, pp. 207-227. See also Paulin's *Ludwig Tieck. A Literary Biography*, Oxford 1985, pp. 271-302.

[23] *Briefwechsel König Johanns von Sachsen mit George Ticknor*, hgb. von Johann Georg Herzog zu Sachsen, im Verein mit E. Daenell, Leipzig und Berlin, 1920.

[24] Rudolf Köpke, *op. cit.*, II, p. 178.

[25] Louise Förster, *Biographische und literarische Skizzen aus dem Leben und der Zeit Karl Förster's*, Leipzig 1846, p. 452-3.

[26] "Lebenserinnerungen", *op. cit.* p. 59.

[27] *Dante Alighieri's Göttliche Comödie. Metrisch übertragen und mit kritischen und historischen Erläuterungen versehen von Philalethes*, Leipzig 1865-66, 3 Theile, *Vorrede zum Inferno*, pp. viii f.

Arnim's *Luisen-Kantate* as Romantic Occasional Verse

Arnim's *Nachtfeier nach der Einholung der Hohen Leiche Ihrer Majestät der Königin. Eine Kantate* (Berlin 1810) must be read against some knowledge of the background of Prussia's historical situation in the year of Queen Louise's sudden death on 19 July, 1810, at the age of 34. This Mecklenburg princess had married the heir to the Prussian throne in 1793 and had been queen since Frederick William III's accession to the throne four years later. The court went into exile during the Napoleonic wars in the course of which Louise herself visited Napoleon in a vain attempt to improve the devastating peace terms imposed on her country; she was a resolute adherent of the Prussian "Reform" movement. The court returned to the defeated capital in December 1809 and the queen died of what seems to have been a sudden lung infection the following summer while she was on a visit to her father in Neustrelitz. As a woman of great personal charm and integrity, she had become the focus and symbol of hope in hard times, and even, by a process of identification not unfamiliar to those living in one of the few remaining monarchies of modern Europe, something of a legend in her own lifetime. This process of myth-making does not necessarily need the special enthusiasm of Romantic poets and artists: it is universal and endemic at all levels where there is still a throne and a crown, more especially when the crown fits a beautiful head.

However, for German Romantic poets such as Novalis, Arnim, Brentano, Kleist, Körner and Schenkendorff, for the generation of an age to remember as one of the most terrible impressions of their younger years the wholesale slaughter of the French royal family, patriotic fervour for the monarchy and identification with its symbolic values was particularly strong. This applied more especially to the noblemen among them who, like Arnim, had boyhood memories of the court and had shared the Königsberg exile of the Prussian royal family. The death of the queen was a personal tragedy for him, its impact on him was more significant than it was, perhaps, for Brentano, a man of different region and family background. But the two friends, sharing a Berlin apartment at the time, set to work immediately and together, writing in the same room to pay poetical tribute to dead royalty: "Ich habe sie aus Kuriosität, wie ich mich bei gleichem Stoff von Arnim unterschiede, in der Hinterstube mit ihm zugleich geschrieben", writes Brentano to the Grimm brothers on 2 November, 1810.[1] In both their poems, feelings and words about a state occasion became, to use Wordsworth's terms, a true "incarnation of thought", giving "to universally received truths a pathos and spirit which readmits them to the soul like revelations of the moment".[2]

The poet's role on such occasions is, as Arnim sees it, to create and provide the common ground of articulation where a common grief can be shared by all and in this way alleviated. The version of the cantata as it is now known is one revised for a reading public; it is not the cantata as it was first heard by the audience at the Royal Opera House in Berlin when it was performed with miming actions on a stage decorated with weeping willows, cypresses and massed hydrangeas, the queen's favourite flowers.[3] "Es ist mir sehr interessant gewesen zu sehen", says Brentano of this revision, "wie man etwas verbessert, was an sich schon vortrefflich ist".[4] Arnim, however, rightly felt that a rather different approach was indicated for the reader of the printed word and the listener to poetry set to music and performed by singers: "Da jedes Gedicht, das der Musik bestimmt ist, ohne Musik seiner wesentlichsten Hälfte beraubt ist, so habe ich durch die für die Musik ausgelassenen Zwischensätze diese Lücken nicht zu füllen, sondern zu decken gesucht", as he wrote in his preface, *An die Leser* (p. 382). Here he also apologizes for the shortcomings of this "musikalisches Gelegenheitsgedicht", written in haste at short notice. Public performance had already given it a public identity expressive of the people's attitude; he had therefore steered clear, in his revision, of a foreign church style, otherwise appropriate for the cantata form, and also of poetical originality: "fremdartiger Kirchenstil und poetische

Eigentümlichkeit sind darin vermieden". A spoken Prologue sets the scene for a portrait bust of the queen to be unveiled on the stage and the audience is reminded that only a few months previously, on Good Friday, Louise herself had in this same house attended the royal command performance of the cantata of Our Lord's Passion.[5] The thought of the Redeemer and the image of the queen herself will be a consolation as the audience remembers the solemn day of her return to her city:

> Der ernste Tag, als diese große Stadt
> Der hohen Leiche schwarz entgegenwallte.
> Es schien die Stadt erstorben überall
> Und alles Leben zu der Leiche hingebannt,
> Die, von den Würdigsten so ernst begleitet,
> Geheimnisvoll verhüllt vorüberzog. (p. 385)

After this introduction the cantata proceeds in dramatic alternation of musically stylized recitative by two solo voices, giving in the main an account of events. This narrative mainly in iambic metre, is then glossed or expanded by the choir in stanza form, usually in trochaic, and occasionally in dactylic metre. Brentano said he found his friend's cantata difficult to read aloud; this is perhaps the measure of the extent to which Arnim had not quite managed, in his revision, to convert the rhythmic emphasis of song into that of speech. The solo voice sometimes speaks in the first person, Arnim himself describing, for instance, his childhood memories of the queen, then of her walks along the sea shore during her exile at Königsberg, his own prayer for faith and hope:

> Ich sah zu ihr empor in so viel schönen Tagen,
> Und jeder Tag vermisset Sie mit anderm Schmerz.
> Wie die Gedanken mich an tausend Gnadenblicke mahnen!
> Als Kind ging ich mit buntem Fähnlein Ihr entgegen,
> Wo ich Ihr hoffte zu begegnen; [...]
> Und feierte als Bürger unter Waffen
> Die letzte frohe Wiederkehr der Hochverehrten:
> Wie weile ich so gern in jenen Tagen! - (p. 388)

> Ich sah die Tränen fließen,
> Als Sie an unserem Meeresstrande weilte [...].
> Ich kam von Preußens meerbestürmter Küste
> Und wollte Ihr des Bernsteins goldne Perlen bringen,
> Die dort das Meer auf Ihrer Tritte Spur,
> Auf die verlassnen Wege,
> Die einst von Ihr betreten grünten,
> An jedem Morgen reichlich streut [. . .]. (p. 387)

The poet sees these amber "pearls" as portents of sorrow and disaster, the tears of fabled spirits of the ocean.

Towards the end of the cantata, after the people have been granted their wish for a last look at the queen in her open coffin exposed to view - for the sake of his poem, Arnim maintained this dramatic but fictitious happening which, in the end, never took place - angels lift her up to heaven where she is welcomed by her three children who have predeceased her. She herself, "Stimme der Königin", then sings a consoling farewell to her loved ones and to her people as she looks down on them where they stand by her coffin. The idea of a queen assumed into heaven by angels "Mit bunten Flügeln hellbeschwingt", and lifting her "auf Weihrauchdüften / Zum blauen Himmel neu verjüngt" [...] .

> Farbig wie ein Regenbogen
> Haben Engel sie umzogen,
> Mondenschimmer Sie umwallt, (p. 398)

might have seemed more in keeping with Brentano's colourful Catholic background. But Arnim as a poet was perfectly prepared to enlist any popular and traditional religious iconography, even in celebrating the memory of his Lutheran queen; moreover, the images of the after life here used were also part of Pietistic thinking by which Arnim in the Berlin of that particular historical moment was not unaffected. J. C. Lavater, for instance, in his *Aussichten in die Ewigkeit,*[6] his popular Baedeker for the heavenly regions, was completely at home with circumstantial speculations about events at the moment of physical death, about the role of language and communication among the blessed and with those yet on earth, and very particularly with phenomena of light and their meaning - a subject the scientific and symbolical dimensions of which had always been of special interest to Arnim.

Arnim has dramatized his cantata, basically a lyrical form, into something like a miniature opera. "Alles Dramatische ist vortrefflich bei ihm", says Brentano of his friend, "und in der Erzählung ist er bloß darum unvollendet, weil er häufig ins Dramatische fällt und alle Übergänge vergißt".[7] The transitions in the cantata are, however, convincingly managed. It is interesting to note that Arnim has instinctively—or even intentionally and on the basis of his wide reading of earlier poetry—followed the traditional sequence and pattern for funeral poetry as originally laid down by Greek rhetoricians and exemplified throughout the genre in Renaissance and baroque verse of this kind.[8] The three stages traditionally traversed by the poet or orator speaking about the dead are praise, lament and consolation, a natural progression of mood and exposition which seems to be demanded of the funeral elegy. The first category, that of praise (επαινοζ), would necessarily include something about the dead person's life and career, the nature of his fatal illness, the circumstances of his death and his attitude to dying - it would not only be an encomium of all his good qualities. This then leads on to the actual sense of grievous loss, the lament proper (δοῆνοζ) which is, of course, present throughout but comes to a climax in this central position. Finally Arnim leads over to his coda, a rousing call to battle on, to work for a new harvest:

> Schaut! es glänzt der Osten helle,
> Schaut! es spiegelt jede Welle,
> Schaut zum Himmel, aus der Nacht
> Steigt der Sonne Herrscherpracht.
> Uns umstrahlet die Entfernte,
> Frisch zur Arbeit, frisch zur Ernte, [...]
>
> (pp. 403-404)

This is the final and essential element of consolation (παραμυδία). In his *An die Leser*, Arnim had already stated his intention "alles Gefühl der guten Seite des Schmerzes, seiner stärkenden, begeisternden Kraft zuzuwenden" (p. 382), and in this he has certainly succeeded: "er endigt mit Halleluja", said Brentano, "und ich mit »meine Seele ist betrübt bis in den Tod«; [...] Es gibt vielleicht kein besseres Beispiel zu zeigen, wie wir divergieren, er so freudig, rührend, tief und hoch, ich in armer, ebner, dunkler, trüber Bahn. Er, der in der zweiten Edition eine Menge dazusetzte, ich, der nichts mehr zu sagen hat [. . .]".[9] It is true that the skilfully varied rhythms and stanza forms of Brentano's shorter and primarily lyrical cantata are less immediate in their impact, more complex in their sequence and have little of Arnim's dramatic impetus. Arnim identified himself with the people, Brentano, in the first instance, with his own personal bereavement, perhaps thinking primarily of the loss of Sophie and of his own dead children rather than of the Prussian queen. Neither does his intricate but more individual poem correspond to the sequence of traditional patterns as does Arnim's, and perhaps the reason for this is Brentano's involvement with the material at a less generalized level. He was also more ambitious in his requirements for the musical setting: before asking Reichardt he approached Beethoven, who, however, refused on the ground that Louise was not known in Vienna and he had no intention of writing exclusively for Prussia and Berlin. Arnim's composer was also to have been Reichardt, but in the end it was G. A. Schneider, a much lesser talent.[10]

While Arnim may not have been so well served by his composer, he, as a poet and certainly in the reading version of his cantata, produced a careful, comprehensive whole, the basic structural pattern of which is the idea of contrast. He points throughout to the dual nature of all events and circumstances connected with the queen and her death, comparing past and present and linking them as being indissolubly enmeshed in a new time dimension. The idea of contrast as a literary stereotype inevitably pervades funeral poetry.[11] In Arnim's cantata contrasting features about Louise's life and death are the actual vehicle of narrative progression. At the very beginning, death's cruel harvest is shown in contrast to the golden season of high summer, and sudden, devastating storms at harvest time are related to her sudden death at this season. Her bridal procession down the Linden to the Brandenburg Gate denuded of its victory goddess by the national defeat, her joyful return from exile in a carriage given by the citizens, - these are contrasted with her funeral cortege down the same street, the hearse followed by this same carriage, now empty; the light and joy of spring, the augury of new life, is contrasted with the gloom of night that now shrouds her unseeing eyes in death. Where Arnim generously lavishes his lines on this, Brentano achieves the contrast by vivid concentration: "Schwarz ist der Leichenzug, ein Schatten / Vom Brautzug in des Himmels Höhn".[12] His statements of contrast are more sparing, sophisticated and subtle, and for that very reason, less immediately effective and popular than Arnim's straightforward antitheses. Louise hastens to follow her own father's invitation, then obeys the summons of her Father in heaven to set out on her last journey of all. The flowers of the triumphal arch welcoming her arrival at her father's home now see her on her way to her last resting place. Flowers and trees - the royal pair is seen in the image of two trees giving one another strength and shelter- grow from earth's dark shroud, but they grow heavenward, "Ätherglanz nach Grabesnacht".

The final emblem of contrast is the Saviour's cross followed by the glory of Easter and the empty tomb; a voice from heaven sings:

In allen euren Jahren
Seid ihr vom Tod umgeben. [...]

In Christus ist das Leben, [...]

In schwerem Liebesschmerz
Tragt ihr das Herz zu Grabe,
Doch mit dem Kreuzesstabe
Durchbricht der Herr den Sarg,
Und was die Erde barg,
Im Herzen bleibt geborgen
Und dringt zum ew'gen Morgen,
Er ist das Herz der Welt,
Das ew'ge Liebe schwellt. (p. 402)

This triumphant cry from heaven is an answer to an earlier voice on earth which had not as yet got beyond the loss of hope:

> Es geht des Schmerzes Abgrund auf,
> Der nimmer sich erfüllet,
> Die Erde scheint ein offnes Grab,
> Das Leben eine Sehnsucht nach dem Tode. (p. 393)

But now the choir falls in, confirming new hope and courage:

> Lobt den Herrn!
> Schaut! es glänzt der Osten helle,
> Schaut! es spiegelt jede Welle,
> Schaut zum Himmel, aus der Nacht
> Steigt der Sonne Herrscherpracht. [...]
> Unser Adler dringt
> Durch die hohe Luft,
> Und die Lerche singt
> Durch den Morgenduft,
> Triumph, Triumph, Sie bleibt uns nah,
> Singt dem Herrn Hallelujah! (p. 404)

This is the happy end, quizzically glossed by Brentano, who, however, is not entirely devoid of hope either at the end of his cantata. His own basic image is the stereotype of the changing seasons and of the flowering and decay of plant life, "Auch Sie war eine schöne Blume [...]". The queen's young but living children, in contrast, perhaps, to the poet's own dead children, peacefully sleep the happy sleep of unconscious childhood amidst all the grief of mourning for their dead mother:

> Selig die Schlummernden,
> Ruhig pochet das Herz,
> Und es gaukelt der Schmerz,
> Ein Traum, über die Wiege hin.
>
> Selig die Unmündigen,
> Bunte Blumen und Flitterglanz,

> Schimmern im Todenkranz,
> Und ihr weinet und lächelt,
> Denn ihr versteht, ihr Unschuldige
> Das unsterbliche Leben![13]

This is an ending which, in its own characteristic way, does have a slight glimmer of hope, and it is fair to add that Brentano's cantata, less successful as a technically "occasional" poem, is better poetry.

But the literary competence and quality of both these cantatas is quite certainly head and shoulders above the kind of verse associated at about this time with command performances on state occasions. It has not been possible for the present writer to unearth the text of any other comparable odes or cantatas on Louise's death, though there certainly were others; Brentano, for instance, tells Wilhelm Grimm that Tiedge wrote one, "[...] wie die Damen sagen, voll Natur, Phantasie, Wahrheit und Liebe, [...] die Himmel komponiert"[14]; and for the first commemorative service in the Berlin Royal Theatre, Iffland himself proclaimed, presumably faute de mieux at such short notice, Klopstock's 1752 ode on the death of Queen Louise of Denmark (omitting verse 5); then after an overture by Gluck, a performance of Mozart's Requiem Mass, introduced by Reichardt, ended up with Handel's Hallelujah Chorus, all of which must have been quite an astonishing artistic potpourri compared with Arnim's unpretentious offering to the Berlin public the following week.[15]

Now in order to give a rough idea of the quality of the verse unselectively used in cantatas even by great composers, one might quote a few sample lines from the beginning and end of the Beethoven cantata on the death of the emperor Joseph II in 1790. The text was probably by one Eulogius Schneider, and (understandably) it has never been published apart from the score in the complete critical Beethoven edition.

> Todt! Todt! Todt! stöhnt es durch die öde Nacht; / Felsen, weinet es wieder! / Und ihr Wogen des Meeres / Heulet es durch eure Tiefen. [. . .] Er schläft, er schläft von den Sorgen seiner Welten entladen [. . .] / Dulder, der große Dulder, / der hienieden kein

> Röschen ohne Wunde brach, / Dulder, der große Dulder, der unter seinem vollen Herzen das Wohl der Menschheit, unter Schmerzen / bis an sein Lebensende trug, / Hier schlummert seinen stillen Frieden der große Dulder. Todt, todt, todt, stöhnt es durch die öde Nacht [...] etc.[16]

Romantic "Zweckdichtung", the writing of which was a matter of conviction and of principle for both Arnim and Brentano, helped to raise standards and the public horizon of expectation in this matter: Kleist, Schenkendorff and Körner also wrote odes to Queen Louise, at least while she was still alive. The death in England of Charlotte, Princess of Wales, only daughter of George IV, called forth, in 1817, an enormous spate of verse; the author of *Imaginary Address of the Princess Charlotte to her Infant,* said of his truly dreadful lines: "They will not bear the severe eye of criticism, but to a feeling heart they must be touching".[17] It is against the background of this kind of thing that one must see these Romantic cantatas and remember Arnim's firm words to his reader that he did not want to stir up sentiment but to instil comfort and courage.

Arnim always, in fact, wrote with vigour and verve about death and as though he relished this kind of composition and his rich elaboration of old and new ideas and words on the subject. "Meine Worte sind Flammenzüge, die mir in der Nacht leuchten", says the poet in *Heymar's Dichterschule* as he tries to find words to describe spring,[18] for spring, too, bears within its glory the seeds of death. In *Das Frühlingsfest. Ein Nachspiel,* planned as part of *Päpstin Johanna,* Beata ecstatically abandons her earthly lover for the god of Spring who draws her to her death in the Rhine. Arnim sees Queen Louise herself as not entirely a stranger to the pull of death; the earth, though she loves it, is in some sense, and of course in the Christian sense, alien territory to this "Blume hell und groß". She plays the part that is expected of her when she is on her visit to her father and family: "Sie überläßt sich froh den heitern Scherzen / Im fremden, luft'gen Lebensmeer", but when the call comes for her to return to her true element, she follows it gladly. At the moment of death, "[. . .] eine Klarheit herrscht in ihrer Seele / Wie in dem Anfang eines neuen Morgenrots", and the chorus sings for her, (a faint echo of Novalis),

> Sehnsucht nach dem heil'gen Lande,
> Das uns Jesus hat gewonnen,
> Löset unsres Lebens Bande,
> Löschet aus der Erde Sonnen,
> Ihre Blumen, ihre Sterne,
> Blickt in tiefe Nacht zur Ferne. (p. 393)

Heine's description of Arnim's benign and almost casual friendliness towards all the characters he had condemned to death in his stories and plays is a locus classicus of Romantic criticism. Where Hoffmann, as Heine says, is himself terrified by his own dead and joins fearfully in their dance of terror, Arnim surveys them affectionately and gives them all a casual, friendly nod of recognition, taking death as a matter of course:

> Wenn aber Arnim seine Toten beschwört, so ist es, als ob ein General Heerschau halte, und er sitzt so ruhig auf seinem hohen Geisterschimmel und läßt die entsetzlichen Scharen vor sich vorbeidefilieren, und sie sehen ängstlich nach ihm hinauf und scheinen sich vor ihm zu fürchten. Er nickt ihnen aber freundlich zu.[19]

But Heine's contention that Arnim was not "Dichter des Lebens, sondern des Todes", is, to say the least of it, debatable; Arnim was simply on good terms with death, which is unusual enough, and perhaps at that point of time not, as yet, Heine's own case.

Arnim's way of integrating death with life in this cantata and in some of his poems is perhaps less akin in spirit to the varying Romantic attitudes of, say, Novalis, Werner or Eichendorff, than to those of some of the English Romantics, notably Wordsworth and Coleridge. In their *Lyrical Ballads* (1798-1802) and in the critical essays explaining their new poetical practice, they analysed ideas similar to the ones the less theoretically minded Arnim presented only in his poetry. The first of Wordsworth's three *Essays upon Epitaphs,* published in Coleridge's periodical, *The Friend,* dates from the same year as the German Romantic *Luisenkantaten.*[20] Although Wordsworth is writing about verse actually engraved on a tombstone, his terms of reference are here much wider, embracing the whole subject of how the poet uses words to "incarnate", as he says, his thoughts and feelings about death with the object of consoling both himself and the bereaved person who does not happen to be a poet. Like Arnim, Wordsworth sees this function of the poet in great moments of human experience as one of his most significant and even divinely ordained responsibilities, the poet's due to mankind.

The first requirement of funeral poetry is that "it should speak, in a tone which shall sink into the heart, the general language of humanity as connected with the subject of death and of life. To be born and to die are the two points in which all men feel themselves to be in absolute coincidence".[21] Wordsworth's "general language of humanity" here corresponds to Arnim's postulate in his *An die Leser* of expressing "Volksgesinnung" and nothing extraneous to that. "The general sympathy", Wordsworth goes on, "should be quickened, provoked and diversified by particular thoughts, actions and images", as Arnim had done in telling the high-light moments of the queen's life and death and linking them with the reflective imagery of choral commentary. "The character of a deceased friend is not seen, no - nor ought to be seen, otherwise than as a tree through a tender haze or luminous mist that spiritualizes and beautifies it [. . .] this is not truth, not a faithful image, [. . .] It is truth of the highest order, hallowed by love".[22] Wordsworth was himself a life-long exponent of the kind of occasional poetry he has analysed in his essays and he succeeded in changing its more formalized eighteenth-century image in England; he would only consent to write, even on public occasions when he was Poet Laureate, if he himself was moved by true and general emotion.

Wordsworth's whole attitude closely resembles Arnim's unified conception of poetry: there was not to be formal state verse on the one hand and popular folk verse on the other: poetry was, and always had been, one unbroken whole, and the poet, as Arnim put it in his *Von Volksliedern* - the nearest he ever came to anything like a theoretical statement - was the universal provider, "Gemeingeist, spiritus familiaris der Weltgemeinde". Like Wordsworth, who wrote much elegaic and memorial verse and also translated Italian Renaissance epitaphs into English because they tallied with his own ideas about this genre, Arnim's lyrical work includes a number of striking poems on the death of friends, on Runge, for instance, who died in the same year as Queen Louise, and also on friends, fallen in battle. Perhaps the most attractive, and the most community-related poem in Wordsworth's sense, is the *Elegie auf den Tod eines Geistlichen,* a Matthias Claudius-like character called Justus Gottfried Hermes of the Gertraudenkirche on the Spittelmarkt in Berlin. He was collected by Freund Hein, as one might say, on 30 December, 1818. The previous year, Arnim had written a kind of elegy about this pastor's church, *Fabel von einer kleinen Kirche in einer großen Stadt;* both pastor and church would have felt perfectly at home in the world of the *Lyrical Ballads* and the *Essays upon Epitaphs* .[23]

But Arnim's cantata on Queen Louise was exceptional in his elegaic poetry because it had the added dimension of being about royalty and all that the idea of sovereignty signifies in the unconscious and conscious thinking of a nation and of the individual subject of a crown. For Arnim, the idea of kingship was a natural corollary to the basically simple political and historical attitude underlying his complex and often chaotic literary utterance. Friedrich von Hardenberg's friend, Kreisamtmann Just, sees the concept of monarchy as the simple basic truth, "einfacher Grund", capable of making history and political theory an intelligible study; he suggested to Hardenberg that this is what had, rather suddenly, turned him into a defender of monarchy in his *Glauben und Liebe-Fragmente* which appeared in the *Jahrbücher der Preußischen Monarchie unter der Regierung von Friedrich Wilhelm III.* in 1798,[24] Hardenberg himself accurately diagnoses and analyses the psychology and appeal of the concept, both in the king himself, "das gediegene Lebensprinzip des Staats [...] was die Sonne im Planetensystem" [...] "ein zum irdischen Fatum erhobener Mensch [...]", and in Louise whom he sees as the archetype of true femininity, carefully trained for her exacting role, Goethe's Natalie being "das zufällige Portrait der Königin [...] Ideale müssen sich gleichen". Arnim's portrait of Louise in his cantata, together with that by Brentano, complements Hardenberg's vision of monarchy in general, and of this particular king and queen whose exemplary marriage transformed the Prussian throne and court in what Hardenberg described as a veritable miracle of transsubstantiation.[25]

Arnim, of course, did not attempt anything more than a generalized portrait of his queen, and would have concurred with Wordsworth that the writer of this kind of poetry "is not an anatomist [...] he is not even a painter [...] his delineation is performed by the side of a grave [. . .] not proud writing shut up for the studious, but exposed to all — to the wise and the most ignorant".[26] Initially, Arnim was writing under the impact of strong emotion, but passion, as he says in his introduction to the *Kronenwächter,* does not make the poet, "vielmehr hat wohl noch keiner während ihrer lebendigen Einwirkung etwas Dauerndes geschaffen". Here too, Arnim's revision of the cantata, which Brentano, who worked no differently himself, saw fit to find astonishing, no doubt helped to make a more successful piece of poetry out of what was originally a hasty improvisation. In Wordsworth's terms, it was "emotion recollected in tranquillity", a good occasional poem in the best and true sense of that often misunderstood term, adequately expressing both a personal and a communal sorrow.

Abbreviations

Arnim	*Nachtfeier nach der Einholung der Hohen Leiche Ihrer Majesstät der Konigin. Eine Kantate.* Berlin 1810. In: *Achim von Arnims Werke.* Ausgewählt und hg. von Reinhold Steig, Leipzig, n. d., 3 vols. Vol. III, pp. 381-404. References below by page number only are to this text.
Brentano	"*Kantate auf den Tod Ihrer Königlichen Majestät, Louise von Preußen* " In: *Clemens Brentano: Gedichte.* Hg. von W. Frühwald, B. Gajek and

F. Kemp. Munich, [2] 1978, pp. 204-217.

Seebaß *Clemens Brentano: Briefe*. Hg. von Friedrich Seebaß. Nürnberg 1951. 2 vols.

Wordsworth *Three Essays upon Epitaphs,* 1810, 1812 and 1814. In: *Prose Works of William Wordsworth.* Ed. W.J.B. Owen and J.W.Smyser. Oxford 1974. Vol.II, pp. 45-119.

---

1 Seebaß II, p. 59.

2 Wordsworth II, p. 83.

3 Reinhold Steig: *Berlin in Trauer um die Königin Luise.* In: *Deutsche Rundschau.* 146, 1910. p. 265 282, p. 274.

4 Letter of 2 November, 1810, to J. and W. Grimm. In: Seebaß II, p. 59.

5 Arnim's note (p. 384) to his lines, "[. . .] Die noch vor wenig Monden hier in Trauer / Den Tod des Welterlösers hat gefeiert", does not name the composer of the cantata. It was Karl Heinrich Graun (1703-1759), the founder of the Berlin Opera, whose *Der Tod Jesu* was performed annually on Good Friday at the Prussian court from 1807 until 1858 when Bach's *Matthew Passion,* not nearly as popular as Graun's in its time, replaced this. cf. MGG *(Musik in Geschichte und Gegenwart)* vol. 5, pp. 703-719. - For the whole genre of the *Kantate,* both in its textual and musical aspects, see RL (Merker and Stammler), vol. 1, and MGG, vol. 5. - For the cantata as occasional verse, see Klaus Conermann in *Gelegenheitsdichtung.* Referate, Gruppe 6, Kongreß des Internationalen Arbeitskreises für Deutsche Barockliteratur. Wolfenbüttel 1976. Eingel. von Wulf Segebrecht, ed. D.Frost and G.Knoll. Bremen 1977. pp.69-109, with a full bibliography. For the Romantic cantata in particular, see G.Schwanebeck: *Die dramatische Chorkantate der Romantik.* (Diss.) Düsseldorf 1938. - For much interesting detail about the performance of Arnim's cantata, see R. Steig (note 3 above). The portrait bust unveiled during the Prologue was probably a cast of Schadow's marble statue of Louise and her sister (1797) as he was also responsible for the stage set. This statue, an important witness of the

Louise cult and myth, is illustrated and discussed in Wolfgang Frühwald: *Das Spätwerk Clemens Brentanos (1815-1842). Romantik im Zeitalter der Metternich'schen Restauration* (= Hermaea NF 37). Tübingen 1977. Illustrations I and 2, and a commentary, p. 393.

6 Publication of this long work began in 1768, but there were many shortened editions, eg. *Aussichten in die Ewigkeit. Gemeinnütziger Auszug aus dem größeren Werk dieses Namens.* Neue Ausgabe. Zürich n.d. The Cambridge University Library copy of this is dated 1841.

7 Letter of 8 May, 1810, to W.Grimm. In Seebaß II, p.43.

8 See O. B. Hardison Jr.: *The Enduring Monument. A Study of the Idea of Praise in Renaissance Literary Theory and Practice.* Chapel Hill, North Carolina 1962. *pp.* 113ff. and Parts V and *VI* as a whole. See also *R*. Lattimore: *Themes in Greek and Latin Epitaphs* (Illinois Studies XXVIII). Urbana 1942, whose classification of themes in epitaphs and epicediums is basic for the understandig of all funeral verse and oratory.

9 Letters of 3 September and 2 November to J. and W. Grimm. In Seebaß II, p. 50 and 59.

10 For a full discussion of Brentano's cantata and its importance to him during the brief years when he was able to identify himself, on Arnim's pattern, with national issues, see Frühwald, (note 5. above), Ch.II, pp.77-85, where there is also an enlightening account of the "Luisenlegende" as a historical phenomenon. - For G. A. Schneider (1770-1839) whom Brentano described as "ein unendlich elender Musikant", whose setting of Arnims's cantata was "für jeden Vernünftigen zum Totlachen", (Seebaß II, p. 50) - though Arnim himself tolerantly made no complaints -, see MGG, vol. II.

11 Hardison, pp. 116ff. (cf. note 8).

12 Brentano, p.216.

13 Brentano, p.217.

14 Seebaß II, p. 59.

15 Steig (see note 3 above), p. 268.

16 *Kantate auf den Tod Kaisers Joseph des Zweiten in Musik gesetzt von L. van Beethoven.* In: *Werke.* Serie 25, Suppl. 264. Leipzig 1888. pp. 1-54. - Eulogius Schneider, originally a Franciscan friar, then a professor of Greek at Bonn and a political agitator in the Reign of Terror, was finally guillotined in Paris in 1794. - The cantata, not performed at the time, lost and then rediscovered in Hummel's "Nachlaß" in Vienna in 1884, was performed on Radio 3 in London in June 1982 by enthusiastic revivalists, an occasion which gave at least one listener a clue why it had fallen into oblivion in Beethoven's life time. It is true that he was only 19 when he composed it.

17 Charlotte, Lady Bury: *Diary Illustrative of the Times of George IV,* (1844), ed. by A. F. Steward. London 1908. 2 vols., vol. I. pp. 147ff.

18 *Ariel's Offenbarungen.* Ed. Jacob Minor. Weimar 1912. p. 148.

19 *Die Romantische Schule.* In: *Heinrich Heines Sämtliche Werke,* ed. by Ernst Elster. Leipzig and Vienna (n.d.). Vol. 5, p. 319.

20 Wordsworth II, p. 49-60.

21 Wordsworth II, p. 57.

22 Wordsworth II, p. 57 and 58.

23 The poem on Hermes' church first appeared in *Der Gesellschafter, oder Blätter für Geist und Herz.* Jg. 1. Berlin 1817. pp. 229ff., a periodical to which Arnim contributed extensively, cf. Mallon, Nr. 95. The elegy on Hermes himself survives in a copy by Bettina; for the text of both poems, see Arnim III, 467ff. and 469ff., more recently in *Gedichte von Ludwig Achim von Arnim,* Zweiter Teil (Nachlaß: Siebenter Band). Ed. Herbert R. Liedke and Alfred Anger. Freies Deutsches Hochstift. Reihe der Schriften, vol 22 Tübingen 1976. p. 223:

Inschriften an den vier Seiten eines Grabmahles

1

Augen der Lieben ich seh euch, ihr hellen lieblichen Sterne,
Aber ihr seht mich nicht mehr und ihr sähet mich gern.

2

Weint nicht ihr Lieben um mich die Thräne einsamer Wehmuth,
Ach es fehlet die Hand, die sie getrocknet so gern.

3

Thränen der Liebe verbrennen das Gras am Grabe der Lieben
Und ich grüne umher, seyet willkommen im Grün.

4

Bring ich Gedeihen der Erndte, den Heerden kühlenden Schatten,
O so erfreut euch darin und ich lebe bey Euch.

24 Letter from A.C. Just to Novalis in Freiberg, 17 and 24 November 1798. In: Novalis: *Schriften*. Ed. Kluckhohn and Samuel. Stuttgart 1960. 4 vols. Vol.IV (1975), pp. 505f.

25 *Glauben und Liebe*, nos. 17, 18, 30, 43, 40; Novalis, vol. II, pp. 488 onwards.

26 Wordsworth II, p. 57 and 59.

Principal publications of

Elisabeth Stopp

'Wandlungen des Tieckbildes. Ein Literaturbericht', *Deutsche Vierteljahrsschrift,* 17 (1939), 252-76

Of Cleaving to God. Translated from the DE ADHAERENDO DEO attributed to Saint Albert the Great, Blackfriars Publications, Oxford, 1948; Mowbrays, London, 1954

E.T.A.Hoffmann, *Meister Martin der Küfner und seine Gesellen,* Cambridge Plain Texts, Cambridge University Press, 1951

'The Romantic Era' and 'The Romantic and Classical Eras' in *The Year's Work in Modern Language Studies,* 1951-53, and 1955, in collaboration with F.J.Stopp

St Francis de Sales. Selected Letters. Translated with an Introduction. (Classics of the Contemplative Life), Faber and Faber, London, 1960, and Harper, New York, 1960

Madame de Chantal. Portrait of a Saint. Faber and Faber, London, 1962, and Westminster Press, Maryland, 1963; Spanish translation (*Ediciones Rialp S.A.),* Madrid, Mexico, Buenos Aires, 1966

'François de Sales and Jeanne de Chantal. Two unpublished letters', *French Studies,* xviii (1964), 17-23

'Jean Goulu and his "Life" of Saint François de Sales', *Modern Language Review,* 62 (1967), 226-37

'"Healing Differences": St Francis de Sales in Seventeenth-Century England', *The Month,* N.S. 38, no. 1 (1967), 51-71

'St Francis de Sales, "Méditations sur l'Église, 1595-6", *Salesian Studies*, 4, no. 4 (1967), 53-69

St Francis de Sales. A Testimony by St Chantal. A Critical Edition from the ms., presented in Translation with an Introduction, Faber and Faber, London, 1967, and Institute of Salesian Studies, Hyattsville, Maryland, 1968

'Musil's *Törleß* : Content and Form', *Modern Language Review,* 63 (1968), 94-118; German translation in *Robert Musil,* edited by Renate von Heydebrand, *Wege der Forschung* 588, Wissenschaftliche Buchgesellschaft, Darmstadt, 1982

'The Metaphor of Death in Eichendorff', *Oxford German Studies,* 4 (1969), 67-89

'Eichendorff's *Die Lerche, 2:* A Textual Problem', *Modern Language Review*, 64, (1969), 809-17

'St Francis de Sales at Clermont College. A Humanist Education in Sixteenth-Century Paris', *Salesian Studies,* 6, no. 1 (1969), 42-63

'"Ein Sohn der Zeit": Goethe and the Romantic Plays of Zacharias Werner', *Publications of the English Goethe Society,* 40 (1970), 123-50

'A Romantic Reaction to *Die Wahlverwandtschaften:* Zacharias Werner and Goethe', *Literaturwissenschaftliches Jahrbuch,* N.F. 11, (1970), 67-85

'Brentano's *Chronika* and its revision', in *Sprache und Bekenntnis, Sonderband des Literaturwissenschaftlichen Jahrbuchs, Hermann Kunisch zum 70. Geburtstag, 27. Oktober 1971*, pp. 161-84

Clemens Brentano, *Die Chronika des fahrenden Schülers. (Urfassung).* Reclams Universal-Bibliothek, Stuttgart, 1971, 'Nachwort', pp. 112-36

'Eichendorff und Shakespeare.' *Festvortrag zur Jahresversammlung der Eichendorff-Gesellschaft,* 7. April 1972, *Aurora,* 32 (1972), 7-23

'Brentano's "O Stern und Blume": Its Poetic and Emblematic Context', *Modern Language Review,* 67 (1972), 95-117

'"Übergang vom Roman zur Mythologie": Formal Aspects of the Opening Chapter of Hardenberg's *Heinrich von Ofterdingen, Part II'*, *Deutsche Vierteljahrsschrift*, 48 (1974), 318-41

'Arnim's *Owen Tudor* and its background', *German Life and Letters*, (Special Number for Trevor Jones), xix, i (October, 1975), 155-66

'Romantic Affinities of Johann Michael Sailer's Kerygmatic Writing', in *Romantik in Deutschland. Ein interdisziplinäres Symposion,* edited by Richard Brinkmann, Metzler, Stuttgart, 1978, pp. 463-74

'Die Kunstform der Tollheit: zu Clemens Brentanos und Joseph Görres' *BOGS der Uhrmacher*', in *Clemens Brentano: Kolloquium im Freien Deutschen Hochstift*, 1978, Niemeyer, Tübingen, 1980, pp. 359-76

'"Ein literarisches Mondkalb": Görres' "Tollgewordener Epilogus" to his "Schriftproben von Peter Hammer"', *German Life and Letters*, (Special number for L.W. Forster), xxxiv, i (October, 1980), 108-16

'Zur bibliographischen Erschließung der Romantik', *Beiträge zur bibliographischen Lage in der germanistischen Literaturwissenschaft.* Kommission für germanistische Forschung, III, Boldt, Boppard, 1981, 111-19

'Joseph Görres' Metaphorical Thinking', in *Literaturwissenschaft und Geistesgeschichte, Festschrift für Richard Brinkmann*, edited by Jürgen Brummack et al., Niemeyer, Tübingen, 1981, 371-86

'Carus' *Neun Briefe über Landschaftsmalerei (1831).* Werk und Form in romantischer Perspektive', *Vortrag auf dem Internationalen Eichendorff-Kongreß*, Würzburg, 15 July 1982, *Aurora*, 43, (1983), 77-91

'Ferdinand von Saar's Austrian Tribute to Goethe in his Poetry', in *Ferdinand von Saar: ein Wegbereiter der literarischen Moderne*, ed. K.K.Polheim, Bouvier, Bonn, 1985, pp. 264-71

'Ludwig Tieck: unveröffentlichte Aufzeichnungen zu Purgatorio VI - XXXIII anläßlich der deutschen Übersetzung von Philalethes, ediert und erläutert', *Deutsches Dante Jahrbuch*, 60 (1985), 7-72

'Ludwig Tieck and Dante', *Deutsches Dante-Jahrbuch*, 60 (1985), 73-95

'Arnim's *Luisen-Kantate* as Romantic Occasional Verse' *Aurora,* 46 (1986), 87-98

'Carl Gustav Carus' Emblematic Thinking', *Bulletin of the John Rylands University Library of Manchester*, 71, 3 (1989), 21-30

'John Henry Newman et Saint François de Sales', *Bulletin de l'Association Française des Amis de Newman,* 5, (1989), 3-14

TABULA GRATULATORIA

Dr. Louise Adey, *Lincoln College, Oxford*
Dr. Jeffrey Ashcroft, *University of St Andrews*
Professor L.J.Austin, *Cambridge*
The Austrian Institute, *London*
Dr. Robert Aylett, *Goldsmith's College, London*

Miss Constance Babington-Smith, *Cambridge*
Professor Alan Bance, *University of Southampton*
Joseph and Colette Barrère, *Stowmarket, Suffolk*
Graham Bartram, *University of Lancaster*
Professor Peter Bayley, *Caius College, Cambridge*
Professor Michael Beddow, *University of Leeds*
David Blamires, *University of Manchester*
Elizabeth Boa, *University of Nottingham*
Patrick Boyde, *St John's College, Cambridge*
Nicholas Boyle, *Magdalene College, Cambridge*
Philip Brady, *Birkbeck College, London*
Peter Branscombe, *University of St Andrews*
Charles and Daphne Brink, *Cambridge*
Prof. Dr. Richard Brinkmann, *Im Rotbad 30, 7400 Tübingen*
Professor Christopher Brooke and Dr Rosalind Brooke, *Caius College, Cambridge*
Brotherton Library, *University of Leeds*
Michael Butler, *University of Birmingham*

Cambridge University Library
Roger Cardinal, *Canterbury*

T.J.Casey, *University College Galway*
Terence Cave, *St John's College, Oxford*
Margaret Chase, *Dial House, Norwich*
Mark Chinca, *Trinity College, Cambridge*
The Rt. Rev. Alan C. Clark, *Bishop of East Anglia*
Tony and Anne Clarke, *Potters Bar*
Rosemary Combridge, S.P.G.S, and *Queen Mary and Westfield College, London*
W.A.Coupe, *University of Reading*
Cecil Courtney, *Christ's College, Cambridge*
The Most Rev. Maurice Couve de Murville, *The Archbishop of Birmingham*
John Cowan, *New College, Oxford*
Dr. J. Cremona, *Trinity Hall, Cambridge*
Geoffrey Cubbin, *Dept of German, University of Cambridge*

Anne Davenport, *Cambridge*
Robert Dolby, *Trent College, Nottingham*
Alison Duke, *Girton College, Cambridge*
David Dumville, *Girton College, Cambridge*
E.E.Duncan-Jones, *16 Amhurst Court, Cambridge*

Toni Ebers, *München*
Eva J.Engel, *Herzog August Bibliothek, Wolfenbüttel*

Elizabeth L. Falconer, *Modern and Medieval Languages Libraries, Cambridge*
Professor Alison Fairlie, *Cambridge*.
James Fegan, *Tokyo*
Konrad and Rahel Feilchenfeldt, *Munich*
The Rev. Dermot Fenlon, Cong. Orat., *Birmingham*

John Francis Fetzer, *Dept of German, University of California, Davis*
Alison Finch and Malcolm Bowie, *Cambridge*
John L. Flood, *London*
Leonard and Jeanne Forster, *Cambridge*
Viktoria and Wolfgang Frühwald, *Munich and Bonn*

Dorothy Gabe, *New Hall, Cambridge*
Peter Ganz, *21 Bardwell Road, Oxford*
Grace Rolleston Gardner, *Liss, Hants.*
Mary Garland, *5 Roseburn Avenue, Exeter*
Howard Gaskill, *University of Edinburgh*
Robert Gillett, *Queen Mary and Westfield College, London*
The Library, *Girton College, Cambridge*
Peter and †Barbara Gray, *Caius College, Cambridge*
Dr. Ron Gray, *Emmanuel College, Cambridge*
Dennis and Margaret Green, *7 Archway Court, Barton Road, Cambridge*
M.C.Green, *Hucclecote, Gloucester*
Philip Grierson, *Caius College, Cambridge*
John Guthrie, *New Hall, Cambridge*

Mrs V.E.Hall, *Cambridge University Library*
Dr. Franz Heiduk, *Würzburg*
Prof. Dr. Arthur Henkel, *Heidelberg*
Marian Hobson, *Trinity College, Cambridge*
Edgar Holloway, *Woodbarton, Ditchling Common, Hassocks*
Ulrike Horstmann-Guthrie, *Cambridge*
Prof. Karl Josef and Mrs Freda Höltgen, *Institut für Anglistik und Amerikanistik, Erlangen*

Prof. Dr. Jochen Hörisch, *Universität Mannheim*
Patricia Howe, *Queen Mary and Westfield College, London*
The Hugh Owen Library, *University of Wales*
Dr. Richard Humphrey, *Universität Gießen*
Alan Hutchinson, *The Glasgow Academy*
Peter Hutchinson, *Trinity Hall, Cambridge*

Margaret C. Ives, *University of Lancaster*
Institute of Germanic Studies, *London*

Harry Jackson, *University of St Andrews*
Edward James, *St John's College, Cambridge*
Peter Johnson, *Pembroke College, Cambridge*
Charlotte Jolles, *24 Stanbury Court, London NW3*
Gillian Jondorf, *Girton College, Cambridge*

Prof. Dr. Helene M. Kastinger Riley, *133 Whittington Drive, Greenville, S.C. 29615*
Prof. Dr. Klaus Kanzog, *Institut für Deutsche Philologie, Universität München*
R.E. Keller, *Manchester*
Raymond Kerby, *St Ives, Cambridgeshire*
Dr. H.R.Klieneberger, *7 Larchfield Road, Dublin 4*
Gerhard Kluge, *Nijmegen*
Norbert and Rosemary Kunisch, *Bochum-Stiefel*

F.J. Lamport, *Worcester College, Oxford*
The Library, *University of Lancaster*
The Library, *University of Leicester*
Professor L.R.Lewitter, *Christ's College, Cambridge*
Professor Richard Littlejohns, *University of Leicester*

Terry Llewellyn, *Christ's College, Cambridge*
Ladislaus Löb, *University of Sussex*
Franz Lösel, *University of Sheffield*
David Lowe, *Cambridge University Library*
Prof. Dr. Paul Michael Lützeler, *Washington University, St Louis*
John Lyons, *Trinity Hall, Cambridge*

W.J.Macpherson, *Caius College, Cambridge*
C.P.Magill, *Aberystwyth*
Prof. Dr. Hans-Joachim Mähl, *Universität Kiel*
The Master and Fellows, *Magdalene College, Cambridge*
The Revd. Dr. Anthony Marks, *Grosvenor Chapel, South Audley Street, London W1*
Graham Martin, *University of Strathclyde*
Eve Mason, *Newnham College, Cambridge*
Prof. Dr. Wolfram Mauser, *Universität Freiburg im Breisgau*
Alan Menhennet, *University of Newcastle upon Tyne*
The Meyricke Library, *Jesus College, Oxford*
David Midgley, *St John's College, Cambridge*
Patrick Miles, *Caius College, Cambridge*
Michael Minden, *Jesus College, Cambridge*
Michael Mitchell, *Alveston Lodge, Stratford-upon-Avon*
Hans Jörg Modlmayr, and Hildegard Modlmayr-Heimath, *Borken-Gemen*
Dr. Renate Moering, *Freies Deutsches Hochstift, Frankfurt am Main*
Hugh and Elisabeth Montefiore, *Wandsworth Common, London SW17*
Estelle Morgan, *Bristol*

Michael Moriarty, *Caius College, Cambridge*
Irene Morris, *Newnham College, Cambridge*
†Beatrice Morton, *Cambridge*
Nevill and Ruth Mott, *Caius College, Cambridge*
Prof. Dr. Walter Müller-Seidel, *Pienzenauer Straße 164, 8 München 81*
Dr. Brian Murdoch, *University of Stirling*

John Neubauer, *Instituut voor Algemene Literaturwetenschap, Amsterdam*
Lisa Newall, *Cambridge*
The Library, *Newnham College, Cambridge*
Fr Aidan Nichols, O.P., *Blackfriars, Cambridge*
Günter Niggl, *Eichstätt*
Barry Nisbet, *Sidney Sussex College, Cambridge*

Dr Denis O'Brien, *Le Château du Chalange, Courtomer, France*
George O'Brien, *King's College, Madrid*
Terence O'Reilly, *University College, Cork*
Dr. M.R.Ogden, *University of Newcastle upon Tyne*
John Osborne, *University of Warwick*
The Modern Languages Faculty Library, *University of Oxford*

Richard Parker, *University of Warwick Library*
Idris Parry, *Manchester*
Roger Paulin, *Trinity College, Cambridge*
Ronald Peacock, *Gerrards Cross, Bucks*
Anthony Phelan, *University of Warwick*
The Revd. Canon Dr Anthony Phillips, *The King's School, Canterbury*
The Ward Library, *Peterhouse, Cambridge*
Hans Popper, *7 Mirador Cres., Uplands, Swansea*

John Porteous, *Caius College, Cambridge*
Helga and Siegbert Prawer, *Oxford*
Judith Purver, *University. of Manchester*

The Library, *Queens' College, Cambridge*

Maurice M. Raraty, *Eliot College, University of Kent*
Frederick Ratcliffe, *Rickinghall Superior, Diss, Norfolk*
Theodore Redpath, *Trinity College, Cambridge*
Professor Hans Reiss, *Bristol*
Peter Rickard, *Emmanuel College, Cambridge*
Dr. Ulfert Ricklefs, *Universität Erlangen-Nürnberg*
Hugh Ridley, *University College, Dublin*
Charlotte and Paul Ries, *Cambridge*
Dr. Ritchie Robertson, *St John's College, Oxford*
Elaine Robson-Scott, *19 Dorset Square, London*
Professor and Mrs B.A.Rowley, *Norwich*

Professor Eda Sagarra, *Trinity College, Dublin*
The Library, *St Andrew's University*
The Library, *St Catharine's College, Cambridge*
Dr. Nicholas Saul, *Trinity College, Dublin*
Olive Sayce, *Somerville College, Oxford*
Prof. Dr. Wulf Segebrecht, *Universität Bamberg*
The Rev. F.J.Selman, *Ely, Cambs.*
Elinor S. Shaffer, *University of East Anglia*
Richard Sheppard, *Magdalen College, Oxford*
Gerhard Schulz, *University of Melbourne*
Susan Sirc, *University of Glasgow*
Peter Skrine, *University of Bristol*
Prof. Dr. Edmund Stegmaier, *Pädagogische*

Prof. Dr. Edmund Stegmaier, *Pädagogische Hochschule, Ludwigsburg*
Prof. Dr. Hartmut Steinecke, *Universität Paderborn*
Jonathan Steinberg, *Trinity Hall, Cambridge*
Sibylle von Steinsdorff, *Institut für Deutsche Philologie, Universität München*
Dr R.H.Stephenson, *University of Glasgow*
†Peter Stern, *St John's College, Cambridge*
Dr A.M.Stewart, *University of Aberdeen*
Dr Mary Stewart, *Robinson College, Cambridge*
Alexander Stillmark, *University College, London*
Marianne Penelope Stopp, *Waterloo, Ontario*
Brigitte Stopp-Krukowski, *Waterloo, Ontario*
Martin Swales, *University College, London*
Erika Swales, *King's College, Cambridge*

Taylor Institution Library, *Oxford*
Peter Thornton, *University of Newcastle upon Tyne*
Edward Timms, *University of Sussex*
James Trainer, *University of Stirling*
The Library, *Trinity College, Cambridge*
The Library, *Trinity Hall, Cambridge*
Prof. Dr. Erika Tunner, *12, rue du Regard, Paris*
Rosemary E. Turner-Wallbank, *University of Manchester*

The Library, *University College, London*

Dr. Johann Vcelak, *Zirndorf bei Nürnberg*

H.M.Waidson, *29 Myrtle Grove, Sketty, Swansea*
Dr. Colin Walker, *The Queen's University, Belfast*

Dr.John Walker, *Selwyn College, Cambridge*
M. O'C. Walshe, *Berkhamsted*
Dr. Joachim Whaley, *Caius College, Cambridge*
Andrew Webber, *Churchill College, Cambridge*
Dr. Barbara Weber (*on behalf of the Krekler Family), Lyon*
Professor David Wells, *University of London*
Professor J.J. and Dr. I.A. White, *University of London*
Margaret Wileman, *Hughes Hall, Cambridge*
Elizabeth Mary Wilkinson, *33 Queen Square, London WC1*
Dr. J. Cameron Wilson, *Jesus College, Cambridge*
Professor R.A.Wisbey, *King's College, London*
Olive Withycombe, *Hucclecote, Gloucester*
Manfred Windfuhr, *Heinrich-Heine-Universität, Düsseldorf*

Gar Yates, *University of Exeter*